Microfinance

This book illustrates the historical, political and economic background to our current knowledge on microfinance. The relationship between its prevailing popularity and the consolidation of neoliberal economic ideology worldwide is fully charted.

Examining current macroeconomic trends, the volume analyzes the historical confluence of microfinance with feminist notions of empowerment and explores the processes and the extent to which gender hierarchies are institutionalized in development. *Microfinance* offers programmatic and procedural guidelines for designing microfinance programs – and for practising development policy more generally – that would engage women's solidarity in order to challenge existing patterns of subordination. This volume also provides valuable insights for, and suggests, new directions for current debates concerning gender and development

This book will prove essential reading for students, academics and practitioners in development economics, gender studies, and social and cultural anthropology.

Jude L. Fernando is a Professor at the Department of International Development, Community and Environment (IDCE), Clark University, Worcester, MA.

Routledge studies in development economics

1 **Economic Development in the Middle East**
   Rodney Wilson

2 **Monetary and Financial Policies in Developing Countries**
   Growth and stabilization
   Akhtar Hossain and Anis Chowdhury

3 **New Directions in Development Economics**
   Growth, environmental concerns and government in the 1990s
   Edited by Mats Lundahl and Benno J. Ndulu

4 **Financial Liberalization and Investment**
   Kanhaya L. Gupta and Robert Lensink

5 **Liberalization in the Developing World**
   Institutional and economic changes in Latin America, Africa and Asia
   Edited by Alex E. Fernández Jilberto and André Mommen

6 **Financial Development and Economic Growth**
   Theory and experiences from developing countries
   Edited by Niels Hermes and Robert Lensink

7 **The South African Economy**
   Macroeconomic prospects for the medium term
   Finn Tarp and Peter Brixen

8 **Public Sector Pay and Adjustment**
   Lessons from five countries
   Edited by Christopher Colclough

9 **Europe and Economic Reform in Africa**
   Structural adjustment and economic diplomacy
   Obed O. Mailafia

10 **Post-apartheid Southern Africa**
    Economic challenges and policies for the future
    Edited by Lennart Petersson

11 **Financial Integration and Development**
    Liberalization and reform in sub-Saharan Africa
    Ernest Aryeetey and Machiko Nissanke

12 **Regionalization and Globalization in the Modern World Economy**
Perspectives on the Third World and transitional economies
Edited by Alex F. Fernández Jilberto and André Mommen

13 **The African Economy**
Policy, institutions and the future
Steve Kayizzi-Mugerwa

14 **Recovery from Armed Conflict in Developing Countries**
Edited by Geoff Harris

15 **Small Enterprises and Economic Development**
The dynamics of micro and small enterprises
Carl Liedholm and Donald C. Mead

16 **The World Bank**
New agendas in a changing world
Michelle Miller-Adams

17 **Development Policy in the Twenty-First Century**
Beyond the post-Washington consensus
Edited by Ben Fine, Costas Lapavitsas and Jonathan Pincus

18 **State-Owned Enterprises in the Middle East and North Africa**
Privatization, performance and reform
Edited by Merih Celasun

19 **Finance and Competitiveness in Developing Countries**
Edited by José María Fanelli and Rohinton Medhora

20 **Contemporary Issues in Development Economics**
Edited by B. N. Ghosh

21 **Mexico Beyond NAFTA**
Edited by Martín Puchet Anyul and Lionello F. Punzo

22 **Economies in Transition**
A guide to China, Cuba, Mongolia, North Korea and Vietnam at the turn of the twenty-first century
Ian Jeffries

23 **Population, Economic Growth and Agriculture in Less Developed Countries**
Nadia Cuffaro

24 **From Crisis to Growth in Africa?**
Edited by Mats Lundal

25 **The Macroeconomics of Monetary Union**
An analysis of the CFA franc zone
David Fielding

26 **Endogenous Development**
Networking, innovation, institutions and cities
Antonio Vasquez-Barquero

27 **Labour Relations in Development**
Edited by Alex E. Fernández Jilberto and Marieke Riethof

28 **Globalization, Marginalization and Development**
Edited by S. Mansoob Murshed

29 **Programme Aid and Development**
Beyond conditionality
Howard White and Geske Dijkstra

30 **Competitiveness Strategy in Developing Countries**
A manual for policy analysis
Edited by Ganeshan Wignaraja

31 **The African Manufacturing Firm**
An analysis based on firm surveys in sub-Saharan Africa
Dipak Mazumdar and Ata Mazaheri

32 **Trade Policy, Growth and Poverty in Asian Developing Countries**
Edited by Kishor Sharma

33 **International Competitiveness, Investment and Finance**
A case study of India
Edited by A. Ganesh Kumar, Kunal Sen and Rajendra R. Vaidya

34 **The Pattern of Aid Giving**
The impact of good governance on development assistance
Eric Neumayer

35 **New International Poverty Reduction Strategies**
Edited by Jean-Pierre Cling, Mireille Razafindrakoto and François Roubaud

36 **Targeting Development**
Critical perspectives on the millennium development goals
Edited by Richard Black and Howard White

37 **Essays on Balance of Payments Constrained Growth**
Theory and evidence
Edited by J. S. L. McCombie and A. P. Thirlwall

38 **The Private Sector After Communism**
New entrepreneurial firms in transition economies
Jan Winiecki, Vladimir Benacek and Mihaly Laki

39 **Information Technology and Development**
A new paradigm for delivering the Internet to rural areas in developing countries
Jeffrey James

40 **The Economics of Palestine**
Economic policy and institutional reform for a viable Palestine State
Edited by David Cobham and Nu'man Kanafani

41 **Development Dilemmas**
The methods and political ethics of growth policy
Melvin Ayogu and Don Ross

42 **Rural Livelihoods and Poverty Reduction Policies**
Edited by Frank Ellis and H. Ade Freeman

43 **Beyond Market-Driven Development**
Drawing on the experience of Asia and Latin America
Edited by Makoto Noguchi and Costas Lapavitsas

44 **The Political Economy of Reform Failure**
Edited by Mats Lundahl and Michael L. Wyzan

45 **Overcoming Inequality in Latin America**
Issues and challenges for the 21st Century
Edited by Ricardo Gottschalk and Patricia Justino

46 **Trade, Growth and Inequality in the Era of Globalization**
Edited by Kishor Sharma and Oliver Morrissey

46 **Microfinance**
Perils and prospects
Edited by Jude L. Fernando

Microfinance
Perils and prospects

Edited by Jude L. Fernando

LONDON AND NEW YORK

First published 2006
by Routledge
2 Park Square, Milton Park, Abingdon, Oxon OX14 4RN

Simultaneously published in the USA and Canada
by Routledge
270 Madison Ave, New York, NY 10016

Routledge is an imprint of the Taylor & Francis Group

© 2006 editorial matter and selection, Jude L. Fernando; individual chapters the contributors

Typeset in Baskerville by Wearset Ltd, Boldon, Tyne and Wear
Printed and bound in Great Britain by MPG Books Ltd, Bodmin

All rights reserved. No part of this book may be reprinted or reproduced or utilized in any form or by any electronic, mechanical, or other means, now known or hereafter invented, including photocopying and recording, or in any information storage or retrieval system, without permission in writing from the publishers.

British Library Cataloguing in Publication Data
A catalogue record for this book is available from the British Library

Library of Congress Cataloging in Publication Data
A catalog record for this book has been requested

ISBN 0-415-32874-8

Contents

List of contributors xi
Acknowledgements xiii

1 **Introduction. Microcredit and empowerment of women: blurring the boundary between development and capitalism** 1
JUDE L. FERNANDO

2 **The global political economy of microfinance and poverty reduction: locating local 'livelihoods' in political analysis** 43
HELOISE WEBER

3 **Disciplining the developmental subject: neoliberal power and governance through microcredit** 64
MORGAN BRIGG

4 **Social capital, microfinance, and the politics of development** 89
KATHARINE N. RANKIN

5 **Rebuilding social capital in post-conflict regions: women's village banking in Ayacucho, Peru and in Highland Guatemala** 112
DENISE HUMPHREYS BEBBINGTON AND ARELIS GÓMEZ

6 **"Banking on culture": microcredit as incentive for cultural conservation in Mali** 133
TARA F. DEUBEL

7	**The darker side to microfinance: evidence from Cajamarca, Peru**	154
	KATIE WRIGHT	
8	**Banking on bananas, crediting crafts: financing women's work in the Philippine Cordillera**	172
	LYNNE MILGRAM	
9	**Microcredit and empowerment of women: visibility without power**	187
	JUDE L. FERNANDO	
	Index	239

Contributors

Morgan Brigg has recently submitted his doctoral thesis at the School of Political Science and International Studies, University of Queensland, Brisbane, Australia. His research interests include the cultural politics of development and conflict resolution. He works as a mediator and his current research pursues ways of reconfiguring knowledge production through cultural difference. His publications include "Post-Development, Foucault, and the Colonization Metaphor" *Third World Quarterly* 23 (3): 421–36 (2002) and "Mediation, Power, and Cultural Difference" *Conflict Resolution Quarterly* 20 (3): 287–306 (2003).

Tara F. Deubel is a doctoral candidate in sociocultural anthropology at the University of Arizona, where she received a master's concentrating in applied anthropology. Her research interests include sustainable development, human rights, literacy, and education with a regional focus in North and West Africa. She has conducted field research on cultural heritage conservation and microcredit in Mali and rural livelihood security in Guinea. Her doctoral research will involve documenting oral traditions to develop community-based literacy materials in Morocco.

Jude L. Fernando teaches at the Department of International Development Environment and Community at the Clark University, Worcester, Massachusetts. His research interests include political economy, international development, NGOs, sustainable development, gender, and human rights in South Asia. Among his publications are published three anthologies by Sage: *Rethinking Sustainable Development, Children's Rights*, and *NGOs, Charity and Empowerment*. He is currently completing a manuscript entitled "A Political Economy of Nongovernmental Organizations: Modernizing Postmodernity" (Pluto Press, UK 2005).

Arelis Gómez has devoted her career to small and microenterprise development, particularly as a finance specialist. Her work has involved extensive exposure to microenterprise lending organizations in Latin America, Africa and Asia. She has worked as an independent consultant

xii *Contributors*

on several short-term assignments devoted to best practices in microenterprise finance. She played a major role in the FINCA village banking program development worldwide, both in the design and the implementation of the financial and administrative strategies. She has also provided services on the microfinance components of the USAID Rural Finance and Income Generation Activities project in Guatemala and the USAID Productivity and Policy Enhancement Project in Honduras.

Denise Humphreys Bebbington is currently the Coordinator for the Latin America Program of the Global Greengrants Fund. She is a founding member and researcher of the Institute for Social and Environmental Transition and has worked on Latin America development issues and on staff of the Inter-American Foundation and Catholic Relief Services. She is presently an Honorary Research Fellow at the Institute for Development, Policy and Management at the University of Manchester.

Lynne Milgram is Associate Professor in the Faculty of Liberal Studies, Ontario College of Art and Design, Toronto. Her research on gender and development in the Philippines analyzes the cultural politics of social change with regard to fair trade, women and crafts, and microfinance. She has co-edited, with Kimberly M. Grimes, *Artisans and Cooperatives: Developing Alternative Trade for the Global Economy* (2000), Tucson, AZ: University of Arizona Press. Her current research explores Philippine women's engagement in the global trade of secondhand clothing.

Katharine N. Rankin is Associate Professor of Geography and Planning at the University of Toronto. Her broad research interests include politics of development, comparative market regulation, planning history and theory, South Asia. She is the author of *The Cultural Politics of Markets: Economic Liberalization and Social Change in Nepal* (2004, Pluto Press and University of Toronto Press) and related journal articles.

Heloise Weber is Lecturer in the Department of International Relations and Politics, University of Sussex. Her research interests are in global political economy, politics of development, development theory, and international political theory. She is currently working on a Monograph on "Global political economy of microcredit."

Katie Wright is a postdoctoral fellow at the department of Economics and International Development, University of Bath, UK. Her interests include: culture and society, microfinance, poverty alleviation, and international migration particularly in relation to Latin America. She is an associate of the ESRC research group "Wellbeing in Developing Countries." http://staff.bath.ac.uk/ecskewk.e.wright-revolledo@bath.ac.uk

Acknowledgements

I would like to thank many people for their assistance and encouragement that made this volume possible. Without the following friends and colleagues, collective and individual thinking about microcredit in the articles included in this volume, would not have evolved into their present form. I am grateful to Caren Zimmerman, Simon Batterburry, Ian Barnes, Dinna Siddiqui, Katharine Rankin, and Lynne Milgram for the assistance they provided me, to articulate the conceptual orientation of microcredit in this volume and reviewing its articles. The insights in this volume also reflect the "random" conversations I had with David Lewis, Heloise Weber, Sangeta Kamaat, Bishawapriya Sanyal, Stuart Rutherford, Amy Mosher, Biju Mathews, Depapriya Bhattacharya, Kushi Kabeer, Kazi Farooq Ahmed, Fr. R. W. Tim, Fr. E. Homric, Stewart Rutherford, David Ludden, Alan Heston, Neil Smith and Lamia Karim. I am grateful to them all.

I would also like to express my sincere appreciation of the valuable comments received from two anonymous reviewers in two different stages of preparing this volume. I am extremely indebted to the contributors to this volume, who patiently dealt with revisions of their individual chapters. I also commend their courage to provide critical accounts of microcredit at a time when such thinking is not so politically fashionable within, and outside the academy. Finally, I am also grateful to many individuals in Mudupur, Bangladesh who assisted me in many ways, to engage critically with microcredit. I hope this will benefit those who consider themselves as politically engaged scholars and practitioners concerned with development and social change.

The editor and publishers wish to thank the following for permission to reproduce previously published material in this book:

Rankin, Katharine N. 2002. "Social Capital, Microfinance, and the Politics of Development," *Journal of Feminist Economics* 8 (1): 1–24. http://www.tandf.co.uk/journals

Chapter 3 has been revised from, "Empowering NGOs: The Microcredit Movement Through Foucault's Notion of Dispontif," originally published in *Alternatives: Global, Local, Political*, 26 (3) July–September 2001. Copyright by Lynne Rienner Publishers. Used with permission.

Chapter 8 was originally published in *Atlantis: A Women's Studies Journal*, 26 (2) spring 2002 (www.msvu.ca/atlantis).

Jude L. Fernando
IDCE, Clark University
20 September 2004

1 Introduction

Microcredit and empowerment of women: blurring the boundary between development and capitalism

Jude L. Fernando

In contrast to Mohammad Yunus, the founder of Grameen Bank, who uses tiny amounts of capital to make a difference in the face of dire poverty, Colin Powell, the U.S. Secretary of the State wants to mobilize "the blessings of Americans' abundant wealth and time" to help the poor and disadvantaged.[1]

By proclaiming 2005 as the International Year of Microcredit, the General Assembly of the United Nations requested that "the Year's observance be a special occasion for giving impetus to microcredit programs throughout the world."[2] This was in response to microcredit occupying a commanding position in economic development and purposive social change as evidenced by its continuing growth terms of volume, geographical coverage, and influence over social, economic and political processes. The 1997 Micro Credit Summit, held in Washington DC, adopted a resolution to reach 100 million of the world's poorest families, especially the women of families with credit for self-employment, and other financial and business services by the year 2005. Globally, the poorest of the poor include 1.2 billion people who live on less than US$1 a day, adjusted for purchasing power parity. As of December 2002, microcredit institutions had reached, approximately, over 67 million clients, 41,594,778 of whom were among the poorest when obtaining their first loan. Of these clients, 79 percent, that is 37,677,0880 in numbers, were women. Assuming an average of five persons per family, by the end of the year 2002, microcredit had reached 41.6 million clients and impacted 208 million family members.[3] In addition, according to the United Nations, in 1998 there were about 3000 microcredit institutions in developing countries.[4] In order to reach 100 million of the poorest by 2005, the movement will need to have a 38 percent growth rate per year. Currently, the growth rate averages just under 37 percent per year.[5] Its coverage has included both developing and developed countries and recorded the highest expansion in regions where the poorest countries are located (see Table 1.1).

According to its proponents, the goals of microcredit extend well beyond the alleviation of poverty. To some, microcredit promises to achieve what previous models of development could not attain. According to Michael Chu, President, ACCION International:

> [t]he confirmation that micro enterprise credit can be managed to achieve economic viability is an accomplishment of revolutionary proportions. This permits an activity motivated by social impact to break free of the structural paradox of most humanitarian efforts, in which the cost of reaching every additional person brings the program closer to its economic limits. Successful microfinance, on the contrary, becomes more self-sufficient with scale.[7]

Others envisage microcredit credit as a social movement, which is likely to mark an important turning point in human history. The Council of Heads of State and Government at the Summit asserted:

> We believe that if we all work together this campaign will become one of the great new chapters in human history and will allow tens of millions of people to free themselves and their families from the vicious cycle of poverty.[8]

The United Nations – General Assembly Resolution 52/194, its recommendations for the rest of the First United Nations Decade for the Eradication of Poverty (1997–2006) – declared that "microcredit programmes have proved to be an effective tool in freeing people from the bondage of poverty, and have led to their increasing participation in the mainstream economic and political process of society."[9] Such claims have been advanced on the grounds that microcredit credit can not only generate financially sustainable lending institutions for poverty alleviation, it can, furthermore, facilitate institutional relations necessary for broad-based social change. In fact, microcredit is a source of empowerment. To some, the term empowerment implies social transformation to be more radical than the conventional term "revolution." The notion of "microcredit revolution" implies that it is a social movement not only superior to but also potentially complimentary to other social movements concerned with social change.[10] The global spread of microcredit movements also makes it a fruitful vantage point to examine contemporary trajectories of social change, which might provide some useful insights to current debates in social theory regarding social change.

Scholarly interest in microcredit continues to proliferate in every discipline, permeating not only those directly concerned with development, but also those concerned with international law, human rights etc.

Table 1.1 Regional breakdown of data[6]

Region	Number of programs reporting	Number of current clients reported, 2001	Number of current clients reported, 2002	Number of poorest clients reported, 2001	Number of poorest clients reported, 2002	Number of poorest women clients reported, 2001	Number of poorest women clients reported, 2002
Africa	811	4,608,407	5,761,763	3,461,632	4,202,280	2,362,172	2,611,650
Asia	1,377	47,891,977	59,632,069	22,340,073	18,098,695	18,098,695	29,423,010
Latin America and Caribbean	246	1,973,357	1,942,005	927,830	643,547	643,547	589,405
Middle East	23	67,770	83,047	36,293	17,324	17,324	12,282
Developing World totals	2,457	54,541,506	67,418,963	26,765,828	21,212,738	21,121,738	32,636,347
North America	47	263,395	47,017	22,469	16,628	16,628	12,450
Europe and NIS	68	127,334	140,100	51,764	31,388	31,338	28,283
Industrialized World totals	115	390,729	187,117	74,233	48,016	48,016	40,733
Global totals	2,572	54,932,235	67,606,080	41,594,778	21,169,754	21,169,754	32,677,080

Perhaps due to the urgency of "doing something good" to address the immediate policy issues in development, current research appears to be less interested in dealing with the *impact* of microcredit on other broader processes of social change. In fact, microcredit has remained somewhat insulated from critical scholarly inquiry and the few existing critical analyses have not been politically popular within academic and policy circles. Harsh critics of claims about microcredit are silenced by labeling them as being idealistic, impatient for results, and as lacking concern for the immediate needs of the poor. These claims imply that there are no other viable alternatives to microcredit credit for helping the poor. Microcredit works!

The methodological and conceptual issues in current studies on microcredit cast serious doubts on the claims about its impact on social transformation. Microcredit has indeed occupied an important place in social development for many centuries. We know little about how credit systems have historically shaped the broader trajectories of social change, nor do we have a great deal of information about their uniqueness today. The most common explanations for the popularity of microcredit emphasize previous development failures on the part of the state and the proven successes of non-governmental organizations (NGOs) to overcome those limitations. Such analyses simply take the claims about the failures by the state and successes of NGOs for granted, rather than grounding them in an adequate theorizing of comparative roles of the state and NGOs in social change.

Most of the positive claims about microcredit credit are based on quantitative indicators, such as number of borrowers and lending institutions, and loan repayment rates. Outcomes measured by these indicators do not reveal the institutional processes through which such outcomes are achieved. Apart from a few notable exceptions, the existing studies have overlooked the possibility that the high repayment rates consistently maintained by women borrowers have not resulted in any changes in the institutions that are oppressive to them.[11] We understand little about how discourse of empowerment through microcredit frames, and is framed by, political and economic structures, and their consequences to women. While microcredit is touted as a global movement, current studies have failed to explore its impact on social, economic, and political processes beyond its immediate project environments: what are the consequences of microcredit on social transformative capacities of NGOs, state formation, gender and development debates, and trajectories of social change in general? This volume is a modest attempt to fill these gaps.

The chapters included in this volume are unique in several respects. Drawing from interdisciplinary theoretical positions and comparative geographical locations, these articles are primarily concerned with understanding the implications of microcredit in the broader processes of social, economic, and political changes. By locating the microcredit in these processes, these chapters examine its impact on empowerment of women, social transformative potentials of NGOs, state formation, and contemporary trajectories of social change mediated by neoliberalism. Their analyses are marked by two important points of departure. First, they recognize that the impact of microcredit on empowerment is diffused well beyond its immediate goals so much so that, "through metaphors of individual and society, it [microcredit] influences the way people construct themselves, their conduct and their relations as free individuals."[12] The discourse of empowerment through microcredit is not simply "purely resources and argument, but resources that may be politically invested by social actors (such as NGOs) to particular ends."[13] A second point of departure is that microcredit as a policy instrument in development stimulates action of multiplicity of institutions through objectification of their subjects and in the process it acquires "seemingly tangible existence and legitimacy."[14] Viewing policy instruments simply as rational and technical instruments with specific goals often overlooks and obscures the fact that "objectification of policy often proceed hand in hand with the objectification of the subject of policy."[15] Consequently, we may never understand how the language of policy cloaks "policy with symbols and trappings of political power" that can be impediments for achieving their intended policy goals.[16]

In order to address these concerns, the contributions to this volume are concerned with the historical processes through which the discourse of empowerment through microcredit evolved as a pivotal social movement in the twenty-first century and how its normative claims frame and represent gender inequalities and empowerment. Rather than viewing this discourse simply as responses to failures of past development policies, this volume is also concerned with exploring how its representation of past failures, and remedies it offers, frame and are framed by structures of political and economic power, and their consequences for poor women. Such an approach will not only provide better insights and more systematic explanations to the current claims about microcredit, but will also prove to be a useful way of understanding the contemporary trajectories of social change.

This volume offers a critical evaluation of the now well-developed field of microfinance, especially in relation to its claims about women's empowerment and their implications for gender and development debates. Several contributors argue that microfinance programs have created opportunities for women's empowerment because they combine access to material resources with strategies for building solidarity and expanding women's agency in the development process. These authors locate their discussion of empowerment not only in relation to interpretations within feminist and development discourses, but also in relation to specific cultural–political contexts of their research. Other authors in this volume present a more skeptical view of the relationship between microfinance and women's empowerment. Their criticism proceeds at two spatial scales of analysis. On the one hand, they examine microfinance in relation to economic globalization and the consolidation of neoliberal capitalism; from this perspective, the "empowerment" in microfinance may be viewed as a governmental strategy consistent with cuts in welfare spending and a market-led approach to development more generally. On the other hand, the skeptics reject claims about women's empowerment on the basis of rich ethnographic analyses of the social and institutional processes through which microfinance programs may entrench, rather than challenge, existing social hierarchies.

The contributors to this volume committed to presenting a selection of fine-grained ethnographic "thick descriptions" of the social processes through which microfinance programs articulate with their local cultural contexts within the larger context of neoliberal political economy. Unlike so many of the academic writings on microfinance, this volume is not a collection of impact studies. Instead of focusing on the conventional quantifiable indicators of program evaluation, such as repayment rates, the contributors analyze the institutional and social processes through which such outcomes are achieved, and their implications for women's empowerment. Concentrating primarily on the NGO sector, the chapters draw on long-term field research in South Asia, Latin America, Africa and the Pacific.

The authors in this volume argue that the increasing involvement of women in staffing, managing, and patronizing microfinance programs has expanded women's agency in the development process. These articles note the role of microfinance, as a new orthodoxy in development, in placing debates about the institutional arrangements for improving the social, economic, and political status of women at the center of the development agenda. In addition to documenting the significant achievements of microfinance programs in terms of geographical coverage, enrolment, repayment rates, and women's enterprise, the contributors also contend that in certain cultural political contexts, microfinance can facilitate social conditions for empowering women. In so doing, they highlight the cross-cultural diversity in interpreting the notion of empowerment itself.

This volume provides a much-needed historical, political, and economic dimension to the current knowledge on microfinance. Collectively, the contributors chart the relationship between the prevailing popularity of microfinance and the consolidation of neoliberal economic ideology worldwide. They demonstrate how microfinance, as a market-friendly approach to development, coincides with the global trend toward diminishing the role of the state in economic development, basic healthcare, education, and welfare. In light of these macroeconomic trends, the contributors analyze the historical confluence of microfinance with feminist notions of empowerment. They note the possibility for women's empowerment to serve an ideological function in the current global economic conjuncture, as well as the programmatic role of microfinance in marrying notions of empowerment with market-led development.

The claims in this volume also focus on empirical analyses of the experience of microfinance in women's everyday lives, but reject the connection between microfinance and women's empowerment so often imputed in the literature. These chapters do not, for example, accept the prevailing view that indicators of the "success" of microfinance programs (e.g. high repayment rates and enhanced productivity of women borrowers) can serve as a proxy for women's empowerment. Instead, they consider microfinance as a social process in articulation with local cultural economies and global political–economic trends. In so doing these chapters stress the processes through which financial services are delivered, utilized, and repaid, and the institutional and power relations shaping and resulting from such processes. The contributors to this volume argue that microfinance, in the contexts they address, has failed to fulfill its promise for women's empowerment. On the contrary, by appropriating the feminist language of empowerment, it disciplines poor women to manage their own welfare through active participation in the liberal economy. The pressure exerted on women to repay their loans, for example, is shown to entrench – not challenge – existing social hierarchies along lines of caste, class, ethnicity, and gender.

This volume offers regional, cultural, and other explanations for the variable assessments of microfinance and empowerment. It then engages the example of microfinance to explore how gender hierarchies get institutionalized in development, and notes the implications of this argument for debates about empowerment. It argues that the fine-grained ethnographic analyses, contained within it, demonstrate foremost the importance of viewing empowerment from the standpoint of those in subordinate social positions. While acknowledging the contingencies of pursuing radical social goals within the constraints of existing institutions, the volume concludes by offering programmatic and procedural guidelines for designing microfinance programs – and practicing a kind of development more generally – that could engage women's solidarity to challenge existing patterns of subordination.

The introduction and majority of the chapters in this volume are critical of microcredit taken from the perspective of empowerment. Their intention is to surface and confront it squarely in consideration of alternative social transformative possibilities for the future, however remote they may seem today. Hence, the critical claims by the contributors do not necessarily imply that the possibility of microcredit as a source of empowerment has been exhausted, and its promise to offer an opportunity to marginalized groups to advance counter hegemonic agendas has ended. For example, C. L. R. James in his *Black Jacobins*[17] shows the ways in which slaves on sugar plantations seized upon Enlightenment discourses as the basis of their struggles for emancipation. Indeed, the notions of empowerment as promised by microcredit could do the same. The contributors to this volume are interested not only in exploring why such impact is not visible in the case of projects concerned with empowerment through microcredit, but also in exploring strategies to make it happen because they believe the political economy of microcredit is underpinned by diverse and contradictory ideological and institutional positions.

The remainder of the introduction broadly outlines the context in which the implications of microcredit are discussed by different authors and their main issues and claims. Its emphasis, however, is on the ideologies, institutions, and development strategies that have shaped the current discourse of empowerment. The unifying theme of its analysis is the positioning of the discourse of empowerment through microcredit in the historical interplay between capitalism, culture, and development. I believe that such a positioning will provide a fruitful perspective to explore the consequences of microcredit for the empowerment of women, state formation, and the social transformative potential of NGOs. By raising more issues than answers, this volume seeks to chart new territories for anthropological and sociological inquiries on role of gender relations in development

Development, capitalism and regimes of credit

For many centuries credit has been used as a means of wealth accumulation, social development, and improvement of the social well-being of the poor. For example, rulers of pre-colonial South Asia used credit as a means of wealth accumulation, and for securing popular legitimacy. Evidence of the use of language such as self-sufficiency, empowerment etc., in programs involving credit, is found in social development programs carried out by nineteenth century Christian missionary agencies. Such programs proved to be a useful means for ensuring the reproduction and sustainability of Christian communities. They served as relief measures for those ostracized after their conversion to Christianity, and relieved them from informal moneylenders and landlords. Missionary agencies also held the belief that improving the entitlement stock of the poor (perhaps anticipating Amartya Sen, who has immortalized the analysis of entitlement) through increases in income was an essential perquisite to minimize their suffering due to famine and drought. The improvement of people's material standards was an integral part of the missionary worldview where spiritual and material well-being were inseparable from each other, and one was expected to be a reflection of the other. In Bangladesh, the credit programs, which were initiated by the mission agencies in the early part of the twentieth century, continue to survive among Christian and non-Christian groups alike.

Capital shortages and chronic indebtedness were matters of serious concern to the British colonial administration in India. Its Central

Banking Inquiry Committee Report of 1930 made several attempts to legislate limits to the "rapaciousness of moneylenders and loss of mortgaged land by small farmers."[18] After independence, in response to the All Indian Credit Survey of 1952, the Indian government launched extensive credit expansion programs. Since then credit has been occupying an important place in every national development plan in all developing countries, and shapes political processes in these countries. Until the end of the Cold War, the failures of these programs were explained in terms of market failure and state failures. The market failures are explained in reference to the culture of market relations, and state failures are explained in relation to political and economic interventions by the state in developing countries.

In the aftermath of the Cold War, particularly in light of the Grameen Bank's experience, there emerged renewed interest in microcredit and the reconfiguration of its role in development and social transformation. As opposed to conventional economic thinking of credit markets in developing countries, cultural variables are now no longer considered significant reasons for market failures. Rather, cultural elements are now considered as highly reliable sources for ensuring the efficiency of credit markets and a means of achieving its broader social goals. Accordingly, the fundamental reasons for continuing poverty lay not with the poor, the social environments within which they live, nor the capitalist system, rather, they were attributed to the failure of development theorists and practitioners to reach the poor, understand their environments, and to recognize their potential to be active participants in the economy. In this regard, microcredit is a promising policy, provided it is institutionalized in a poor-friendly manner.

F. J. A. Bouman's 1990 book describes microcredit credit as "small, short and unsecured" – microfinance is the provision of very small loans that are repaid within short time periods, and is essentially used by low income individuals and households who have few assets that can be used as collateral.[19] Historically, there has been a great deal of diversity in credit systems in terms of their orientation, functions, embeddedness, scales, social meanings, and the institutions and ideologies that governed them. Bouman notes that many of the current microfinance practices, in fact, derive from community-based mutual credit transactions, which were peer-driven, based on trust, and on non-collateral borrowing and repayment. Transactional (e.g. moneylenders), mutual (e.g. ROSCAs), or personal (e.g. friends and neighbors) credit suppliers have always lent to the poor, providing the right quality and quantity of credit at the right time and place, to low-income households.

The historical continuity of the remarkable similarities, continuities, and discontinuities of credit models suggests that the uniqueness of a given program of credit at a given moment can best be defined by the context within which it evolved and is embedded. Given the existence of many different types of microcredit programs in most given contexts, the notion of "credit regime" is a useful analytical category. It implies the coexistence of diverse systems of credit in a given setting. Within a regime, some models have been more influential than others in terms of their scope of operations, and have gained popular and institutional recognition. Then, how does one system of credit become more influential, hegemonic if you like, than others? Systematic analysis of social and economic processes, which define the context in which such hegemonic formations emerge and function, is crucial not only for an understanding of the uniqueness of a given microcredit program, and but also to evaluate its wider impacts.

Indeed, experiences of microcredit in Bangladesh played a pivotal role towards gaining its current worldwide popularity. At the time when Grameen-type credit evolved into an influential model in international development, Bangladesh was a painful testimony to the impasse in development theory and practice. The pressures to find ways out of it were so intense that calls for the abandonment of "development" or liberating development from its roots in an enlightenment project of modernity, gained considerable academic reception by post-developmentalists, post-colonialist and post-structucturalists.[20] According to the Mexican activist Gustavo Esteva, "[i]n Mexico, you must be either numb or very rich to notice that development stinks. The damage to persons, the corruption of politics, and the degradation of nature, which recently were only implicit in development, can now be seen, touched and smelled."[21]

Although calls for an abandonment of development have not carried any influence as a counter-hegemonic force or translated into radical change in mainstream development policy, their challenges have had significant influence on development thinking. One important challenge is that development now has to accommodate the demands of multiple interest groups (e.g. feminists, environmentalists, human rights activists, cultural relativists, indigenous communities etc.), collectively known as new social movements. Microcredit is considered as an important instrument of social mobilizational efforts and sustenance of these movements. These movements are organized around multiple identities and demands. Their "democratic struggles encompass not just political system but also future of development and eradication of social inequalities."[22] These movements combined democracy and development as inseparable goals and the processes of achieving them are not "homogeneous, but rather internally discontinuous and uneven: different spheres and dimensions have distinct rhythms of change leading some analysts to argue that these processes are fluid and inherently disjunctive."[23] They are organized around everyday "practices and interpersonal networks of everyday life" that "sustains them across mobilizational ebbs and flows that infuse new cultural meanings to political practices and collective action."[24] They give voice to "subaltern" groups whose voices have been marginalized by the political processes of modernity and mobilize them towards social change within paradigms that "cannot be strictly defined within the paradigms of Western modernity."[25] These movements also "configure new interpersonal, interregional, and political and cultural linkages with other movements" and foster "alternative modernities."[26] Microcredit as a social movement attempts to redefine the trajectory of development by privileging the empowerment of women in it, which entails the enactment of cultural politics of empowerment, which, as this volume will show, can help shed light on the economic, cultural, and political consequences of microcredit not only for women, but also for other social struggles over social change. However, it is important to recognize several limitations of the cultural logic of social movements theories in light of their impact on development and capacity to address the concerns raised in this volume.

By emphasizing the textuality of development, and its representation, power, and dominance, post-structuralist and post-developmentalists conceptualize development as a discourse that has its origins in the West. Historically, its purpose is to dominate the so-called Third World or transform it according to the image of the West. However, the discursive idealism in the category of development discourse is self-contradictory. These theorists have overlooked the fact that "development has a mode of thought has contained critical versions," that they are evidence of a highly contested nature of development "which stems from various opposition to" dominant paradigms of development.[27] As Maya Unnithan and Kavita Srivastava have documented, such self-constructed notions of development have "difficulty in encompassing the wide range of responses and agendas among Indian women working in and for development."[28] Discourse analysis provides an artificial unity and homogeneity to development by bringing conflicting positions of development into one whole in the name of representation, power, and dominance. According to Arif Dirlik, "intended as a critique of ideology, it becomes itself an ideological articulation of contemporary situation."[29]

Post-structuralist positions on development are derived from simplistic assumptions about the distinctions between West and Third World, culture and economy, and fail to explain how these diverse positions are produced and coordinated by the expansionary logic of capital. The descriptors of post-structuralism such as "repudiation of unified subjectivity and binaries in favor of 'hybridity' and 'multiculturalism' and in its affirmation of fluid and transportable subject positions, reads very much like life under global capitalism that they failed to comprehend and theorize."[30] The conceptualizations of development by Arturo Escobar and James Ferguson that privilege dominance, power, and representation and those of Amartya Sen,[31] emphasize that freedom, opportunities, and capabilities are important means and ends of development and have provided numerous possibilities for neoliberal institutions to play a hegemonic role in framing the discourse of empowerment through microcredit in ways counter productive to its goals: their formulations have the *effect* of simultaneously "provincializing" and politically marginalizing the centrality of class relations in our understandings of economic and social inequalities and social mobilizations against them.

Under these influences, the current discourses of gender and empowerment, by virtue of their failure to recognize the multiplicity of voices in development and by privileging dominance, power, and freedom as opposed to the logic of capital, remain rather feeble and restricted in their potential to address gender inequalities. They have imprisoned the scope of empowerment through microcredit within the narrow confines of neoliberalism, partly because their formulations are not grounded in a theory of social change that is radically different from that of the capitalist modernity.[32] The main problem of the current analysis of empowerment projects, hence, can be "summarized as a problem akin to liberating discourse(s) that divorces itself from the material conditions of life, in this case global capitalism as the foundational principle of contemporary global society."[33]

Capitalism is growth oriented via the expansion of surplus value. Expansion via the accumulation of surplus is a dynamic and crisis-ridden process that is manifested in multiplicity of social relations. Crisis is internal to the logic of capital itself. At a more fundamental level, crisis "flows from a single barrier defined by the unequal relationship between the workers as producer and the worker as consumer."[34] In order to produce surplus value, workers must produce more than they consume and the capitalist class cannot consume the entire surplus, since a portion of the surplus value needs to be reinvested. If both the capitalist and working classes together cannot provide an adequate market, "then even though exploitation has taken place and surplus value has been extracted, that value cannot be realized."[35] According to Marx, "the more productivity develops, the more it comes into conflict with the narrow basis on which the relations of consumption rest."[36] As Michael Hardt and Antonio Negri note, "[t]he restrictive character of capital constitute an ever present point of crisis that pertains to the essence of capital itself: Constant expansion is always inadequate but nonetheless necessary attempt to quench an attempt to insatiable thirst."[37] In order to overcome these barriers, capitalism requires sufficient dynamism to transform relations and forces of production. This also means it cannot function within a fixed territory and population, but always overflows its border and internalizes new spaces. As Marx explained, "[t]he tendency to create a global market is directly given in the concept of capital itself. Every limit appears as a barrier to overcome."[38] Capital, therefore, must penetrate into every society in order to exercise not only "open exchange with non-capitalist societies or appropriate their wealth; it must also transform them into capitalist societies themselves."[39]

The expansionary logic of capitalism does not transform the world into a homogenous entity, rather it configures, disciplines, and manages the highly diverse, and fluid social relations in ways conducive to the realization of surplus value. Surplus value, although measured in monetary terms, is a commodified social relation, realization of which has been spatially and time specific. Rudolf Hilferding, while referring to the geographical aspects of capital, particularly in the context of finance capital, used the notion of "export of capital" to refer to "export of value which is intended to breed surplus value."[40] Hardt and Negari have correctly interpreted its meaning by asserting that "[w]hat is exported is a relation, a social form that will breed and replicate itself. Like a missionary or vampire, capital touches what is foreign and makes it proper."[41] "Making it proper" means the configuration and disciplining of social and economic diversity of the world in ways conducive to the realization of surplus value, rather than an attempt to transform the world as a homogeneous entity. To do so is contrary to the logic of capital itself because reproduction of diversity and difference is internal to the self-realization of capital.

Capitalism's successes in securing conditions for its expansion through changes in structures of production and their representation depends on the ways in which it manages its dual crises, i.e. accumulation and crisis of legitimization. The "crisis of accumulation" refers to barriers to the expansion of surplus value due to the increasing costs of production, resources, and the technological limits to production, while "crisis of legitimization" describes the social, economic, and political crises generated by continuing accumulation that limits its expansion. The continuing reproduction of capital rests on the simultaneous management of the two crises. At the most fundamental level, this requires changes in the institutions that give meaning to these crises and solutions to them. However, institutional change under capitalist development is not an easy task as there are standard formulae to guide them. The crisis of accumulation and legitimization functions as a vicious circle. Often, the policies used to resolve one crisis, undermine the effectiveness of another. A given ideology, and institutional forms that were conducive to its reproductive needs of capital at one time, can be an obstacle for it at another time. In other words, once institutions and the discourse that frame their meanings get rooted in the society, the given meaning(s) of development or relations between state and society do not immediately change in response to the new conditions necessary for reproductive needs of capital.

Continuing reproduction of spatially uneven development globally is simultaneously a product of and a barrier to capitalist expansion.[42] Unevenness is manifested in diverse social and institutional formations, and most importantly in the worldwide differences between state formations. Hierarchy of nation states in terms of their control over global economy and political power is one important institutional manifestation of the uneven development of capitalism.[43] In the final analysis the popular legitimacy of the state lies in how it manages the tensions between popular and particular interests of the society, which in turn determines the *nature* and *form* of the state. These tensions take a variety of forms due to the spatially uneven development of capitalism and how they are managed by different states and non-state institutions in them.[44] These management strategies in turn impact the outcomes of microcredit programs. The bipolar division of the world's state system during the Cold War period was a manifestation of how different states and ideological formations came to terms with the spatially uneven development of capitalism.

Development, given its universal goals, and being a project of the nation state was "up for grabs" by states divided into two ideological blocs. For example, the global initiative taken by the United States under President Harry Truman, to spread development in developing countries, had overlapping goals. On the one hand, development was used to secure conditions for reproduction of capital under North American hegemony and preventing economic inequalities legitimating the claims of communists. On the other hand, development under the influence of dependency and world systems theories showed tendencies to constrain the expansionary scope of capitalism and to be an instrument of communist expansion.

Development during the Cold War period, therefore, was partly shaped by the struggle between socialist and capitalist blocs and the struggles for political and economic independence. The state remained as the leading agency in developing countries that either wanted to be an ally of one of the two ideological power blocs or that aimed to claim autonomy from them. This partly explains the reasons for the dominant role played by state planning in developing countries. During this time, the capitalist countries were more than willing to tolerate the so-called "inefficiencies of the state" in developing countries to the extent that they were beneficial to the political and economic interests of their countries.

Compared to the credit schemes discussed in this volume, the numerous credit schemes that existed during the Cold War period, however, were less rigid in terms of their commercial orientation, and they were an integral part of the state-led development plans. The conditions for the rapid commercialization of credit neither existed in developing countries, nor were easy to create. Moreover, the space of capitalist expansion and its structural needs did not require such a rapid expansion of credit in developing countries. The state-led development in Third World countries was more or less conducive to the interests of those states, which occupy a commanding position in the global economy. Hence, there was no urgent political necessity to rethink the role of credit in developing countries. Although over-determination of political expediency of credit programs frequently led to their inefficiencies and collapse, this was not a serious concern of those controlling the development process in Third World countries. That is to say, "the state as the main cause for failures in development" thesis did not attract much political force until the end of the Cold War. Claims about failure of the state in the post-Cold War period was not so much about its performance in the area of development, rather that they provided the ideological legitimacy for the need to restructure the state–society relations according to the imperatives of capital.

Since the end of the Cold War there have been dramatic changes in the capitalist mode of production and in the ways in which different states are structurally integrated with it. These changes were in response to the expansion reaching serious limitations due to the increasing costs of production and the narrow basis of consumption, the opening of new opportunities for expansion after the collapse of the Socialist blocs, and the necessity of consolidating its control over the energy producing countries. Expansion of capital under these new realities required a more aggressive creation of institutional conditions conducive to the "free" mobility of capital, labor, and commodities across the globe.

In response to acute crisis and aggressive demands of capitalism, development now more than ever has become a direct target of capitalist control given that a majority of the world's population and the various social and natural environments are still under the hegemony of development. The majority of the world's population experience capitalism through the language and practices of development. Historically, development has taken different forms in terms of how it was ideologically and spatially positioned within and between states. Such positioning needs to be understood in terms of how different states responded to the reproductive needs of capital. It is important to emphasize that development has never been a monolithic project. Historically, it has shown the tendencies to be an instrument through which capitalist relations penetrated into and were resisted by the third world. Such contradictory positioning of development is a manifestation of how the international state system managed the accumulation and legitimization crisis of capitalism.[44a] The discourse of microcredit and empowerment of women could be viewed in terms of both these trends because it was a result of convergence of neoclassical and feminist thinking in development during the post-Cold War period. During the post-Cold War period it became essential to blur the boundary between development and capitalism. Hence, "development" needs to be conquered, reconfigured, and disciplined according to the imperatives of capital. This also means the reconfiguration of relations (both real and representational) between capitalism and development. The objective of development policies is to remove the obstacles for commodification of social life and the natural environment.

Sustainable development, the most socially and environmentally progressive notion of development, needs to trickle down from the "inevitable" success of capitalism. Environmental degradation, multiple forms of social inequalities, and exclusions resulting from this process, are either ignored or considered temporarily to be capable of resolution within the capitalist framework itself. Development will deliver its promises as long as it can facilitate the reproductive needs of capital. Development needs to improve the entrepreneurial capabilities of people. The best chance for development to fulfill this promise now depends on the ability of the state and society to create conditions for the expansion of capitalism. This really means development's obligation to maximize its capacity to generate surplus value and the further blurring of the boundaries between development and capitalism.

Historically, development has never been a monolithic project (or Orientalist project as suggested by Arturo Escobar), rather it has taken diverse forms and shapes; it has been contextually specific and a nuanced process.[45] Development has also shown the potential counter-hegemonic force against capitalism and to be a means of achieving radical social change. In fact, for some, microcredit-led development was expected to do the same. However, several case studies in this volume demonstrate how the roles of microcredit programs are progressively reduced to connecting, coordinating and disciplining the diverse social transformative possibilities of development, to function according to the reproductive needs of capital. This volume explains such predicaments faced by ideologically and operationally diverse micro-credit programs in terms of their relations with totality of capitalist development. The notion of 'totality' implies a structured unit constituted by relations between its constituting elements. According to George Lukacs:

> The category of totality does not reduce its various elements to an undifferentiated uniformity, to an identity. The apparent independence and autonomy which they posses in capitalist system of production is an illusion only so far as they are involved in a dynamic dialectical relationship with one another and can be thought of as the dynamic dialectical aspects of an equally dynamic and dialectical whole. The result we arrive at says Marx "is not that production distribution, exchange and consumption are identical, but they are all members of one totality, different aspect of a unit".[46]

Paradoxically, capitalism achieves its totalizing character or homogeneity through the continuing production of social heterogeneity, for example, by developing needs and creating new identities, so that it can ensure the continuity of consumption, the driving force in contemporary forms of surplus accumulation. Diversity and fluidity of social relations are encouraged as long as they help to resolve the accumulation and legitimization crises of capitalism. Systematic analysis of the relationship between microcredit and development, and its consequences for gender inequalities, needs to be grounded in an analysis of how it impacts the accumulation and legitimization crises of capital. Such an analysis of microcredit as a social movement would also shed light on the current debates concerning the impact of so-called "new social movements."

The uniqueness of the post-Cold War microcredit regime needs to be located within the "radical" rethinking of the link between capitalism and development by NGOs. For example, Professor Mohammad Yunus, a trained mainstream economist and the co-founder of Grameen Bank, echoing Milton Friedman's *Capitalism and Freedom*,[47] popularized the notion that development could be achieved through humanizing capitalism. This means providing opportunities for the poor to unleash their hidden entrepreneur potential and enabling them to actively participate in capitalist development, and benefit from it. The identity of the poor in development was reconfigured as "new entrepreneurs." The explicit message is: we need to bring capitalism to the homes of the poor! Underdevelopment is a result of the failures of conventional theories and practices to reach the poor and to understand their social and cultural environments, hence neglect and suppression of their entrepreneurial potential. These arguments provided a "new life" to the decade old argument in the mainstream development theory about the lack of capital to be the main obstacle for development.

Some 80 percent of the world's 6.4 billion people live in low and lower-middle income countries and have no access to formal credit. Of these, close to 3.5 billion people (the average household size is five and a half people) account for unmet demand for commercial credit or savings. This is known as the "absurd gap," referring to the difference between the demand and supply of credit.[48] An important reason for this is that the majority of these households are located in the informal sector, whose financial demands are ignored by the formal sector financial institutions. Historically, the existence of the informal sector indicated the relative inability of the formal economy to absorb the labor force, or constituted a form of disguised unemployment. The conventional economic rational was to expand the formal sector to absorb the labor from the informal sector. Such understanding of the informal sector was no longer conducive to the new demands of capital for the following reasons: (1) the expansion the informal sector due to the dismantling of state investment in social welfare and development, (2) structural adjustments and stabilization policies, (3) massive rural migrations, and, most importantly, (4) a decline in overall living standards. The way out of this dilemma was not to expand the labor absorptive capacity of the formal sector, but to improve the "legality, security, and financing of the formal sector."[49]

The informal sector in mainstream development circles is now considered to be a permanent rather than a temporary condition and is unlikely to disappear from the economy. It is, in fact, an inevitable structural outcome of neoliberal economic policies. The very survival of the formal sector now hinges on the market's friendly activities towards the informal sector. The latter is important for the former in a number of respects. Under neoliberal economic reforms, the informal sector absorbs the cost of adjustments, provides cheap labor subcontracting services to the formal sector, creates new markets, and subsidizes the low wages paid in the formal sector. At the same time, neglect of the informal sector will lead to political instability given that the distributional struggles are mostly located in it.[50]

The proponents of these views about the informal sector argued, that the "widespread informal sector finance suggests that it is well-suited to most of the rural conditions" and "most informal lenders provide valuable services at a reasonable cost to the borrowers."[51]

> The role and strength of informal finance agents in small-scale rural economics ... and their importance to low-income households should not be underestimated ... The informal sector allows low income people access to services ... at a relatively low cost. It can do so because the informal sector is the normal environment for the rural people.[52]

In neoliberal discourse the informal–formal dichotomy is no longer viewed as an abnormal or temporary condition, but rather as an inevitable outcome of the expansion of capital. Indeed, it is seen as a reality that needs to be managed according to the needs of capital. The constituents of the informal should be active producers and consumers in the "new economy," without depriving the capital of the benefits them being located in the informal sector. The sector needs to be disciplined, (or empowered, in the language of NGOs), without undermining its structural relations with the formal sector. Failure to do so will undermine the survival of the formal sector, both economically and politically.

These alternative formulations of the role of the informal sector in mainstream development also coincided with a methodological debate in mainstream economics as to why theories of market imperfections resulting from information asymmetries and other imperfections, leads to the clearing of markets at Pareto-inefficient levels. This resulted in "new micro-foundations" or "new information theoretic economics,"[53] that incorporated market imperfections as a viable method of theorizing the efficient allocation of resources. According to Ben Fine, "instead of taking the social as given, the social is now open to explanation, despite the continuing dependence upon optimizing individuals."[54] The social is reduced to/equated with market imperfections, and market imperfections are endogenized in ways compatible with endogenous theories of economic development.[55]

The very organization of micro-credit programs provides ample raw material for mainstream economists to begin their analysis of market imperfections (e.g. peer group pressure, informal local institutions and social networks as a means of optimizing utility), instead of perfect market conditions, without sacrificing the fundamental ideological basis and methodological individualism of neoclassical economics. The methodological emphasis on market imperfection is in turn used to explain both economic and non-economic phenomenon, resulting in the marginalization of class, power and conflict issues that are central to empowerment. In other words, explanations and solutions to these issues of political economy are sought through models of market imperfections.

The combined marginalization of these issues in mainstream economics and studies concerned with gender and empowerment, is an important reason for the colonization of the latter by the former. These shifts, to use Ben Fine words, is tantamount to "economic imperialism" further consolidating neoliberalism's control over progressive and counter hegemonic trajectories of social change.[56] The appropriation of "social" by mainstream economics via equating social with imperfect market conditions is further provided legitimacy for restructuring of state-society relations according to the imperatives of neoliberalism. The state is in turn able to reproduce its capitalist nature by changing its form in accordance with the reproductive needs of capital. Such changes in the form of the state is further aided by NGO advocacy regarding their comparative advantages vis-à-vis the state, in development.

Meeting these challenges institutionally meant radical definition of the role of the state in, and its relationship with, the economy and society according to the imperatives of capitalist development. Now the state, similar to the poor, is expected to be an entrepreneur and function according to the logic of market rationality as coordinated by global centers of capitalism, e.g. the World Bank, the International Monetary Fund (IMF), the World Trade Organization (WTO), and those countries that control their functions.[57] The important consequences of the neoliberal restructuring of the state have been progressive dismantling, scaling back and privatization of social welfare systems, exercising direct state investments in development, and reducing the economic costs of the state apparatus. The underlying rationale of these policies is that a strong capitalist economy will make permanent state-driven social policies unnecessary. State social welfare expenditure constitutes an unproductive government expense, not a productive investment. Unless such expenditure promises to generate short-term profits, they are simply condemned as unproductive social compensation. The government-controlled social security and social safety networks need to improve their efficiency making them opportunities for the expansion of capitalist accumulation.

Historically state interventions in social development have varied from one context to another. This partly explains reasons for differences in *form* of the state formations in different developing countries, while their *nature* has always been capitalist.[58] The diversity of state formations then, is a result of negotiation between *form* and *nature*, in response to the strategies used by the state to manage the accumulation and legitimization crises. Diversity of state formation around the world cannot be explained outside the context of global expansion of capital. As Bukharin noted, "the internationalization of capital was simultaneously its nationalization (in the sense that a national economy and a national capital are developed), and they together provide the specific economic foundation for the capitalist nation state."[59] The uneven development of capital that we experience in terms of nation states, binaries between the center and the periphery, developed and under-developed, and region and "global village" are different ideological and spatial "fixes" that secure conditions for the continuity of accumulation of surplus value.[60] In the final analysis, the society experiences these "fixes" in terms of how they are institutionalized in the domains of the state.

In the neoliberal phase of capitalist development, the boundaries between *nature* and *form* appear to have blurred as the role of the state has, to date, more directly evolved into an agency responsible for organizing and disciplining the social order, according to the imperative of capitalist development. Despite a considerable decline in state "autonomy" from the society and the market, the state remains the primary agency responsible for managing accumulation and legitimization crises of capital. This means that it has to continue to reproduce its capitalist *nature* by changing its *form* in socially acceptable ways, unless it is willing to use force as opposed to consensus.

The restructuring of the state is also accompanied by the blurring of differences of economic policies between different interest groups competing for state power. They cannot rely on the neoliberal economy to take care of the general interest of the society. Loss of employment, job insecurity, violence, urban congestion, rising common crime, and growing social inequality, are linked increasingly with the expansion of capital. These groups cannot seek popular legitimacy for their respective agendas by identifying purely as an instrument of capital, or claiming to have faith in the trickle-down benefits from the "new economy." At the same time state continues to be the guardian of the general and particular interests of the society. In the final analysis, even the so-called "third way" represented by NGOs and new social movements seek to address their grievances within and through structures of the state.

Even if significant improvement of the economy occurs under neoliberal economic reforms it consistently leaves a trail of victims among small and medium business owners, employees, urban wage earners, women, rural communities, and children. Neoliberalism marginalizes and expels people at a greater rate than these programs can compensate. The state enjoys less flexibility to deviate from the neoliberal economic policies. Under such conditions, those groups competing for state power cannot articulate differences between them in terms of their economic policies. The challenge is to secure new modes of representation and legitimization of their agendas and differences between allows them, on the one hand, to disguise their helplessness under the conditions of neoliberal economy and, on the other hand, to subvert social resistance against them. In this regard the language of self-reliance, self-sufficiency and empowerment through microfinance appear to be extremely productive given that they simultaneously provide legitimacy for the withdrawal of the state from development, and creates conditions for capitalist expansion.

These transformations in the state formation are also closely intertwined with the "radical" challenges to capitalist modernity emerging from religious and secular social movements. For example, in a number of developing countries, religious nationalism has become the dominant legitimizing ideology of the state, while there is no significant deviation from the commitment of these states to pursue development within the neoliberal capitalist framework. The evolving chasm between the ethno-religious nationalist orientations of the state and their commitment to neoliberal economic policies in Bangladesh, Pakistan, Sri Lanka, and petroleum rich Middle Eastern countries, are good examples of this trend. Social and political processes transpire from the interplay between bifurcations of legitimizing ideologies of the state which have placed the state in a precarious position within the neoliberal economy by simultaneously making it (interplay) a necessity and a barrier for its own reproduction. Some NGOs, on the one hand, use microcredit as a means of social mobilization against regimes whose religious-nationalist ideologies are oppressive to women. And on the other hand, they also use local power relations as a means of managing their credit programs. Current studies have given limited emphasis on links between such NGO interventions and political processes at the national level.

Such complexity of articulation on the role of the state in development was also a response to a "cultural turn" in development, which in turn has a significant impact on popular legitimacy of microcredit in development. This particularly applies to those countries where religious nationalism is an important determinant of the relations between NGO, state, and society. Culture in neoliberal discourse is not simply a means to, but also an end product of, development.[61] Correspondingly, multiculturalism and ethical relativism led development to favor culture-friendly and diverse development practices as opposed to monolithic, top-down ones. Even neoclassical economists, who once despised or ignored cultural variables on the grounds in which they constituted major factors contributing to market imperfections and failures, are now in search of ways to use them as instruments to correct such failures. Simultaneous maintenance of cultural diversity and its commodification have led to even more serious political and economic contradictions and crises as they assume different meanings in different cultural locations and in turn impact the activities of NGOs and the new social movements in them.

One noteworthy outcome of the search for empowerment through diverse institutional formations centered on diverse identities and interests is the marginalization of class relations in the theorization of contemporary patterns of social change and political mobilization. This trend is rather puzzling given the fact that no social struggle can escape from the logic of class relation in the reproduction of capital as a central force of contemporary social change. Consequently, the social mobilizations of "politics of identity" have taken dominance over politics of distribution.[62] It was not that these social mobilizations were entirely uninterested in class inequalities, rather, they do not assign adequate emphasis on how class relations are implicated in their respective struggles.

Another important influence of cultural turn in development is its emphasis on diversity and ethical relativism as opposed to "universal truth" claims of modernity. Such privileging of the diversity and relativism in the normative claims that underpin the contemporary development interventions, raises several important issues. How does one reconcile the tension between the universal and relative interests of women, without falling into the trap of the tyranny of universalism or cultural relativism?[63] Do microcredit programs' reliance on peer group pressure and local culture and traditions reproduce the internal institutions and power relations that oppress women and consequently deprive them from the benefits of social change induced from outside that are based on universal norms and values of progress and social justice? How does microcredit reconfigure public and private? What are the consequences of these configurations? The answers to these questions should be grounded, in the first instance, in an analysis of the institutions and power structures that shape the discourse of empowerment through microcredit.

If diversity is the underlying logic of social change, the question is, "Where is the locus of social agency?" A post-structuralist would answer, it is "everywhere." "Who are the agents of social change? Again the simplest answer is every one every where."[64] No one denies that social change is diverse and complex due to the multiplicity of social actors involved in it. Nor is it possible to deny that diversity is coordinated by a multitude of trans-local forces and by the hybridity of cultures. Within the context of reproduction of capital on a global scale, one cannot escape from grappling with the issue as to "How are all these diverse potentialities and possibilities controlled and disciplined to produce permanence in the circular structures and systems encountered daily in that entity we call 'society'? How are the stabilities of a historically and geographically achieved social order, crystallized from within the flux and fluidity of social processes?"[65] To explain social change in terms of multiple agents in diverse locations is simply to overlook the centrality of class relation to social reproduction. The global spread of microcredit and the universal regulatory frameworks associated with it could be analyzed as "correspondence rules between different" social locations "to guarantee the stability" in them so that they function according to the reproductive needs of capital.[66] Studies in culture and development are mostly concerned with the preservation or utilization of culture in the process of development, rather than with the production of culture in practices of development. This raises several issues relevant for our current efforts to understand the impact of microcredit on social change: how does the discourse of microcredit frame, and how is it framed by, the interplay between diversity of cultural formations and worldwide reproduction of capital? What are the consequences for the empowerment of women? Do the current practices of microcredit credit lead to the reproduction of cultural practices and institutions that are oppressive to women? How does the discourse of empowerment through microcredit frame the reproduction of class relation as the central means of expansion of capital in different locations of microcredit?

Answers to these questions need to be grounded in systematic analyses of the links between microcredit and production of spatial relations, as we now understand that the notion of self-regulation of market is an impossible utopian project and that the economy is "structurally embedded in networks of social relations that collectively makeup the social structure."[67] Intellectually, we are now better equipped to do so in the light of the consensus regarding the "near impossibility of" viewing culture as a bounded concept and mapping the concerns into some spatial grid.[68] However, I do not think that this implies any possibility of entirely rejecting the bounded nature of culture as analytically irrelevant because diverse elements that structure society through practice occur in "concrete" spaces. As Bashkow has pointed out, "we readily equate bounded culture with problematic essentialism, even though boundaries offer the sole basis for constructing entities in a nonessentialist way."[69] Therefore, we cannot escape from the boundedness because "socio-cultural entities can be created entirely through a process of bounding, by yoking together particular sites of difference to form apparently enclosing frontier."[70] These theoretical concerns are extremely useful in understanding the consequences for empowerment of women, resulting from framing of their "cultures" by the discourse of empowerment via microcredit, and for mapping the interfaces between such framing and women borrowers' own perceptions of empowerment.

Feminists' encounters with microcredit credit

The majority of the world's poor are women. Despite the fact that women constitute approximately 50 percent of the world's working population, and do roughly 67 percent of the world's work, they earn only 10 percent of the world's wages, and hold 1 percent of its wealth. The type of work performed by women is similar to that by men, yet women share a greater burden of poverty within the household. Their work remains invisible, unpaid, and unaccounted for in studies concerned with economic development. After a decade of criticism of the gender-blind conceptualizations and practices of development and advocacy, it was only in the 1970s that interests in gender became a central concern in mainstream development.[71] Since then conceptualization of women's position in development has been shaped by perspectives, ideas, and debates that are thematically expressed in notions such as Women in Development (WID), Women and Development (WAD), Gender and Development (GAD), Women, Environment and Development (WED), and Postmodernism and Development (PAD).[72] By the mid-1980s there emerged rather "uneasy" consensus among the proponents of these perspectives regarding the usefulness of microcredit as a promising means of addressing the gender inequalities and empowerment of women. Microcredit as a moment of women's struggles against gender inequalities also coincided with the marginalization of radical socialist feminism in gender and development debates in the midst of consolidation of neoliberalism worldwide.

The position of women in the neoliberal phase of capitalist expansion is shaped by three overlapping factors. First, from the point of view of the capitalist class, women are an under-tapped resource as sources of labor, and as consumers. It is not that they were not actively participating in global production as consumers and laborers, rather, their participation was relatively less-commodified and, as such, represented a barrier that ought to be overcome in relation to the reproductive needs of the neoliberal economy. As Barrett notes, "oppression of women is not pre-given by logic of capitalist development, [but] became necessary for the ongoing reproduction of the mode of production in its present form."[73] Second, gender relations have to be configured in ways conducive to the expansionary needs of capitalism. This may be partly a response to mainstreaming of gender in development, and a way of subverting the social struggles focused on gender inequalities becoming a threat to the expansion of capitalism. Third, explicit desire to address the gender inequalities is an important, if not an inescapable source, of popular legitimacy for any social production. The gender inequalities, that historically capitalism and development overlooked and contributed to, now appear, simultaneously, as barriers to overcome and an opportunity for the expansion of surplus value. The framing of gender relations in the discourse of empowerment through microfinance appeared as a sound compromise for feminists concerned with both gender inequalities and capital to achieve their respective goals. Microcredit was also a response to tensions between "First World" and "Third World" feminists, resulting from the neglect of poverty-related issues in developing countries by the former, and a general call for "materially engaged, transformative politics."[74] Within a short matter of time, microcredit proved to be an instrument of building worldwide consensus between not only between feminists with different ideological perspectives on empowerment, but also between them and the governments, World Bank, and commercial banks.

Not all NGOs voluntarily accepted microcredit. During my initial field work in Bangladesh and Sri Lanka in the late 1990s, many organizations were quite apprehensive about microcredit. Their opposition, however, did not carry much political weight and some of them were forced by their donors to introduce a microcredit component to their empowerment projects. Even at the field-level, the organization's ability to provide credit became an important source of their credibility among their members. Eventually, many of them came to terms with the fact that microcredit is simply a strategic instrument improving the economic standards of women, as it is an essential prerequisite for other forms of empowerment of women.

Within a short time span, the extensive involvement of women in microcredit programs and the remarkably high repayment of credit by women became a living testimony of the positive correlation between microcredit and empowerment. Yet, these indicators do not sufficiently explain the institutional processes, through which women borrow, invest, and maintain high loan repayment rates; neither do they reveal their impact on gender relations in their localities. There is something astonishingly different about how gender-theorists/feminists approach the impact of microcredit credit and other development interventions, e.g. the structural adjustments and free-trade zones on women. They appear to be more complacent and less critical about the former than the latter.

Since the WID debate, the meaning of empowerment has become broader as it has incorporated concerns of culture, the economy, and politics.[75] The different objectives of empowerment are not only ambiguous and often contradictory, but also limited in terms of its usefulness. First, it is not grounded in a theory of social change that allows us to comprehend the centrality of global capitalism for comprehending the contemporary global transformations. Second, there has been limited emphasis on the ideologies and institutions that frame the meanings of empowerment and their consequences for women. Third, privileging of diversity in the current formulations of diversity and analysis, outside the context of its embeddedness, has marginalized radical criticism of neoliberalism. Fourth, such formulations have failed to articulate clearly the type(s) of social, economic, and political relations (e.g. property rights, production and exchange relations, distributive justice etc.) which should mirror a typical ideal of social order(s) they consider as "empowered." Current debates on empowerment have simply excluded these concerns and share the optimism that empowerment will trickle down from microcredit programs, similar to the trickle-down theory of neoliberal economics.

From a methodological point of view there are several doubts about the current claims on the impact of microcredit on the empowerment of women. The systematic analysis of microcredit reveals evidence that directly contradicts the current claims about the impact of microcredit on empowerment of poor women. These claims are based on highly problematic (mis)representations of important characteristics that define the uniqueness of microcredit. Some of the important characteristics used in microcredit programs are collateral-free lending, low interest loans, reaching the poorest of the poor, and peer group pressure. Consequently, other than a few notable exceptions, current studies conceal rather than reveal the "real" implications of microcredit on empowerment.

Microcredit loans primarily target the poor who cannot provide types of collateral required by conventional banks. Instead, it uses peer group pressure as a substitute for collateral. Peer group pressure in practice, however, does not mean the absence of conventional types of collateral as an important determinant of assessing creditworthiness. Given that both the group leaders and the NGO officers are responsible for ensuring regular rates of repayment, they both retain a good deal of flexibility to screen the creditworthiness of borrowers and to further impose a complex array of conditionality and punishments on borrowers. Credit does not reach the poorest of the poor women due to the self-selection of creditworthy borrowers, determined according to their likely ability to repay.

My field work in Bangladesh and Sri Lanka revealed that in order to assess creditworthiness, group leaders make detailed assessments and inventories of household wealth, e.g. bicycles, flashlights, rickshaws, furniture, trees in the gardens, the number of chickens owned, electric goods, presence of at least one income-earning male member, the number of unmarried daughters and widows in the household, the ability to obtain employment and to borrow from the moneylenders. Borrowers are forced to surrender the freedom to manage their domestic economy and social life to the NGOs and local institutions. This, in turn, blurs the boundary between the public and private domains of the lives of the borrowers. The so-called collateral-free lending practices of NGOs not only exclude the poorest of the poor but, even more strikingly, also function as a mechanism of controlling and disciplining the lives of the borrowers, than would the conventional banks and informal lending institutions.[76]

High repayment rates do not necessarily mean that there is an increase in the borrowers' incomes. The nominal identity of the borrower and the repayment rates do not reveal how and where the credit is invested, the sources of repayment, and the final beneficiaries of credit. These practices involve a complex social network, rather than a simple transaction between the lending agency and the borrower. Such institutional networks are important to the borrowers, as they assist them to become creditworthy, provide employment, and provide emergency funds to make timely repayments. These networks limit the borrowers' control over their loans and the income. They are also means through which income and repayments are appropriated by the moneylenders, traders and the NGOs, and the NGO which, in turn, transfers them to families and localities that promise better long rates of repayments. This exacerbates the economic inequalities within the communities and between different localities.

The positive outcomes of micro credit are also explained by indicators of women's increasing responsibility and numerical visibility in micro credit related activities and their participation in credit related meetings that occur outside their homes. We know little about the economic and social costs, and the hardships they endure due to them bearing the entire responsibility for loan repayments and their forced participation in mandatory group meetings organized by the NGOs. Current studies do not reveal the structure and activities of these meetings where women meet, nor the social, economic and political cost implications for women.

The case studies on Bangladesh illustrate the numerical visibility of women (or to put it in the language of NGOs "traditional women coming out of their homes") in these meetings is not a sufficient indicator of positive changes in their lives. For women, do the costs of participation in these meetings outweigh the benefits? There is no systematic ethnographic analysis of the power dynamics underpinning these meetings, particularly how these dynamics are linked with the emerging global political economy and consequences for women.

Numerical visibility of women in microcredit programs is a highly misleading indicator of qualitative dimensions of their empowerment. The numerical strength of women in these credit programs does not automatically translate into qualitative changes in their social status. It is not logical to argue that the public domains of women now framed by microcredit programs are more empowering than their traditional public and private spheres. In the light of the findings in most of the chapters in this volume, I argue that the institutional relations that women experience in the public sphere after they join the microcredit programs have resulted in further impediments for their empowerment. In fact, the institutional relations that underpin the microcredit programs may suppress the potentialities of local sources of empowerment. Current studies take the superiority of public domain over private domain for granted, instead of examining how the institutional relations within and between them are framed by microcredit and the resulting consequences for women. Ironically, such claims about private–public boundaries are often associated with those that are vehemently committed to uncovering the liberating potentials of those at the margins of the society or the subalterns through indigenous knowledge and strategies of resistance.

Peer group pressure, the substitute for conventional collateral, is derived from existing institutional and power relations. The issue at stake from the point of view of empowerment is whether the use of peer group pressure weakens or strengthens the institutions that are oppressive to women. The field officers of NGOs, women, and those institutions that are implicated in microcredit programs, are aware of the fact that their mutual survival depends on the ability to maintain the required rates of loan repayment. The exerting of any pressures on potential defaulters are legitimate actions sanctioned by the community. Lives of women and their households enjoy less "autonomy" from the larger society, resulting in serious consequences for women in terms of their economic and social well-being as they bear the ultimate responsibility for repayment of loans.

According to NGOs, the average monetary value of their loan per person is smaller compared to the commercial banks. Women consider microcredit loans as another addition to their overall portfolio, or simply as another source of income. Often, the loans from the NGOs are supplemented with additional borrowings from the moneylenders and traders. In the processes of becoming creditworthy and engaging in the utilization and repayment of loans, borrowers also enter into various contractual agreements with moneylenders and traders. These agreements involve investing credit in enterprises that are owned by moneylenders and traders, purchasing of inputs for investments from and selling of produce to them, and use of credit to pay outstanding debt owed to them. In practice, on the one hand it means the actual value of the loan is inflated in the NGO records, and on the other hand, the amount directly utilized by the borrowers (or that benefits the borrowers directly), is less than recorded by the NGOs.

Theoretically, the interest rates charged for NGO loans, is much smaller than those implicated by informal lending agencies. Yet, this seems to disguise the real cost of the interest rates to the borrowers. First, NGOs calculate interest rates based on the assumption that borrowers have access to the exact amount of credit stated in the records of NGOs. Often, the field officers and NGO officers informally retain a certain amount of the loan as collateral in order to ensure the regularity of repayments and to settle outstanding debts to the NGO. Group leaders also retain a certain amount to make an income, supposedly for the benefit of the entire group, by lending to non-NGO members. It is simplistic to assume that the NGOs calculate the interest rate based on the nominal amount of the loan stated in their record and that their interest rates are lower than that of the moneylenders or that the actual cost of the loan for borrower from the NGOs is lower than the moneylenders. When loans from the NGO are supplemented by other sources, not only do women end up paying interest to two sources, but they also sell their products at lower prices to these other sources, given the nature of contractual obligations between them. From the women's perspective, the real interest rate charged by the moneylenders may be less than that of the NGOs when the other reciprocal and long-term contractual relations between them and the moneylenders and the flexibility of timing and means of repayments to the latter are taken into consideration. In some Bangladeshi villages, the NGOs are known as "new Zamindars" and "New East India Company," indicating that they are purely interested in squeezing the "blood" from the poor.

The borrowers do not consider NGOs flexible institutions in comparison to other local ones. According to them, the criteria for evaluating creditworthiness, the timing and size of loans, and other methods used by the NGOs, are rigid, and borrowers have little control over them. Often, in the case of NGO loans, there is no grace period for beginning loan repayments, even in cases where the investment takes a long time to generate income. We know very little about the impact of the pressure to generate cash for loan repayments on a weekly basis on the consumption, health, leisure, and education of the borrowers and their families. In times of cash shortages, families sell their food reserves and force their school-going children to either work for cash, or otherwise to take care of domestic work while parents work for extra cash. Female children often become the primary victims of these situations.

Current studies have overlooked the impact of microcredit on the well-being of women in relation to the "commodification" of relations and forces of production in the local and national economy in response to neoliberal economic reforms and the need to generate cash to repay NGO loans. While commodification might increase productivity in some instances, for several reasons it nevertheless also creates systemic scarcities and social inequalities. First, commodification forces people to produce a certain type and quantity of goods to maximize the *exchange values* as opposed to *use values* or simply to maximize profit. Second, commodification reallocates resources from meeting basic subsistence activities to cash-income generating activities and forces people to purchase their subsistence needs from the marketplace. Third, scarcities may also arise due to the determination of the quantity of produce and levels of consumption according to "market values" and loan repayment requirements. The need to generate cash flow forces them to sell their basic food reserves usually allocated for use during periods of floods and slack periods. Finally, in an indirect way, when repayments are made by moneylenders and traders on behalf of the borrowers, the latter are forced to work long hours for less pay and even sell their produce at lower prices to the former, including the interest for additional borrowing from them.

Within credit groups, women are internally divided along the lines of economic inequalities between their families. The visibility of women in microcredit programs as an indicator for group solidarity or as a sign of their collective empowerment is misleading. One study shows that microcredit programs, which utilize the group solidarity approach, "promote unprecedented levels of indebtedness and [...] low levels of default figures mask unprecedented misery."[77] Moreover, in rural settings, the family remains the basic economic unit, and women evaluate the successes and failures of their participation in microcredit credit programs in terms of the costs and benefits to the family. Claims about the links between lending to women and their ability to maintain high repayment rates, may well be due to the economic differences between the families and the social status they occupy within their community, rather than some unique (essentialist, if you like) characteristics of women borrowers themselves.

The discourse of empowerment through microcredit is another example of the remarkable capacity of capitalist interests to utilize the language and practices of its opponents for its own reproduction. Just like the discourse of modernity (or Orientalism, if you like), it frames the subjectivity of poor women, in an essentialist way and articulates their empowerment within the fundamental parameters of capitalist modernity. A way out of this historical predicament requires a politically committed analysis of the processes through which the subjectivity of women and gender are constructed and framed according to the logic of class relation (or reproductive needs of capital) by the very projects that seek to address gender inequalities. As Michael Burawoy noted, while capitalism may diverge in its expression across different social identities and social relations, such divergences are interconnected *in order to realize effects of class relation.*[78] The challenge is to "to find commonalities within difference, and to develop a politics that is genuinely collective in its concerns, yet sensitive to what remains irreducibly distinctive in the world today."[79]

The NGOs, state and capital: the unholy trinity

In many developing countries, the states, commercial banks and diverse locally-based organizations continue to play an important role in providing credit for the poor. However, the post-Cold War microcredit regime is mainly associated with the popularity of NGOs as leading actors in development and the claims about their ability to institutionalize credit in ways more friendly towards the poor, especially women. This is attributed to the claims that NGOs hold an advantage over the state according to their ability to respond to the needs of the poor due to their flexibility in accordance with their ideological and operational orientations, their ability to reach the poorest of the poor, and their commitment to values and goals, as opposed to bureaucratic imperatives. The proponents of these claims view NGOs as more accountable and transparent institutions.[80] Through microcredit NGOs have not only have enhanced the credibility of claims about them, but also have built national and global alliances between themselves, new social movements government agencies, and market institutions. Indeed, efforts of NGOs have contributed towards providing much needed visibility to women and facilitated a greater gender sensitivity in development theory and practice.

NGOs' encounter with microcredit initially led to conflict between them on ideological grounds, often backed by their respective donors. NGOs that do not share the optimism of benefits for empowerment through microcredit are subject to enormous pressure from their donors to use microcredit in order to be financially self-sufficient and produce measurable results by criterion easily understandable to the commercial sector. As a result, many of these leading NGOs that are mainly interested in social transformation through changes in institutions and power relations (or in other words, they privilege structure over the agency), have cautiously accepted the idea that economic empowerment through microcredit is an essential and viable prerequisite for cultural and political empowerment. These NGOs also consider credit as a way of reaching communities and marginalized groups such as those less open to change.

Current literature is mostly concerned with the benefits of NGOs as opposed to other institutions as implementers of microcredit. These studies uncritically take the widely believed comparative advantages of NGOs vis-à-vis the state for granted. Such uncritical use of "differences" between NGOs and the state in current studies, instead of theorizing how differences are institutionally produced and legitimized, casts several doubts over the legitimacy of their claims about the institutional superiority of the NGO over the state. Such doubts also result from the failure to explore the complementary roles of NGOs and the state in development, and the impact of development interventions by the latter on the former and vice versa.

The popularity of NGOs as the "third sector" in development occurred along with the worldwide consolidation of neoliberalism. On the one hand, NGOs are front line critics of the failures of the state and the markets to respond to the needs of the poor. On the other hand, the institutional and organizational reforms within NGOs, governments and commercial sectors continue to blur the boundaries between them as they are being subjected to common policy and regulatory frameworks guided by the imperatives of market rationality. Consequently, NGOs are subjected to the global trend towards standardization and harmonization of development interventions and to evaluating their outcomes by the same criteria used in the evaluation of market-oriented institutions. In fact, in the name of accountability and transparency, NGOs and states are in the forefront of compelling each other to adopt these universal standards for measuring the effectiveness of their development interventions. In other words, microcredit has proved to be an effective instrument to coordinate the activities of NGOs, governments and the commercial organizations under a common policy framework.

As a consequence, financial self-sufficiency of NGOs involved in microcredit has become an important concern in development policy. A recent policy document by the United Nations underscores these trends and pointed out that, "[m]uch of the enthusiasm rests on the notion that the institutions of micro-finance, and foremost, the non-governmental organizations (NGOs), are not only effective in reducing poverty, but also sustainable as market entities."[81] The proof of such trends "is often found in the conversion of many successful NGOs into Banks and the involvement of commercial banks into micro-lending operations."[82] The policy makers consider the formalization of the regulatory framework necessary for several reasons. First, it allows the microcredit institutions to improve their credibility and scope, and remove constraints they face from the donors, governments, and other outsiders, and effectively serve the poor. Second, improvement of services attracts a larger clientele and improves the credibility of the institution. Third, existence of a market-friendly regulatory environment allows NGOs to attract private investors and banks to invest in microcredit and NGO operations. Currently, it is a concern among the donors and development think tanks that, "the majority of the NGOs yet do not fulfill the criteria set by the investors" to ensure "sustainability." The proponents of these views believe that commercial viability is crucial for NGOs, because, "institutions unable to ensure commercial returns are destined to live always off the uncertain charity of development aid and other external funding."[83] In this sense, Gonzalez-Vega (1994) points out that, "sustainability generates compatible incentives for all those with an interest in its [organizations] survival, such as clients, managers, and staff, because it underpins the perceptions of microfinance organization's supremacy."[84]

The push towards financial sustainability has several other consequences for NGOs. The extent to which the microcredit institutions can be sustainable is determined by factors beyond the control of individual organizations. Robinson's study on "a paradigm shift" in microfinance, has pointed out that the "Grameen model of micro-lending institution, though it has been successful for many years, is not globally affordable. Moreover, the most experienced and even the successful NGOs have found themselves exposed to external conditions."[85] In fact, in Bangladesh, microcredit institutions, including Grameen Bank have outstanding repayments more than $500 million in total. The costs for survival of the organizations range from $100 million a year and BRAC needs an estimated amount of $50 million of additional funding to get back on its feet.

In response to needs of financial sustainability, NGOs are rapidly transforming their internal organizational practices in the areas of recruitment, management, decision making, and evaluation of performance. NGOs increasingly hire technocratic-minded professionals at high salaries and compensation packages. This has led to tensions within NGOs (i.e. between the highly paid technocratic professionals and those who still believe in "radical social change") and even to their disintegration. The organizational practices are hierarchically structured in response to loan repayment becoming the main determinant of the sustainability and credibility of organizations. The programs for improvement of human resources couched in the language of efficiency often disguise their impact on changes in the organizational norms and values and their implications for social transformative capacities of NGOs. The policy and training manuals by NGOs used in microcredit programs cannot be viewed simply from instrumentalist and programmatic points of view, but as instruments to objectify the subjects of development, according to predetermined notion(s) of development. The language of efficiency and civility often do not reveal the interests of institutions that formulate them and how they frame the intended outcomes at the field-level. Current studies do not examine the impact of technocratic investments in NGO programs on the goals of empowerment.

The programs intended to improve the quality of human resources within organizations, that are often couched in the language of efficiency, disguise their impact on the norms and values of organizations and their social transformative capacities. The use of NGOs' policy and training manuals in microcredit programs cannot be viewed simply from instrumentalist and programmatic points of view. They are, rather, instruments for objectifying the subjects of development in accordance to predetermined notion(s) of development. The language of efficiency and civility that often figure in management training programs in NGOs do not reveal the interests of institutions that formulate them and how they frame the intended outcomes at the field-level.

Generally, NGOs have attempted to resolve these tensions either by suppressing the social objectives until the organization and their beneficiaries become financially self-sufficient, or by defining the subjectivity of their members in response to the organization's financial targets. Collectively, these practices treat all borrowers as clients, or, in other words, relations with women borrowers are simplistically configured as "client relations." Thus, effects of the "clientification of gender" are in many ways similar to those created by *homo economicus* in neoclassical economics, and class relations in capitalism.[86] The material and ideological impact of this has profoundly impacted the current global political economy. Materially, it contributes to the expansion of surplus value and has transferred it from relatively more productive centers to less productive centers. Ideologically, it provides popular legitimacy to neoliberal economic reforms by the state, particularly by "provincializing" and "marginalizing" social movements reacting directly against the class inequalities. In this regard, neoliberalism has been successful using the language and practices of its opponents to subvert and suppress opposition against it. In other words, the effects of gendering of *homo economicus* (a process that can also be referred to as the feminization of the rational, utility-maximizing economic man) end up being politically beneficial for neoliberal economic policies. Current studies on microcredit have overlooked how capitalism has historically realized the "effects class" relation through diverse "nonclass relations."[87] Microcredit opens the lives of economically-disadvantaged women to be controlled by institutions which ostensibly assist them in maintaining regular loan repayments to NGOs. Thus, for such women, these processes have simultaneously increased their visibility in development and at the same time, deprived them of means for self-empowerment. The consequences of this process, which I refer to as the feminization of capitalist modernity is similar to the consequences of the feminization of poverty.

The push towards financial sustainability has increased interventions by the government and the international donors in NGO affairs. Such interventions are responses to a number of factors. Public complaints about microcredit and the donor pressures on the government to provide a regulatory framework for efficient management of microcredit programs are now used as an excuse by the government to probe into NGOs that are suspected of being anti-government. For instance, the government of Bangladesh has decided to closely monitor the microcredit credit disbursement operations conducted by the NGOs in the country with a view to ensuring transparency in NGO activities. It has formed the Cabinet Committee on Micro Credit, a 12-member committee headed by Bangladesh Bank Governor Dr Fakhruddin Ahmed, to formulate a regulatory framework for disbursing microcredit. The government, while making the announcement of the regulatory framework, noted that "if any NGO wants to run on commercial interests, they have to abide by the existing rural and regulations."[88] In response, Cooperatives Minister, Abdul Bhuiyan told reporters, that "The government does not feel any necessity for ADAB, which has no legal grounds for representing NGOs."[89] Such government intervention is, partly, a direct consequence of NGOs giving priority to financial sustainability over other social goals and restructuring them according to universal technocratic rationality and regulatory framework that emphasize commercial sustainability, transparency, and accountability. These practices have further erased the differences between NGOs and have undermined their relative autonomy. Technocratic language is not value neutral, but intended to discipline social relations to serve the interests of those institutions that shape them.

The blurring boundaries between NGOs and the state in relation to commercial imperatives of microcredit programs have further constrained their ability to engage in development within the imperatives of the neoliberal economy, and have increased the tensions between the NGOs and the state. At the same time, donors use the state to bring NGOs to a common regulatory framework and the NGOs use the state intervention to ensure the timely repayments by their borrowers. The NGO criticism of the state, however, provides ideological justification for demands by institutions of neoliberalism to reduce state spending in areas contrary to market interests. NGOs, however, do not even marginally compensate for social welfare losses suffered by the poor due to the withdrawal of state subsidies.

The studies that attribute the positive outcomes of microcredit to NGOs have often overlooked the impact institutions (e.g. the state) have contributed towards the successes of microcredit programs. Proponents of microcredit claim that high repayment rates are attributable to the "efficiency of NGOs," while their failures are attributed to state intervention, borrower experiences with conventional banks, and various informal sector organizations. Current studies have not considered the possibility that the different degrees of success in different credit programs are predicated on the past and ongoing investments by the state, and the other NGOs in the areas of healthcare, education, and infrastructure for production. In such situations, the credit for success in maintaining high repayment rates belongs as much to the state and to other agencies, as to the NGOs concerned. Within the context of neoliberal restructuring of the state we also need to explore: how do people compensate for the loss of state assistance, such as agricultural subsidies, particularly when they are crucial for the livelihoods of the microcredit credit borrowers? Is it possible that the main beneficiaries of microcredit are those who have benefited from the neoliberal restructuring of the state?

The absence of studies dealing these issues provides undue legitimacy for the arguments of institutions such as the World Bank, the IMF, and the WTO, who attribute the failures in development, to the state.[90] There is little evidence to suggest that marginalized people are increasingly reliant upon NGOs to meet their needs. In the final analysis, they consider the state as the final guardians of their basic needs. During periods of economic downturn, social protests are most likely to be against the state rather than against the NGOs. In an event of mass default of microcredit, it would be easier for the NGOs to exit from their projects. Unless the state cannot escape from pressures from the international donors, it is unlikely to assist NGOs to achieve their financial goals. The state will weigh the political and economic costs and benefits of acting against the borrowers as opposed to NGOs. In such situations, it would be easy for the NGOs to abandon their programs, whereas the state will not have such a privilege. Compared to microcredit, it takes a long time and effort to rebuild development programs in the areas of healthcare, education, awareness building, and social mobilization.

While the NGOs are critical of the state and organize social protests against its policies, they have not put forward a theory of the state that has radically different characteristics from the neoliberal state. Not only their legal identity is defined by the state, they are imprisoned within the political economy of the neoliberal state. Consequently, use of microcredit by the NGOs has shaped the discourse of development, and mobilized diverse interest groups who have a stake in it, in ways that do not threaten the interests of the neoliberal state.[91] The outcomes of microcredit programs demonstrate how NGOs have contributed to the structuring of the state according to the interests of neoliberal capitalism. This is also a direct consequence of the ambiguity of the notion of empowerment in the NGO sector, particularly the disjuncture between various components of empowerment and how they are prioritized in their microcredit projects.

Reasons for these limitations of current studies on the comparative role of NGOs and the state in empowerment projects are not grounded in theorizing of NGOs in social change, particularly within the context of the uneven development of capitalism. Even though the boundaries between

NGOs, the state, and markets are blurring, the continuing production of differences between them is crucial for their respective identity and legitimacy. Finally, there has hardly been an analysis regarding the question of how neoliberal capitalism has hijacked and subverted the potentiality of NGOs to become a counter hegemonic social force, through the medium of microcredit credit. That is to say, the current emphasis is limited as to how the NGOs can utilize microcredit to liberate the poor from the oppressiveness of the state and the markets, rather than on exploring how NGO interventions in microcredit are used as a means of reproducing the state–market–NGO nexus according to the imperatives of capital and their consequences for poor women.

Author contributions

Heloise Weber's chapter challenges the conventional assumptions about the role of microfinance in poverty reduction, as well as discourses about associated social empowerment, through an analysis of the way in which the approach is instrumentally embedded in the global political economy. She argues that the microfinance and poverty reduction agenda is primarily oriented towards facilitating the drive for financial sector liberalization on a global scale, and is generally conducive to neoliberal restructuring. Her analysis further elaborates and provides critical insights into the social impact and political consequences of microfinance programs as implemented within the neoliberal political economy.

Drawing on the post-development literature, and Michel Foucault's notion of "*dispositif*," Morgan Brigg's chapter demonstrates how and why the critical tools for understanding the shifts in development projects need to be extended beyond those approaches that center around economic relations, and emphasizes the need to make some adjustments for the use of this concept to date. She argues that the outcomes of microcredit programs cannot necessarily be viewed as emancipatory, but instead need to be considered in terms of the complex mix of effects they generate. These effects can just as readily include the reinforcing of conventional developmentalist modalities, the integration of subjects into the development *dispositif*, and the displacement or writing out of other subjective modalities, as they can include the easing of economic hardship and the dispersion and proliferation of subjective modalities beyond developmentalism.

Katharine Rankin's chapter takes the issue of social capital a step further in terms of its implications for feminist objectives of social transformation. She evaluates prevailing ideas about social capital (rooted in rational choice theory) against three alternative approaches; by utilizing Marxist social capital theories (*à la* Pierre Bourdieu), neo-Foucauldian governmentality studies, and her own feminist-oriented ethnographic research on the social embeddedness of economic practices in a merchant community of Nepal. She brings these critical insights to bear on possibilities for designing microfinance programs, and practicing a kind of development more generally that could engage women's solidarity to challenge dominant gender ideologies.

Arelis Gómez and Denise Humphreys Bebbington examine the links between microcredit and social capital in post-conflict societies. The authors argue that micro-lending programs have become popular because they are quick to reach significant numbers of very poor people while producing immediate results – specifically, increased family income. The success of these programs, however, depends either upon the prior existence of practices and relationships of *confianza* and social capital, or on the ability of the program to develop these relationships quickly. The main question probed in this paper is how the restoration of social capital occurs in zones emerging from conflict. It specifically analyzes the process of rebuilding *confianza* and the expansion of social networks among rural and semi-urban, marginalized women in Ayacucho, Peru and Highland Guatemala, resulting from their participation in village banking programs.

Tara Deubel's case study of the *CultureBank*, a village-level initiative in rural Mali, demonstrates how it employs credit as an incentive for the conservation of rapidly disappearing material culture in the Dogon region of Mali. This strategy has abated the widespread sale of valuable heirlooms to foreign tourists and Malian antique brokers. *CultureBank*, while successful in augmenting household revenues from loan-assisted commerce, has had an impact on decreasing the commodification of objects of cultural value, and raising awareness at multiple levels of the society, essential for conservation of culture and reproduction. While the strategies of *CultureBank* have prevented the commodification of cultural artifacts in the commercial sense, it does not seem to have had as much success addressing the gender imbalances existing in society, as Tara's analysis reveals that the overall benefit to women, outweigh that of men.

Katie Wright's chapter is based on field research conducted in Peru and highlights evidence of the "darker" side to microfinance. By providing a systematic understanding of the linkages between microfinance and wider social structures the paper reinforces the arguments by other critiques, that social structures based on kinship and patron–client relationships in rural communities directly affect the ways in which these programmers operate. Rather than understanding utilization as a vehicle to challenge these unequal structures, microcredit groups reinforced existing hierarchies and inequalities. Though disillusioned members may spread rumors to exaggerate the number of presidents who use the loan for personal gain, there is nevertheless strong evidence to suggest that this practice does exist: there is no smoke without fire. Furthermore, the issue is not so much that embezzlement by the leaders goes undetected. Rather, microfinance organizations do not see it as their role to intervene, but as an issue internal to the microfinance group.

Lynne Milgram's chapter, drawing on ethnographic research in the Philippine Cordillera, argues that microfinance projects have embedded social change objectives in initiatives driven by market-led forces, thereby failing to realize social justice for women. She argues that microfinance projects have the potential to create more realistic opportunities for women and to develop a collective social criticism of gender and class inequality. Provided they promote broader debates within microfinance initiatives, as well as within other affirmative approaches, microfinance can provide a foundation for operationalizing a more normative agenda for development. These debates should facilitate more transformative interpretations of women's needs within the parameters of their lived experiences.

Jude Fernando's chapter explores the historical processes that shaped the post-Cold War microcredit credit regime and its consequences for empowerment of women, state formation, and social transformative potentials of NGOs. By utilizing actor-oriented methods and analysis combined with Marxist structuralist perspectives, he demonstrates how high repayment rates of microcredit credit programs are predicated on the very institutions that are oppressive to women. The current popularity of microcredit demonstrates the remarkable capacity of capitalism to make use of the language and practices of its critics and opponents to secure conditions for its own reproduction. Microcredit programs have increased the costs of capitalist development incurred by women. Consequently, gender relations in the discourse of empowerment are framed within the ideological and institutional parameters of neoliberal capitalism: gender relations are nothing but a de facto class relation. In the final analysis, such institutional framing has contributed towards "feminization of capitalist modernity" in ways detrimental to expectations of those engaged in gender and development. In searching for ways out of this predicament, he suggests Capitalism and Gender (CAG) ought to be the thematic and policy focus of debates concerning gender and development.

Notes

1 Walters, K. (2000) "Muhammad Yunus, Colin Powell: Two Paths to the Same Vision," State of the World Forum, 2000 State of the World, Inc, http://www.simulconference.com/clients/sowf/dispatches/dispatch13.html. 4–10 September, p. 1.
2 United Nations Resolution 53/197 of 15 December, http://www.gdrc.org/icm/iym2005/.
3 Sherine, M., McConnell, B. and Rao, D. S. K. State of Microcredit Summit Report (2003) http://www.microcreditsummit.org/pubs/reports/socr/2003/SOCR03-E[txt].pdf, pp. 2–3.
4 Bulletin on Eradication of Poverty (1998) Volume 5, United Nations, http://www.un.org/esa/socdev/poverty/documents/boep_05_1998_EN.pdf.
5 Druschel, K., Quigley, J. and Sanche, C. (2001) The State of Microcredit Campaign Report, http://www.microcreditsummit.org/pubs/reports/socr/2001/SOCReport2001.doc, p. 26.

Introduction 39

6 Source: Harris, S. D. (2003) The State of Micro-Credit Summit Campaign Report, http://www.microcreditsummit.org/pubs/reports/socr/2003/SOCR03-E[txt].PDF, p. 21.
7 Microcredit Summit, (1997) 5–7 February, Washington DC, http://www.microcreditsummit.org/declaration.htm#Preamble, p. 2.
8 Ibid. p. 6.
9 United Nations – General Assembly Resolution 52/194, 1997, http://www.gdrc.org/icm/iym2005/un-note.html, p. 1.
10 Robinson, M. (2001) *The Microfinance Revolution: Sustainable Finance for the Poor*, The World Bank, Washington, DC.
11 Rahman, R. I. (1986) "Impact of Grameen Bank on the Situation of Poor Rural Women" Working Paper, No. 1, Grameen Bank Evaluation Project, Dhaka, Bangladesh Institute For Development Studies; Fernando, J. L. (1997) "Disciplining the Mother," *Ghadar*, a bimonthly publication of the forum of Indian leftists, 1 (1), 1 May, p. 37; Fernando, J. L. (1997) "Nongovernmental Organizations, Microcredit and Empowerment of Women," in Jude Fernando and Alan Heston (eds) *The Role of NGOs*, Annals of the American Academy of Political and Social Science, Sage, Thousand Oaks, CA. pp. 150–76; Goetz, A. M. and Sen Gupta, R. (1995) "Who takes the credit? Gender, Power and Control over Loan Use in Rural Credit Programs in Bangladesh," *World Development*, 24 (1): 45–63; Fernando, J. L. (2002) "Perils and Prospects of Microcredit. Cultural politics of Empowerment," 16 May 2002, Paper presented at a conference "Livelihood, Savings and Debt in a Changing World: Developing Anthropological Perspectives" Wageningen International Conference Centre, Wageningen, the Netherlands; Rahman, A. (1999) "Microcredit Incentives for Equitable and Sustainable Development: Who Pays?" *World Development*, 27 (1): 67–82.
12 Seidel, C. and Vidal, L. (1997) "The implications of 'medical,' 'gender in development' and 'culturalist' discourse for HIV/AIDs Policy in Africa" in C. Shore and S. Wright (eds) *Anthropology of Policy: Critical Perspectives on Governance and Power*, Routledge, London.
13 Shore and Wright (1997) p. 10.
14 Ibid. p. 4.
15 Ibid. p. 5.
16 Ibid. p. 6.
17 James, C. L. R. (1989) *Black Jacobins: Toussaint L'Ouverture and the San Domingo Revolution*, Vintage, second edition, New York.
18 Halim, A. M. (1993) *Social Welfare Legislature in Bangladesh*, Dhaka University Press, Dhaka, p. 233.
19 Bouman, F. J. A. (1989) *Small, Short and Unsecured: Informal Rural Finance in India*, Oxford University Press, Delhi, p. 6.
20 Escobar, A. (1995) "Imagining a Post-Development Era? Critical Thought, Development and Social Movements" *Culture and Anthropology*, 3: 428–43; Rehama, M. (1977) "Towards post-development: Search For Signposts, a New Language and New Paradigms" in M. Rahnema and V. Bawtree (eds) *The Post-Development*, Zed Books, London; Sachs, W. (1992) *Development Dictionary, Guide to Knowledge as Power*, Zed Books, London.
21 Esteva, G. (1987) "Regenerating Peoples Spaces" *Alternatives*, 12: 133.
22 Alvarez, S. E., E. Dagnino and A. Escobar (2002) *Culture of Politics: Re-visioning Latin American Social Movements*, Westview Press, Boulder CO, p. 2.
23 Ibid.
24 Ibid. p. 11.
25 Ibid. p. 15.
26 Ibid.

40 *Jude L. Fernando*

27 Peet, R. and Hartwick, E. (1999) *Theories and Development*, Guildford Press, New York, p. 155.
28 Unnithan, M. and Srivastava, K. (1997) "Gender Politics, Development and Women's Agency in Rajasthan," in R. D. Grillo and R. L. Stirrat (eds) *Discourses of Development: Anthropological Perspectives*, Berg Publishers, Oxford, p. 157.
29 Dirlik, A. (1994) *After Revolution: Waking to Global Capitalism*, Wesleyan University Press, Hanover and London, p. 99.
30 Ibid. p. 97.
31 Escobar, A. (1995) *Encountering Development: The Making and Unmaking of the Third World*, Princeton: Princeton University Press; Ferguson, J. (1990) *The Anti-politics Machine: "Development," Depolitization, and Bureaucratic Power in Lesotho*, University of Minnesota Press, Minneapolis.
32 Escobar (1995).
33 Dirlik (1994) p. 99.
34 Marx, K. (1973) *Capital*, Vintage Press, New York.
35 Ibid. p. 224.
36 Ibid. p. 225.
37 Hardt, M. and Negari, A. (2000) *Empire*, Harvard University Press, Cambridge MA, p. 222.
38 Marx, K. (1973) *Grundrisse*, Vintage Press, New York, p. 408.
39 Ibid. p. 407.
40 Hilferding, R. (1981) [1910] *Finance Capital: A study of the latest phase of capitalist development*, in T. Bottomore (ed.) (trans. M. Watnick and S. Gordon), Routledge, London; Hardt and Negari (2000) p. 226.
41 Hardt and Negari (2000) p. 227.
42 Smith, N. (1990) *Uneven Development: Nature, Capital and the Production of Space*, Oxford University Press, Oxford, p. 142.
43 Ibid.
44 Smith, N. (1984) *Uneven Development: Nature, Capital and the Production of Space*, Blackwell, UK.
44a Clark, S. (1992) *The State Debate*, Macmillan, London, pp. 22–49.
45 Grillo, R. D. and Stirrat, R. L. (eds) (1997), *Discourses of Development: Anthropological Perspectives (Explorations in Anthropology)*, Berg Publishers, UK.
46 Lukacs, G. (1993) *History and Class Consciousness*, Rupa Publishing and Co., Delhi: 14.
47 Friedman, M. (1962) *Capitalism and Freedom*, University of Chicago Press, Chicago.
48 The phrase "absurd gap" is used by Michael Chu, the President of Accion International, at a conference on "Building Healthy Financial Institutions For the Poor," sponsored by the U.S. Agency for International Development and held in Washington, DC, in September 1994. op. cit. in Laurance Hart and Judith Brandsma "Making Microfinance Work Better in Middle East and Africa," http://www.worldbank.org/wbi/devdebates/MENA/brandsma_hart.pdf.
49 Ibid. p. 10.
50 For discussion on the relationship between informal sector and capitalist development see, Tabak, F. and Crichlow, M. A. (2000) *Informalization: Process and Structure*, Johns Hopkins University Press, Baltimore, MD.
51 Von Pischke, J. D., Adams, D. W. and Donald, G. (1983) *Rural Financial Markets in Developing Countries: their use and abuse*, Economic Development Institute, Baltimore.
52 Gonzalez-Vega, C. and Chaves, R. A. (1993) "Indonesia's Rural Financial Markets," A Report for the Financial Institutions Development Project and USAID, Jakarta, Indonesia, revised January 1993, p. 9.
53 Stiglitz, J. (1994) *Wither Socialism*, 1994, MIT Press, Cambridge, MA.

54 Fine, B. (2000) "Economic Imperialism and Intellectual Progress: The Present as History of Economic Thought?", *History of Economic Review*, 32(1): 13.
55 For endogenous theories of economic development see Mare, D. (2004) *Motu Economic and Policy Research*, 2004, "What do Endogenous Models Contribute?" http://econwpa.wustl.edu/eps/dev/ papers/0412/0412002.pdf; Sadoulet, L. and Carpenter, S. *Endogenous Matching and Risk Heterogeneity: Evidence on Microcredit Group Formation in Guatemala*: http://homepages.ulb.ac.be/ ~sadoulet/pdf/opthet0105.pdf.
56 Ibid, p.15
57 Peet, R. (2003) *Unholy Trinity: The IMF, World Bank and WTO*, Zed Books, London.
58 For a discussion on form and nature of the state in capitalist development see, Clarke, S. (1992) *The State Debate*, Macmillan, London, pp. 26–47. Clark has pointed out that the state is not, in the strictest sense, necessary to capitalist reproduction, nor can it be "logically derived from the requirements of the capitalist social reproduction. It is not formal or abstract; it is an historical necessity, emerging from the development of the class struggle, as a collective instrument of class domination: the state has not developed logically out of the requirements of capital, it has developed historically out of the class struggle." The problem of conceptualizing the state is then the same as the problem of conceptualizing the class struggle resulting from capitalism's drive toward self-realization.
59 Smith, N. (1990) *Uneven Development: Nature, Capital and the Production of Space*, Oxford University Press, Oxford, p. 142.
60 Ibid.
61 Allen, T. (2000) "Taking Culture Seriously," in T. Allen and A. Thomas (eds) *Poverty and Development into the 21st Century*, Oxford University Press, Oxford, pp. 249–67.
62 For a discussion of "Politics of Recognition" and "Politics of Redistribution" see Fraser, N. (1996) *Justice Interrupts: Critical Reflections on the "Postsocialist" Condition*, Routledge, New York.
63 For a discussion on the tension between Universal and relative rights see, Booth, K. (1999) "Three Tyrannies" in T. Dunne and N. J. Wheeler (eds) *Human Rights in Global Politics*, Cambridge University Press, Cambridge, pp. 11–71.
64 Harvey, D. (1996) *Justice Nature and the Geography of Differences*, Blackwell Publishers, p. 106.
65 Ibid. p. 105.
66 Ibid. p. 105.
67 Granovetter, M. (1985) "Economic Action and Social Structure: The problem of embeddedness" *American Journal of Anthropology* 91: 481–510; Stiglitz, J. (2001) "Forward" in K. Polyani, *The Great Transformation*, Beacon Press, Boston, MA, vii–xvii; Block, F. (2001) "Chapter 3" in Polyani, K. *The Great Transformation*, Beacon Press, Boston, MA, xviii–xxxvii.
68 Gupta, A. and Ferguson, J. (eds) (1997) *Culture, Power, Place: Explorations in Cultural Anthropology*, Duke University Press, NC.
69 Bashkow, I. (2004) "New-Boasian Conception of Cultural Boundaries," *Journal of The American Anthropological Association*, 106 (3), September: 453.
70 Abott, A. (2004) *Time Matters: On Theory and Method*, Chicago University Press, Chicago; Bashkow (2004): 453.
71 Moser, C. (1993) *Gender Planning in Development, Theory, Practice and Training*, Routledge, London; Kabeer, N. (1994) *Reserved Realities: Gender Hierarchies in Development Thought*, Verso, London; Visvanathan, N. (1997) "Introduction" in N. Visvanathan, L. Duggan, L. Nisonoff and N. Wiegerasma (eds) *The Women, Gender and Development Reader: Writing on Gender and Development*, Zed Books,

42 *Jude L. Fernando*

London, pp. 17–32; Young, K. (1993) "GAD and WAD" in V. Desai and R. Potter (eds) *The Companion to Development Studies*, Arnold, London, pp. 321–5.
72 For a detail discussion on the evolution of the notion of empowerment see Kabeer (1994); Rai, S. M. (2002) *Gender and Political Economy of Development*, Polity Press, Cambridge, Chapter 2; Peet and Hartwick (1999) pp. 163–94.
73 Barrett, M. (1988) *Women's Oppression*, London, p. 248.
74 Papart, J. (1995) "Post-modernism, Gender and Development," in J. Crush (ed.) *Power of Development*, Routledge, London, pp. 253–65; McEwan, C. (2001) "Post-colonialism, Feminism and Development: Intersections and Dilemmas," *Progress in Development Studies*, 1 (2): 93–111.
75 Kabeer, N. (1999) The Conditions and Consequences of Choice: Reflections on Measurements of Empowerment," UNRISD Discussion paper 108. Geneva: United Nations Research Institute For International Development.
76 Fernando (1997) p. 167. Fernando, J. L. (2002) p. 32.
77 Lawrence, S. (1997) "Micro-Credit's Dark Underside: Problems of Bangladesh's Grameen Bank," *The Next City*, Winter 1997.
78 Italics are my emphasis.
79 Burawoy, M. (2001) "Neoclassical Sociology: From End of Communism to End of Classes," *American Journal of Sociology* 106: 1118.
80 Clark, J. (1991) *Democratizing Development: The Role of the Voluntary Organizations*, EarthScan Publications, London; Farrington, J., Bebbington, A., Wellard, K. and Lewis, D. J. (1993) *Reluctant Partners: Non-governmental Organizations, the State and Sustainable Development*, Routledge, London; Sanyal, B. (1991) "Antagonistic Cooperation: A Case Study of Non-governmental Organizations, Government and Donors" Relationship in Income-Generating Projects in Bangladesh," *World Development* 19 (10): 1367–79; Tandon, R. "The Relationship between the NGOs and the Government," paper presented to the Conference on the Promotion of Autonomous Development, New Delhi: PRIA [1998], mimeographed. Fernando, J. and Heston, A. (eds) "NGOs between States and Markets, and Civil Society," ANNALS of American Academy of Political and Social Science, Volume 536, May 1998.
81 "Formalizing Microcredit: Crossing The Bridge Between Non-Governmental Organizations and Commercial Banks" (1999) Technical Paper, ST/ESA?PAD.5, Department of Economic and Social Affairs: Division For Public Economic and Public Administration, United Nations, New York, p. 4.
82 Ibid.
83 Ibid. p. 5.
84 Gonzalez Vega, C. (1994) "Stages of the Evolution of Thought on Rural Finance: A Vision from the Ohio State University," Economic and Sociological Paper, NO. 2134. The Ohio State University, Columbus, Ohio, p. 23; Op. cit. Formalizing Microcredit (1999).
85 Robinson, M. (2002) "A Paradigm Shift in Microfinance: A Perspective From HIID," Occasional Paper, Harvard Institute For International Development-HIID, Boston (Source: http:///www.hidd.bellanet.org/partners/mfn).
86 Fernando, J. L. (2002).
87 Ibid. p. 20.
88 Saleem Samad (2003) "New Policy Bans Political Activities of NGOs" Daily Times (26 April 2003), p. 2.
89 Association of Development Agencies of Bangladesh is the apex body of NGOs in Bangladesh, which is historically controlled by NGOs not so sympathetic towards microcredit and by individuals with more left-wing political sympathies.
90 Ibid., Formalizing Microcredit (1999) p. 5.
91 Ibid. p. 10.

2 The global political economy of microfinance and poverty reduction

Locating local 'livelihoods' in political analysis

Heloise Weber

Introduction

My concerns in this chapter are twofold: first, to provide a critical political analysis of microcredit and microfinance programmes implemented as poverty reduction schemes. My task, in critically examining debates around microcredit (and microfinance schemes) is to show how such schemes are a part of a wider process of political restructuring and to locate their ideological underpinnings within a neoliberal trend to advance and consolidate in particular – in formal legal terms – the current conjunctures of capitalism on a global scale. I pursue this analysis through an evaluation – and interpretation – of the social–legal and political frameworks constructed to deliver microfinancial services for the poor on a global scale *not* in terms of a 'development' agenda, but rather, in terms of a governance – or more specifically – a disciplinary approach which aims to 'lock in' local livelihoods in accordance with the imperatives of the restructuring of capitalism on a global scale. Implications of the latter include the re-regulation of legislation for the financial sector – that is, re-regulation conducive to neoliberal restructuring – at national, local and in some cases, regional levels. I show how this is achieved at the cost of social deprivation and social and political discipline. Second, my analysis entails a critical engagement of the methodological approaches that have informed conventional analyses of microfinance programmes. Through such an engagement I am able to identify the political dimension of specific methods that have been applied to the production and analysis of evidence in support of microfinance- and microcredit-based poverty reduction schemes. Together, these frame the conventional discourse about microfinance. Thus, a political analysis of microfinance schemes necessarily ought also to entail a critique of methodological choices upon which stories of their 'success' rest.

A few words clarifying my study of microfinance are necessary. My overall analysis is based on a study of microfinance-based poverty reduction schemes that are directly or indirectly connected, influenced or contingent upon the procedures of the policies of the World Bank (WB) and the International Monetary Fund (IMF). In this context, I address the emergence of microcredit as a policy for poverty reduction in the WB by considering its political significance initially for structural adjustment programmes (SAPs) and now for the comprehensively revised Poverty Reduction Strategy Paper (PRSP) Initiative. Although I focus on the role of the WB and the IMF in global political restructuring, my argument aims to demonstrate the potential global impact and more importantly global dimension of what are often conceived of as locally embedded poverty reduction schemes.

The chapter is organised in to three parts. Part one briefly considers the political context in which microcredit programmes emerged within key global institutions and demonstrates how they came to be appropriated to facilitate, consolidate and manage the contradictions of neoliberal global governance. Part two considers conceptual and theoretical issues central to analyses of the microfinance approach. Part three engages methodological aspects and analytical problems underpinning the study and evaluation of microfinance. The chapter concludes with a few thoughts on the social and political limits of attempts to 'embed' the neoliberal variant of capitalist restructuring through a poverty reduction discourse.

The global political context of the 'local' poverty reduction agenda

Since the 'crisis' of the 1970s global political restructuring has proceeded on an unprecedented scale (Amin, 1997; Ruggie, 1995). With the end of the so-called 'embedded liberal' compromise the original Bretton Woods agreement was brought to a close (Ruggie, 1982). This meant that Keynesean welfare politics was drawn back in favour of the norms and values advanced by the rise of the new right, reflected in Reaganomics and Thatcherite social and political policy. The consequences of this were global in scale, effecting political regulation within both the so-called 'developed' and 'developing' states. 'Adjustment' to the political-economy imperatives that were perceived to be a necessary response to the crisis of the 1970s has since been high on the global political agenda. In this context, various strategies that emerged from the 'new right' set out to provide a political framework for the construction of neoliberal governance on a global scale. In the development context, the framing discourse for this since the 1980s came to be referred to as the 'Washington Consensus' (WC).[1] By the late 1990s, the policies implemented under the WC were considered to be in need of reform in order to take explicit account of the persistence of poverty and rising inequality. This shift in focus – from macro-political re-regulation to micro-political aspects encompassing a focus on agency – came to be referred to as the post-Washington Consensus (post-WC). It is against the background of these developments that the global poverty reduction agenda of the twenty-first century is best located and evaluated. It is in this context also, that the political significance of the specific example of microfinance can be located and analysed.

In order to both develop and locate my argument with reference to the institutional policy shift away from a macro-political focus to that of poverty and poverty reduction, in what follows, I engage in more detail first, the socio-political implications of the WC, and then that of the post-WC.

Adjustment, resistance and governance

Adjustment to the imperatives of the new economy by many of the southern ('developing') countries often occurred in conjunction with the implementation of policies advanced by the IMF and the WB: specifically such polices were attached as conditionalities to funds borrowed by the 'developing' states. The central focus of the WC, while often conceived in terms of fiscal austerity, was actually lodged more within the progressive development of 'new constitutionalism' with its associated neoliberal discipline (Gill, 2002). In practice, this meant re-regulating domestic legislation in ways so as to bring about global convergence conceived in terms of 'private' international *commercial* law (Cutler, 1999a and b). The overt pressure involved in driving this agenda forward led to social and political resistance as a consequence of ever more obvious 'externalisation' of social risk and in particular because of its impact on the least advantaged. Indicative of this struggle, were widespread protests against SAPs with mounting political pressure on the implementing governments to redress such trends (e.g. Walton and Seddon, 1994). Reflecting wider concerns, analysts of development policy from the 'North' swung towards the advocacy of 'adjustment with a human face' (Cornia, Jolly and Stewart, 1987). These initial calls which often reflected concerns with specific policy implications of a SAP were followed by the gradual rise of social movements and political protests expressing general disquiet with the neoliberal political project on a global scale (e.g. Teivainen, 2002; Weber 2004a: 194–6). The concerns of the latter are not necessarily limited to particular adjustment policy or political processes confined to particular countries but is increasingly reflective of a broader global (transnational) counter-coalition to the project of global (transnational) neoliberal restructuring. Thus, since the 1990s there has been an overt political expression of a crisis of legitimacy in world politics.

The emergent focus on the 'poor' together with discourses of global poverty reduction can be seen as part of the response to this crisis of legitimacy. Such discourses present development and poverty reduction as a *core* objective of global politics (World Development Movement, 2001: 1); as such, this objective is ostensibly said to be the reason for the comprehensive remaking of forms of governance on a global scale. It is this shift that is said to characterise the normative and policy framework of the 'new' post-WC. This agenda is being worked into policy revisions within the World Bank, while similar concerns are being 'written' into institutional objectives of the IMF and even the World Trade Organisation (WTO, 2001: 2). Although previously, poverty reduction did not figure as an explicit and direct objective of the IMF and the WTO, both institutions are now consolidating, coordinating and unifying policy (together with the WB and other relevant institutions) *for* poverty reduction on a global scale (World Bank, 2000; Ben-David *et al.*, 1999; MDBs/IMF, 2000; OECD, 2000). These trends are reflected in concrete terms in the key poverty focused decisions taken in 1999 by the boards of the IMF and the WB. They include the strengthening of the link between international debt relief and poverty reduction policy, reflected in the enhanced Heavily Indebted Poor Country Initiative (HIPC2), as well as in the creation of the IMF and WB joint poverty focused conditionality, the Poverty Reduction Strategy Paper (PRSP) initiative (see Weber, 2004a). However, continuity of *content* rather than paradigmatic change with regards to the normative premises of the WC ensues – together with a more constrained political *form* – through the post-WC.

In this context, through a critical analysis of the examples of microcredit and microfinance schemes, it is possible to illustrate how political discipline mediated through social relations and formalised in legal terms has been advanced and consolidated since the late 1980s primarily against the backdrop of a poverty reduction discourse. For example, although microcredit schemes appear as a popular 'poverty reduction' policy in the post-WC context, they evolved within WB policy during attempts to manage social and political risks associated with SAPs. The context of the origins of microcredit schemes within key global institutions in terms of a targeted poverty reduction strategy, and their relatively advanced institutionalisation across levels from the global to the local, makes them a good example for the study of ways in which livelihoods are increasingly enmeshed within objectives of emerging global governance in the logic of efforts to construct a 'global constitution' for capitalism.

Global political restructuring and the institutional origins of microcredit

The institutional origins of microcredit schemes can be argued to date back to the 1970s during which small-scale credit-based projects existed in various forms under the rubric of rural development and in particular the development of rural financial markets. However, it is only since the mid-1980s that it really acquired the degree of scale and scope as reflected in the institutional policy framework of the 1990s and beyond. This occurred in the context of novel 'experimentations' in appeasing and/or disciplining popular protest and general disquiet directed at neoliberal restructuring: the appropriation of microcredit schemes under such circumstances involved – and evolved – together with attempts directed at legitimacy building to make SAPs in particular and neoliberal restructuring more generally, politically feasible and acceptable in an era of global 'democratisation'. The origins of microcredit credit schemes in such contexts can be illustrated by drawing on the Bolivian experience.

The Bolivian experience and political discipline: social funds and microcredit schemes

In the context of the emergence of (early) resistance to SAPs both the IMF and the World Bank recognised the need to counteract any such tendencies (Denters, 1996: 135). The pertinence of such a need became further evident in the context of one such experience: this was the Bolivian experience with the implementation of the 1986 Bolivian 'Structural Adjustment Program' under the broader rubric of the New Economic Programme (NEP). Attempts to implement the NEP encountered a substantial degree of political and social risk to which counteraction was deemed necessary for politically expedient reasons. Together with key Bolivian governmental representatives and prominent Bolivian businesspersons, the WB and the IMF set up an Emergency Social Fund (ESF) as a 'bottom' up micro-level strategy to complement the political restructuring at the macro-level. The ESF project was designed as a 'quick-disbursing mechanism for financing small, technically simple projects' (Jorgensen *et al.*, 1992: 6). Of the four types of projects considered suitable for ESF funding one included the provision of credit, 'through NGOs to *microenterprises* producing in the informal sector and to cooperatives in mining and agriculture' (Jorgensen *et al.*, 1992: 6).[2] Microcredit schemes constituted a large part of the ESF. The ESF approach was a departure from more traditional public-welfare programmes, such as those lodged within a policy of public provision of services and service subsidies set up to cushion so-called 'market-failures' under the period of embedded liberalism. This new approach, with its focus on *individualism* and *entrepreneurialism* suited the objectives of the NEP well: a WB evaluation of the ESF concluded that 'the ESF philosophy was consistent with the macroeconomic framework' (Jorgensen *et al.*, 1992: 120). The approach had, as an explicit focus, 'empowerment' of the 'poor' in both urban and rural areas. This was complemented by a widespread public discourse about the new 'public' support for the creation of an entrepreneurial culture within Bolivian society. Such a culture was presented as key to the construction of a vibrant Bolivian economy.

The World Bank and the encounter with dissent: 'mainstreaming' microcredit schemes

Although strategies which 'targeted the poor', in the sense of the ESF and possibly other similar examples, were already being implemented since 1986, it was not until 1988 that a distinct 'poverty focus' evolved in the World Bank. This was also the year the IMF acknowledged the political need for the inclusion of 'confidential standard instructions' in the context of adjustment programmes. The IMF acknowledgement entailed a commitment that WB and IMF staff proactively take on board considerations of the social and political impact of SAPs and suggest an appropriate response to the respective government concerned. As part of what was evolving as a wider poverty strategy during this time, it was decided that the WB would develop (further) an 'involvement with NGOs, poverty programmes, women's programmes, and *micro-enterprises*', (Kapur *et al.*, 1997: 368). This decision occurred in the context of the Bolivian ESF experience.

The political value of the ESF strategy generally – and the microcredit component in particular – was deemed important particularly because 'the timeliness and businesslike design of Bolivia's programme helped make it a model for replication for the World Bank. Other Social Emergency Funds were soon created, especially in Latin America and Sub-Saharan Africa' (Kapur *et al.*, 1997: 365). The ESF and ESF-type policies were supposedly originally designed as temporary measures to bridge the period between economic adjustment and recovery ('adjustment with a human face'). Meanwhile, however, the ESF policy framework has been adopted and transformed into a 'long-term' development and poverty reduction strategy (Ribe *et al.*, 1990). Since the Bolivian case the WB has rapidly increased its portfolio for Social Fund type programmes. At the end of fiscal year 1996, the World Bank had approved 51 Social Funds in 32 countries. All but five were IDA-financed (Narayan and Ebbe, 1997: 2–3).

The Bolivian ESF effectively set the precedent for the development of more comprehensive poverty focused targeted interventions at the policy level of the World Bank (World Bank, 1996). By the early 1990s clear policy was intact in the WB regarding targeted poverty interventions, and in 1991 the Operational Directive 4.15 (on Poverty) was approved. (This is now being redrafted in terms of OP 4.15). In practice, an increase in 'poverty targeting' has meant an increase in the application of Social Fund-type policies. Thus, a WB sponsored study stated that social funds were,

> *the most common and most popular means of extending credit to the very poor and are often set in countries undergoing major social adjustments.* Included in the characteristics of social funds is a focus on income generation or microfinance. Delivery of credit is usually through government agencies or NGOs using group delivery mechanisms.
>
> (emphasis added, CGAP, 1998a)

It is in this context that the appropriateness of microcredit schemes as an intervention into poverty reduction came to be placed on the global political agenda. Similarly, broader neoliberal restructuring has continued to be advanced 'in the name of the poor' with public discourses maintaining that *poverty reduction* is the primary objective of economic growth (e.g. World Development Movement, 2001; WTO, 2001).

The World Bank, IMF and SAPs: financial sector liberalisation and microcredit schemes

What makes microcredit schemes a particularly 'novel' example is that in addition to their commercial orientation more generally, they are financially driven. This means that as a strategy they have the potential to facilitate a core objective of neoliberal restructuring; that is, the liberalisation of the financial sector and the development of the financial *services* market. The latter aspect has been an important objective of the World Bank since the 1990s, together with the IMF and now also the WTO. For example, at the International Monetary Fund's annual meeting in Hong Kong SAR in September 1997,

> the Interim Committee issued a *Statement on the Liberalization of Capital Movements Under an Amendment of the IMF's Articles of Agreement*... to make the liberalization of capital movements one of the purposes of the IMF and extend, as needed, the IMF's jurisdiction in this area.
> (IMF, 1998: 74, 77)

As the WB and the IMF consolidate and intensify policy unification for 'poverty reduction', their mandates and operational guidelines are being simultaneously redrafted accordingly to reflect the emerging global financial framework (Key, 1999).[3] In this context, in some cases the 'tracks have already converged' with the 'trade in financial services' agenda of the WTO. 'In future, for all countries, routine IMF surveillance will be expanded to cover national financial systems, including both liberalization and prudential regulation' (Key, 1999: 73). Simultaneously, in the context of the division of labour between the IMF and WB,[4] Key notes that '[t]he World Bank is continuing to address these issues through its structural lending programs for the financial sector and its technical assistance programs' (1999: 72).

Closer analysis of IMF and WB cooperation shows how this agenda has developed historically both within and between these institutions. More recently, it becomes clear how this macro-political agenda has come to relate to the poverty reduction agenda, and the way in which it has shaped and informed the design and implementation of 'poverty reduction' programmes. (To be sure, the 'top-down' policy framework has being influenced by analyses of 'local' social and political struggles.) In the context of the institutional division of labour between the WB and the IMF, the

WB 'should focus in practice on the *reforms of administrative systems, production, trade and financial sectors*' (Denters, 1996: 160). Since the 1980s, policy began to emerge in pursuit of this objective, although it became more defined in the 1990s. The WB's strategy of advancing financial sector reform has been reflected in both the drafting and the redrafting of its policy for financial sector operations. For instance, an Operational Directive (OD) for the financial sector (OD 8.30) adopted in 1992 set out the broad policy agenda for financial sector operations. The redrafting of OD 8.30 in 1998 in the context of a general shift in WB policy from Operational Directives to Operational Policies (OP) does however reveal more than a shift from 'directive' to 'policy'. OP 8.30 outlines the way in which the new 'macro' level financial agenda is to be realised in practice (this aspect or lack thereof was considered to be a major limitation of OD 8.30). In the new revised policy for financial sector operations (OP 8.30) the strategy for policy *implementation* is clearly outlined, articulated in terms of discourses of poverty reduction with an emphasis placed on the development of microfinance schemes. Microfinance schemes figure quite significantly in the overall strategy of financial sector liberalisation and can be seen to guide the stages of implementation. In this sense, presented in terms of an approach to poverty reduction, they legitimate the establishment of the macro-level policy framework for the development of financial intermediary lending; this, in effect, enables the re-regulation of financial policy in accordance with the emerging trend to consolidate legislature for the trade in financial services. The 'implementation' aspect of the revised policy for the financial sector is a new addition that was not written as such in the former OD 8.30. To complement the WB's direct policy implications vis-à-vis microfinance and financial sector liberalisation, the WB Group and a donor consortium have established the Consultative Group to Assist Poorest (CGAP). The task of the CGAP is to develop 'best-practice' on microfinance, act as the global 'hub' to oversee adherence to appropriate policy and bring about enhanced, complementary linkages along the continuum of macro–micro financial policy. Detailed illustration of this has been provided elsewhere (Weber, 2004a).

Having examined the global context under which the mainstreaming of the scale and scope of microcredit programmes developed, we can move on to examine debates specific to the theoretical aspects as well as impact of such programmes.

The microcredit and microfinance agenda: what is in the detail?

Basic framework of microcredit programmes

The microcredit approach to poverty reduction is premised on the provision of small loans to individuals, usually within groups, as capital investment to enable income generation through self-employment. Microcredit programmes are usually complemented by the extension of microfinancial services, which may include, for instance, options for insurance schemes or savings. Microfinance departs significantly from other approaches to poverty reduction in that it is commercial in a fully-fledged sense. The approach institutionalised – and thus also the one being globalised – is minimalist in that it entails the offer (supply) of credit only: it entails no skills advancement or training schemes (capabilities enhancement) as part of the package.

Assumptions and premises examined: a neoliberal approach to poverty

The microfinance approach is premised upon a particular notion of poverty. Modern poverty is not seen as a consequence of a particular way in which society is organised through relations of power and domination. Neither is it seen as the consequence of the role that political decisions and specific ideas play in the production and reproduction of wealth and capital accumulation. Rather, the advocates of microfinance as an approach to poverty reduction view conditions of poverty (material insecurity and livelihood struggles) as the consequences of unfulfilled market potentials. The response from this latter perspective then becomes one of creating the appropriate market conditions, which, according to the theory at least, ought to empower all, and the poor in particular. Primacy is here accorded to enhancing entrepreneurial potential for which capital investment in turn becomes necessary. Through microfinance this problem is presumed to be resolved. The predominant focus thus becomes one about the *supply* of credit (microfinance) to the poor. In order to establish an enabling policy environment to enhance the supply of credit, the removal of what is termed as 'access barriers' to the credit provision is pursued. This entails the effort to replace rules, norms and laws deemed inappropriate for microfinance programmes with those more conducive to a liberal political order. These include the removal and/or replacement of barriers and include (perceived) socio-cultural constraints such as Islamic perspectives on interest, legislation that may reflect redistributive foci, anti-competitive practices (ceilings on interest rates, barter, collectivism) or ideological inhibitors to 'marketisation'. The latter could simply encompass discourses that critique neoliberal politics as exploitative and argue that the idea of progress for all is an ideological myth contrived to construct legitimacy for neoliberal political restructuring. Thus, the evangelical discourses of microfinance advanced by its proponents can be seen as a counter-discourse engaged in ideological struggle (Rogaly, 1996).

Theory and practice: complementary aspects of governance

In policy practice, as indicated above, microfinance has direct implications for the financial sector – and financial liberalisation in particular –

given that microfinance schemes are extended in terms of a fully-fledged commercial approach. In keeping with this logic, the preferential interest rates for microfinance usually are the optimal market rates. In some cases it is a condition that NGOs or Microfinance Institutions (MFIs) do *not* lend to the poor below a given commercial rate (World Bank, 1996: 51). Microfinance is also generally provided in the absence of conventional forms of collateral. Instead, group guarantee mechanisms such as peer monitoring and peer pressure are employed as a form of social collateral. However, emerging new laws, such as the Policy Framework Paper (PFP) in Bolivia is setting the precedent to set meagre belongings and/or even capital-worth possessions, such as land, as collateral against microfinancial services. It is also emerging that savings (on a weekly, monthly or on some other basis) are becoming mandatory rather optional and that such 'savings funds' will also serve as collateral against the provision of microfinance.

Contending discourses on the virtuous impact of microfinance and the politics of method

From the perspective of its proponents microfinance is said to result in a 'virtuous cycle': the transformation of the conditions of the poor from a 'vicious circle of poverty' to a 'virtuous cycle'. Such an understanding is based on the notion that the credit taken will be invested, which in turn will generate profits which together with more credit could lead to bigger investments, which will in turn lead to a repetition of the credit cycle (Otero and Rhyne, 1994; Schneider, 1997). Other perspectives on microfinance have been somewhat cautious about the 'virtuous outcomes' but have nevertheless not challenged the concept or its implications in political terms (Hulme and Mosley, 1996; Wood and Sharif, 1997). Generally, popular images and conventional wisdom maintain a positive correlation between microfinance and poverty reduction. The 1997 Microcredit Summit inaugurated a global microcredit campaign which committed to an 'action plan' to target 100 million poor families with microcredit by the year 2005 (RESULTS, 1997: 2). Thus, it is generally assumed that through microfinance people will become self-employed and thus self-sufficient.

Yet, there have been some studies that challenge the conventional wisdom of microfinance, including that of the Grameen Bank in Bangladesh (Benjamin and Ledgerwood, 1999; Khandker, unpublished; Rahman, 1998, 1999; Khondkar, 1998; Todd, 1996; Weber, 2002).[5] Moreover, the World Bank's own impact assessment studies have cautioned on the 'band-wagoning' of microcredit for poverty reduction (Benjamin and Ledgerwood, 1999: 12; Khandker, unpublished: 2). Despite such injunctions, as demonstrated in part one of this chapter, the microfinance agenda has continued to be consolidated at policy level across global institutions. The normative force underpinning discourses about the 'virtuous' impact of microfinance continues to legitimise the expansion of the agenda. At the same time, policy makers have reacted to critical impact assessment findings by changing the terms of reference in a way that both avoids engaging with the social impact and implications and allows for a privileging analysis of the success of microfinance in terms of *institutional* success. Thus, as long as institutional sustainability obtains, it has been fairly common practice among the policy makers – and their commissioned researchers – to interpret financial viability as indicative of the social, political and economic success of microfinance programmes.

Where the widespread use of microcredit for purposes other than for investment or self-employment prevails, policy makers now refer to such practices as 'consumption smoothing'. The equally widespread practice of poor clients borrowing from one NGO or MFI to pay off the other is simply referred to as 'cross-borrowing' or 'over-lapping'. The taking out of further loans to service repayment of old loans is referred to as a 'pyramid loans' system. Such narrow interpretations of the impact and implications of microfinance minimalism avoid engaging with highly problematic social and ultimately political consequences of the agenda. These narrow interpretations are a consequence of the analytical bias in interpreting the social impact in a way that accords a privileged status to an evaluation of 'success or failure' of microfinance in terms of institutional success. Such an approach is possible *because this* (i.e. institutional success) *has already been established as the criterion for assessing the success or failure of microfinance as a poverty reduction strategy*. It is assumed that measurements of institutional financial viability will necessarily reflect enhancement of social and political well-being. Economic indicators are thus drawn upon to tell a story about the development of emerging building blocks for 'future empowerment'. (Alternatively, one could also read the debt-laden survival [livelihood] struggles as a empowering process itself, although, it is not one which I myself would advance.) Thus, we can identify the relationship between method of inquiry and a broader ontological premise; establishing competitive financial institutions ought to be the primary objective as they are best suited to reduce poverty because they provide the foundation for entrepreneurial success. Such premises constitute the ideology and practice of neoliberalism.

If one changes the method of inquiry and the criteria of assessing success or failure one gets another interpretation of the social and political impact as well as consequences of microfinance. If, for example, we deconstruct the term 'consumption smoothing' we open up a different discourse that reveals these same practices and experiences from a contrastively different perspective. We encounter people taking the credit, often as a last resort to meet immediate and basic needs; we encounter people struggling to pay back their debts and resorting in desperation to more borrowing from other NGOs or MFIs. We encounter people resorting to the offer (sometimes from the same NGO of MFI which he or she is a member of) to take out new loans to pay off older ones. These newer loans would have to be larger or simply be used to make payments against the accrued interest rates. We encounter social pressure and in some cases physical violence directed at the 'debtors' to ensure that repayments are sustained. Meagre belongings if set as collateral against the credit are expropriated to ensure institutional success. From this alternative perspective on the world of microfinance, the starting premises for the criteria of assessment of success or failure are the *social* impact and the social *experiences* of microfinance. This reading could *explain* institutional success as a *consequence* of social immiseration. Moreover, from this perspective, the continued drive to entrench the compulsion of the pursuit of institutional success is seen as a process by which social struggle is intensified. In short, it can be seen as a political process that disciplines and exploits the social lifeworld in order to entrench and legally consolidate capitalist restructuring. Such an interpretation of this 'alternative' reading of microfinance (although it does not necessarily follow) could reflect ontological premises which maintain 'development' and the development of capitalism to be inherently contradictory.

What does this mean for the argument advanced so far? First, that the conventional story about microfinance has relied on a particular method through which it becomes possible to privilege a *particular* methodological approach. In our case, it is that of new institutionalism. Authoritative claims about the conventional story about microfinance emanate from analyses grounded in such an approach; the critical *experiences* of microcredit schemes are rendered even inexplicable from such analytical premises.

There is now some degree of official recognition of a 'crisis' in repayments and even of crisis of the microfinance industry (Cohen, 2002; Meyer, 2002; Woller, 2002). This has set challenges to the hitherto institutional viability of microfinance generally and the broader micro-base-level support such initiatives provide for the wider global financial liberalisation project. Yet, this crisis has not translated into a critical analysis of the social and political consequences of the poor clients. Rather, the discourse has once again shifted; it is now framed in terms of basing the next steps by listening to and meeting the needs of the poor. This 'new approach' includes a commitment to improve their facilities to save, which is now claimed to be one of the 'core' needs of the poor. This shift in discourse has continued to maintain a privileged focus on the MFI and the idea and practice of legalising and extending the Financial Intermediary (FI) in its neoliberal logic. In this sense, the 'new' savings agenda – in so far as it relies on the broader framework of the FI – continues to provide the bottom-up catalyst for the broader global financial services agenda.

Against this background, the question continues to arise: why is the microfinance minimalist approach still pursued, despite the discrepancies between its public image and the actual impact on poverty? The strategic embedding – dual function – of microcredit in the global political economy provides a substantial explanation for understanding not only the disjunction between the purported normative claims and actual experience, but moreover, *why* microfinance continues to be consolidated even under the 'adjusted' version of the WC. In other words, through such a process it is possible to advance social discipline and appease social and political resistance while simultaneously facilitating and entrenching neoliberal forms of governance.

Social consequences of the politics of methodological choices

In this section, by examining closely methodological underpinnings of analyses of microfinance schemes, my aim is to elucidate their political dimension and thus also the relevance of subjecting methodological choices themselves to critical political scrutiny. Through such an engagement I can identify specific *methods* that have been applied in the production and analysis of evidence in support of microfinance- and microcredit-based poverty reduction schemes. Together, these frame the conventional discourse about microfinance. Three aspects are particularly obvious in this regard;

1 Normatively, there is the association of the notion of empowerment with the taking of credit by 'the poor' for investment purposes, conceived in the broadest terms. In this context, social and political benefits – i.e. the normative 'goals'– as stipulated outcomes, serve to legitimise the global organisation of microfinance programmes.
2 Empirically, the evidence mobilised in support of microfinance and microcredit programmes in the realisation of the normative goals is selective. It is very much limited to that which relates to the measurement of institutional success, in terms of, for instance, loan (credit) repayment rates. Often, these indicators are then used to justify or to read off them a corresponding story about social empowerment.
3 Analytically, there is a tendency to explain the impact of microfinance by locating the strategy within the confines of the 'local'. The normative and empirical aspects outlined above are then brought together in ways that frame the overall analysis within these confines. The deployment of conventional sociological/anthropological methodology, which operates on the basis of *spatially* compartmentalised notions of the 'local' forecloses the possibility of engaging the impact as well as implications of microfinance schemes as mediated in terms of sets of *social relations* generally, *and* in terms of their constitution within a *global* rather than *local* space. This point is of paramount importance for understanding what is increasingly emerging in terms of a globally organised and globally regulated political system, in which microfinance schemes are embedded within a system of global financial circulation.[6]

Through a critical engagement with methodology and method, one is able to engage the discourses according to which microfinance and microcredit schemes are legitimated in ways that can draw attention to the ideological underpinnings of the criteria used to support this legitimation.[7] These discourses I take as politically constitutive practices that privilege particular methods of analysis on the basis of their compatibility with the broader neoliberal trend. For example, what constitutes valid 'knowledge' about microfinance and microcredit is biased in favour of the three aspects identified above. This means that the discourse of justification attached to microfinance is hierarchically structured, privileging certain types of evidence, experiences and ideas whilst marginalising others. The methods that underpin such analyses are conducive to the conventional methodological approach that informs overall analysis of microfinance programmes. Thus, a critical analysis of microfinance is also inevitably involved in a critique of the politics of – as well as the political consequences of – methodological choices.

My approach to microfinance analysis (as demonstrated above, but also in Weber 2002, 2004a, 2004b) is premised on the notion that livelihoods in specific locales can only be wholly comprehended when conceived of in their global context. This is particularly relevant for capturing the problems involved in studying localised livelihood effects of a global medium such as money/credit/finance. The latter, understood as constituted by *global social relations,* cannot be grasped in terms of a state-centric approach (i.e. the development benefits of microfinance interpreted as for example in terms of 'the development benefits of Bangladesh'). Nor can it be wholly captured merely in sociological or anthropological terms (i.e. without reference to the political economy imperatives that often underpin the emergence of such programmes). The approach I have outlined above in order to expose the strategic-embedding of microfinance in the global political economy and the associated disciplinary aspect, enables an analysis that can take full account of the way in which contemporary ideas and structures of governance – of which microfinance is a part – are mediated through *global social relations* and legitimated in terms of 'public' policy. For example, the social power relations which shaped the 'Bolivian experience of social and political struggles', or indeed the case of Bangladesh and the implementation of microcredit programmes in that country, can only be fruitfully captured through an appreciation of transnational social relations which mediate and reproduce the 'structures' and constitutional arrangements of global capitalism. This brings into view the globally constituted political order behind the emergence of what *appear to be* several locally-conceived microfinance schemes.

Thus, even those methodological approaches which retain a focus on the social but accord privileged analytical status to the 'social site of the local' in analyses of the success and failure of microfinance schemes are limited in the sense that they fail to acknowledge the *scale* of the *connectivity* of such schemes: the global flows of credit and finance regulated via emerging forms of global governance. Thus, the conventional 'development studies' approach, which among other things adopts a methodological territorialist conception of impact and implication assessment, fails both to retain an adequate focus on *social relations* as well as to appreciate the way in which 'local' livelihoods are shaped and influenced – and in turn, shape and influence – the current phase of capitalist restructuring on a *global scale*. Increasingly, 'local' livelihood struggles – and indeed the ways in which those struggles become played out and managed – reflect an interplay between:

1 the agendas and objectives of key global institutions which themselves are sites for the consolidation and extension of the ruling ideology (in our case, capitalism, expressed through neoliberalism), and
2 globally refracted social and political struggle to the ideological as well as substantive practical implications of neoliberal restructuring.

Thus, the 'micro-political' focus of anthropological and sociological inquiry into poverty would be richer if they were to be complemented with critical scrutiny of the trajectories of a wider range of social relations with an eye to revealing how such conditions are constituted by and reproduced through a global ideology of 'international development'. This in turn means that a radical rethinking is needed of the boundary of the 'international' and what it means for the demarcation it offers in terms of an infrastructure for development indicators (Brenner, 1999).

What I have attempted to advance here is that a critique of methodological choices in analyses of poverty and poverty reduction strategies is a necessary precondition for a critical study of the *global* organisation of microcredit schemes. What my empirical study has demonstrated is that the narrow framework of analysis employed by most development studies as well as some international relations scholars for the study of poverty in world politics need a radical work-over if we are not to reproduce – unwittingly – the architectural follies of politically naive analysis. Thus, a substantive critique of microfinance schemes ought to properly appreciate the global political economy embedding of what appear to be 'local' schemes and locate the analysis of the same within the context of capitalist restructuring. To understand the disciplinary and governance aspects which underpin microcredit schemes, social and political struggles ought to be located in terms of sets of global social relations and not taken in terms of a spatial framing of the political: this means moving from a spatial to a social cartography of development (Robinson, 2002; Weber, 2004a). Finally, we need to reconcile discourse with forms of governance; we need to relate discourses of emancipation more comprehensively to concrete practices of domination and ongoing efforts to entrench new as well old forms of property rights. In this way, will we be able to deconstruct what is claimed to be the 'intrinsic' value of microfinance for the 'poor' (Martin and Halstead 2004: 288), ask how such 'value' is mediated via social relations and inquire into what such value constitutes in concrete practical terms: from the basis of such premises we can properly start to engage with struggles of domination, exploitation and dispossession in terms of *political* analysis.

Notes

1 The term 'Washington Consensus' is meant to capture the dominance of the orthodoxy of what is referred to as the neoliberal turn in global capitalism during the late 1970s to the 1990s. For an account of the social implications of neoliberal policy prescriptions, see Caroline Thomas (Thomas, 1999).
2 The other three cited include: (1) economic infrastructure–infrastructure closely related to productive activities, such as road upgrading, urban improvement irrigation, flood control and reforestation; (2) social infrastructure – infrastructure for health and education, water and sanitation and basic housing; (3) social assistance – recurrent costs in education and training, vaccinations, school breakfast and production of school materials. It is interesting to note that as the focus was the implementation of 'labor intensive' activities, little attention was paid to the capabilities of the workers in relation to the projects. With reference to an assessment of the technical quality of works, the following was identified, 'In 1988, strong concerns arose that the technical quality of the physical works was so low as to jeopardize their value' (Thomas, 1999).
3 Sydney J. Key (1999) provides an account of the roles of the IMF and the World Bank in the process of financial liberalization under the General Agreement on Trade in Services (GATS) (*Services 2000*), in the WTO.
4 The World Bank is obliged by statute to design its operations in accordance with IMF objectives (see Article V Section 8 of the IBRD statutes). Article V Section 8 (b) Clause: 'In making decisions on application for loans or guarantees relating to matters directly within the competence of any international organization of the type specified in the preceding paragraph and participated in primarily by members of the Bank, the Bank shall give consideration to the views and recommendations of such organization'. Denters states that this implicitly points to the Fund and that there is no equivalent in the Fund's Statutes (1996: 153).
5 See for example, Benjamin and Ledgerwood (1999). This study is based on research conducted by the World Bank under the Sustainable Banking with the Poor (SBP) project, other literature on microfinance and their (authors) own experience over the last 15 years. On the issue of loan use, this study confirms that cross-borrowing is a part of survival strategies of the poor (i.e. where money is borrowed from one NGO to pay off the other); Shahidur Khandker (unpublished) has also noted that 'microcredit induced self-employment is a complement to child labor and that self-employed activity financed by a microcredit program may facilitate child employment' (p. 48); Aminur Rahman (1998, 1999) draws attention to the adverse social implications of microcredit programmes, as does Mubina Khondkar (1998). See also Helen Todd (1996); Weber (2002). My own field work in Bangladesh confirms the critical research findings.
6 I am thinking here of the example of the World Trade Organization (WTO). See for instance Markus Krajewski (2003a) and Howse and Nicolaides (2003).

7 I will simply use the term microfinance to imply microfinance-based poverty reduction schemes. I assume here that most microcredit schemes can now fall under the header of microfinance given that financial services now constitute the make-up of such schemes.

Bibliography

Altvater, E. (2002) 'The Growth Obsession' in Panitch, L. and Leys, C. *Socialist Register 2002 – A World of Contradictions*, London: Merlin.

Amin, S. (1997) *Capitalism in the Age of Globalization*, London: Zed Books.

Ben-David, D., Nordstrom, H. and Winters, L. A. (1999) *Trade, Income Disparity and Poverty*, WTO Special Study No. 5, Geneva: WTO.

Beneira, L. and Mendoza, B. (1995) 'Structural Adjustment and Social Emergency Funds' in Vivian, J. (ed.) *Adjustment and Social Sector Restructuring*, Geneva: UNRISD.

Benjamin, M. and Ledgerwood, J. (1999) 'Case Studies in Microfinance, Non-Governmental Organizations (NGOs) in Microfinance: Past, Present, Future – An Essay' available at www.esd.worldbank.org/sbp/end/ng.htm.

Brenner, N. (1999) 'Beyond State-centrism? Space, Territoriality, and Geographical Scale on Globalization Studies' *Theory and Society* 28: 39–78.

Bullard, N., Bello, W. and Malhotra, K. (1998) 'Taming the Tigers: the IMF and the Asian Crisis' *Third World Quarterly* 19 (3).

Burnham, P. (1994) 'Open Marxism and Vulgar International Political Economy' *Review of International Political Economy* 1 (2).

Cameron, A. and Palan, R. (2004) *The Imagined Economies of Globalization*, London: Sage.

Cerny, P. G. (1993) 'The political economy of international finance' in Cerny, P. G. (ed.) *Finance and World Politics: Markets, Regimes, and States in the Post-Hegemonic Era*, Cheltenham: Edward Elgar.

CGAP (Consultative Group to Assist Poorest) (1995a) *CGAP – A Policy Framework for the Consultative Group to Assist the Poorest*, Washington DC: World Bank.

—— (1995b) *Micro and Small Enterprise Finance: Guiding Principles for Selecting and Supporting Intermediaries* (the 'pink book', Washington DC: World Bank.

—— (1996) 'Newsletter-Issue 2', Washington DC: World Bank.

—— (1997a) 'Newsletter-Issue 3', Washington DC: World Bank.

—— (1997b) 'A Review of the World Bank's Microfinance Portfolio', Washington DC: World Bank.

—— (1998) *CGAP Phase II*, Washington DC: World Bank.

—— (1998b) *The Status Report – Consultative Group to Assist the Poorest 1995–98*, Washington DC: World Bank.

—— (1999) *Annual Report – July 1998–June 1999*; available at www.cgap.org.

Cohen, M. (2002) 'Making Microfinance more Client-led' *Journal of International Development* 14: 335–50.

Cornia, G. A. (2001) 'Social Funds in Stabilization and Adjustment Programmes: A Critique' *Development and Change* 32.

Cornia, G. A., Jolly, R. and Stewart, F. (1987) *Adjustment with a Human Face*, Oxford: Oxford University Press.

Cutler, C. (1999a) 'Public meets Private: the International Unification and Harmonisation of Private International Trade Law' *Global Society* 13 (1): 25–48.

—— (1999b) 'Locating "Authority" in the Global Political Economy' *International Studies Quarterly* 43 (1).
Deacon, B. (2000) 'Social Policy in a Global Context' in Hurrell, A. and Woods, N. *Inequality, Globalization and World Politics*, Oxford: Oxford University Press.
Denters, E. (1996) *Law and Policy of IMF Conditionality*, The Hague: Kluwer Law International.
DFID (2000) *Eliminating World Poverty: Making Globalization Work for the Poor*, Norwich: The Stationary Office.
Dunkerley, J. (1990) *Bolivia – Political Transitions and Economic Stabilization, 1982–1989*, London: Institute for Latin American Studies.
Engberg-Pedersen, P., Gibbon, P., Raikes, P. and Udsholt, L. (eds) (1996) *Limit of Adjustment in Africa. The Effects of Economic Liberalisation, 1986–94*, Copenhagen, Oxford and Portsmouth, Centre for Development Research, Copenhagen: James Curry).
Germaine, R. D. (1997) *The International Organization of Credit – States and Global Finance in the World Economy*, Cambridge: Cambridge University Press.
Gill, S. (2002) 'Constitutionalizing Inequality and the Clash of Globalizations' *International Studies Review* 4 (2): 47–65.
Glaessner, D. J., Lee, K. W., Sant'anna, A. M. and St Antoine, J. J. (1994) *Poverty Alleviation and Social Investment Funds – The Latin American Experience*, Washington, DC: World Bank.
Helleiner, E. (1992) *States and the Re-emergence of Global Finance*, Ithaca, NY, Cornell University Press.
—— (1993) 'When Finance was the Servant: International Capital Movements in the Bretton Woods Order' in Cerny, P. (ed.) *Finance in World Politics*, Cheltenham: Edward Elgar.
Howse, R. and Nicolaides, K. (2003) 'Enhancing WTO Legitimacy; Constitutionalisation or Global Solidarity?' *Governance* 16 (1): 73–94.
Hulme, D. and Mosley, P. (1996) *Finance against Poverty*, (2 Vols), London: Routledge.
IMF (1998) *Annual Report 1998*, Washington DC: IMF.
Jayarajah, C., Branson, W. H. and Sen, B. (1996) *Social Dimensions of Adjustment – World Bank Experience*, Washington DC: World Bank.
Johnson, S. and Rogaly, B. (1997) *Microfinance and Poverty Reduction*, Oxford: Oxfam.
Jorgensen, S., Grosh, M. E. and Schacter, M. (1992) *Bolivia's Answer to Poverty, Economic Crisis and Adjustment – The Emergency Social Fund*, Washington DC: World Bank.
Kapur, D., Lewis, J. P. and Webb, R. C. (1997) *The World Bank – Its First Half Century*, Washington DC: Brookings Institute.
Keane, J. (1984) 'Introduction' in Offe, C. *Contradictions of the Welfare State*, London: Hutchison.
Key, S. (1999) 'Trade Liberalization and Prudential Regulation: the International Framework for Financial Services' *International Affairs* 75 (1).
Khaled, M. H. (1998) 'Overlapping Problems in Microcredit Operations' *The Microcredit Review* 1 (1).
Khandker, S. (1995) 'Fighting Poverty with Microcredit' unpublished research paper (World Bank, Poverty and Social Policy Department).
Khondkar, M. (1998) *Women's Access to Credit and Gender Relations in Bangladesh*, PhD Thesis, University of Manchester.

Kindleberger, C. (1987) *Marshal Plan Days*, Boston: Allen & Unwin.
Krajewski, M. (2003a) 'Public Services and Trade Liberalization: Mapping the Legal Framework' *Journal of International Economic Law* 6 (2); 341–67.
—— (2003b) *National Regulation and Trade Liberalization in Services*, The Hague: Kluwer Law.
Lacher, H. (1999) 'Embedded Liberalism, Disembedded Markets: Reconceptualising the Pax Americana' *New Political Economy* 4 (3): 343–60.
Leroux, H. E. (2002) 'Trade in Financial Services under the World Trade Organization' *Journal of World Trade* 36 (3).
Martin, L. M. and Halstead, A. (2004) 'Attracting Micro-Enterprises to Learning in Community' *Work & Family* 7 (1): 29–70.
MDBs/IMF (2000) Global Poverty Report to G8, July 2000, available at www.worldbank.org.html/extdr/extme/G8_poverty2000.pdf.
Mendoza, M. R. (1989) *Uruguay Round-Papers on Selected Issues*, Geneva: United Nations.
Meyer, R. L. (2002) 'The Demand for Flexile Microfinance Products; Lessons from Bangladesh' *Journal of International Development* 14: 351–68.
Mishra, R. (1999) *Globalization and the Welfare State*, Cheltenham: Edward Elgar.
Mittelmann, J. H. (2002) *The Globalization Syndrome: Transformation and Resistance*, Chichester: Princeton University Press.
Narayan, D. and Ebbe, K. (1997) *Design of Social Funds-Participation, Demand, Demand Orientation, and Local Organizational Capacity*, Washington DC: World Bank.
Nusbaumer, J. (1986) 'Preface' in Giarini, O. (ed.) *The Emerging Service Economy*, Oxford: Pergamon Press.
OECD (2000) *The DAC Journal – International Development* 1 (1), Paris: OECD.
Offe, C. (1984) *Contradictions of the Welfare State*, London: Hutchison.
Otero, M. and Rhyne, E (eds) (1994) *The New World of Micro-finance Enterprise – Building Healthy Financial Institutions for the Poor*, London: Intermediate Technology Publications.
Palan, R. (1999) 'Global Governance and Social Closure, or "Who is to be Governed in the Era of Global Governance"' in Hewitt, M. and Sinclair, T. (eds) *Approaches to Global Governance Theory*, Albany: SUNY Press.
Preston, L. T. (1994) 'Partnership to Fight Hunger' in World Bank, *Overcoming Global Hunger*, Washington DC: World Bank.
Rahman, A. (1998) *Rhetoric and Realities of Micro-Credit for Women in Rural Bangladesh*, PhD Thesis, University of Manitoba.
—— (1999) 'Microcredit Initiatives for Equitable and Sustainable Development: Who Pays?' *World Development* 2 (1).
RESULTS (1997) *Microcredit Summit Report, Feb 2–4 1997*, Washington DC: RESULTS.
Ribe, H., Subbarao, R., Habib, M., Raney, L. and Carvalho, R. (1990) *How Adjustment Programs Can Help the Poor*, Washington DC: World Bank.
Robinson, W. I. (2002) 'Remapping Development in the Light of Globalization: from a Territorial to a Social Cartography' *Third World Quarterly* 23 (6): 1047–71.
Rogaly, B. (1996) 'Microfinance Evangelism, "Destitute Women", and the Hard Selling of a New Anti-Poverty Formula' *Development in Practice* 6 (2): 100–12.
Ruggie, J. G. (1982) 'International Regimes, Transactions, and Change: Embedded Liberalism in the Postwar Economic Order' *International Organization* 36 (2): 379–415.

—— (1995) 'At Home Abroad, Abroad at Home: International Liberalisation and Domestic Stability in the New World Economy' *Millennium* 24 (3).

Rutherford, S. (2002) 'Microfinancial Services' *Journal of International Development* 14: 273–94.

Sachs, J. D. (1990) *Developing Country Debt and Economic Performance: Volume 2*, London: University of Chicago Press.

Saurin, J. (1995) 'The End of International Relations? The State and International Theory in the Age of Globalization' in MacMillan, J. and Linklater, A. (eds) *Boundaries I Question – New Directions in International Relations*, London: Pinter.

—— (1996) 'The Promises of Modernity' *Millennium* 25 (3): 657–80.

—— (2001) 'The Global Organisation of Disaster Triumphant: the Unintended Consequences of Enlightenment' Discussion paper presented at the ISA Convention, February 2001.

Schefer, K. N. (1999) *International Trade in Financial Services: The NAFTA Provisions*, London: Kluwer Law.

Schneider, H. (1997) *Microfinance for the Poor*, Paris: IFAD/OECD.

Stewart, F. and van der Geest, W. (1995) *Adjustment and Poverty – Options and Choices*, London: Routledge.

Teivainen, T. (2002) *Enter Economism, Exit Politics: Experts, Economic Policy and the Damage to Democracy*, London, Zed Books.

Thomas, C. (1985) *New States, Sovereignty and Intervention*, Hants: Gower.

—— (1987) *In Search of Security – The Third World in International Relations*, Sussex: Harvester.

—— (1999) 'Where is the Third World Now?' *Review of International Studies* 25.

—— (2000) *Global Governance, Development and Human Security*, London: Pluto Press.

Todd, H. (1996) *Women at the Centre: Grameen Borrowers after one Decade*, London: Westview Press.

Vivian, J. (ed.) (1995) *Adjustment and Social Sector Restructuring*, Geneva: UNRISD.

Waller, G. (2002) 'From Market-Failure to Marketing Failure: Market Orientation as the Key to Deep Outreach in Microfinance' *Journal of International Development* 14: 305–24.

Walton, J. and Seddon, D. (1994) *Free Markets and Food Riots: The Politics of Global Adjustment*, Oxford: Blackwell.

Weber, H. (2002) 'The Imposition of a Global Development Architecture: the Example of Microcredit' *Review of International Studies* 28 (3): 537–56.

—— (2004a) 'Reconstituting the "Third World"?: Poverty Reduction and Territoriality in the Global Politics of Development' *Third World Quarterly* 25 (1): 187–206.

—— (2004b) 'The "New Economy" and Social Risk: Banking on the Poor?' *Review of International Political Economy* 11 (2): 356–86.

Woller, G. (2002) 'The Promise and Peril of Microfinance Commercialization' *Small Enterprise Development* 13 (4): 12–21.

Wood, G. D. and Sharif, I. A. (1997) *Who Needs Credit? Poverty and Finance in Bangladesh*, London: Zed Books.

World Bank (1992) 'Financial Sector Operations – OD 8.30' *Operational Policy Manual* available at www.worldbank.org.

—— (1994) *Bangladesh – Privatization and Adjustment*, Washington DC: World Bank.

—— (1995) 'World Bank News – International Donors provide big backings for small loans', available at www.worldbank.org/html/extcs/wbn0720.htm.

—— (1996) *Bangladesh, Poverty Alleviation Microfinance Project*, Washington DC: World Bank.

—— (1998) 'Financial Intermediary Lending – OP 8.30' *Operational Policy Manual*, available at www.worldbank.org.

—— (1999) *Poverty Reduction and the World Bank – Progress in Fiscal 1998*, Washington DC: World Bank.

—— (2000) 'The World Bank Group Operations Policy and Strategy, "Poverty Reduction Strategy Papers Internal Guidance Note"', available at www.worldbank.org.

World Bank/IMF (1999) 'Overview: Transforming the Enhanced Structural Adjustment Facility (ESAF) and the Debt Initiative for the Heavily Indebted Poor Countries (HIPC) Initiative – Strengthening the Link between Debt Relief and Poverty Reduction' Policy paper, Washington DC: IMF/World Bank.

World Development Movement (2001), available at www.wto.org.uk/campaigns/Genoa.htm.

World Trade Organization (2001) Ministerial Declaration, Doha, available at www.wto.org/english/thewto_e/minist_e/min01_e/mindecl_e.htm.

3 Disciplining the developmental subject

Neoliberal power and governance through microcredit

Morgan Brigg

The provision of targeted credit has been a longstanding strategy in national development efforts in the South or Third World. In Bangladesh, the birthplace of microcredit through the now famous and globally influential Grameen Bank, rural credit was touted as central to development efforts in the 1970s.[1] However, neoclassical economists, who argued that such practices resulted in a distortion of the market for scarce investment funds, identified subsidised credit as a failure from the mid-1970s.[2] During this same period, a number of Non-Government Organisations (NGOs) experimented with mechanisms for the alternative delivery of credit. These 'microcredit' initiatives involved the provision of collateral-free small loans to jointly liable people for the purposes of income generation and self-employment. The recipients of loans were typically not eligible for credit from commercial lenders, and were predominantly women. Microcredit programmes expanded rapidly in Bangladesh generating a wave of enthusiasm in development circles with the Microcredit Summit Secretariat (MCS) launching a 'global movement to reach 100 million of the world's poorest families, especially the women of those families, with credit for self-employment and other financial and business services, by the year 2005'.[3]

Amid the enthusiasm for microcredit the critical response from development studies has been somewhat muted. This is in part a corollary of the 'impasse' of the 1980s,[4] and the fact that development studies is still coming to terms with the rise of NGOs and the proliferation of associated notions such as autonomy and empowerment in the shifting development project. As development studies is informed by both a strong economic orientation and attempts to address the realities of poverty, microcredit is further insulated from critical inquiry as an initiative which promises both a commonsense good such as 'empowerment' and a better standard of living for the poor. This chapter assists in addressing this lacuna by developing a critical analytical framework for considering the place of NGOs and notions of empowerment in a shifting development project, and analysing the operation of microcredit as a technology of developmental discipline and governance.

I first show that the critical tools for understanding the shifts in the development project need to be extended beyond those approaches that centre economic relations. To begin to address this need I develop one aspect of post-development literature by drawing on Michel Foucault's notion of *dispositif* and making some adjustments for the use of this concept to date. The *dispositif* is particularly useful for allowing the fluidity and heterogeneity of the development project, and for considering of relations of knowledge, power and subjectivity alongside the economic. To address the question of the rise of NGOs and associated notions of autonomy and empowerment, I draw upon Foucault's notion of governmentality to demonstrate that the rise of NGOs is not necessarily emancipatory. Rather, I show that apparently apolitical practices and initiatives that effect simultaneously individualising and totalising operations of power are central to liberal governance and that with a shifting development project these operations can penetrate into and result in a neoliberal governmentalisation of the Third World. I then examine the Grameen Bank and the microcredit movement showing that this neoliberal approach to poverty effects a governmentalised operation of power that links individual Third World subjects with First World capital markets in an operation of developmental discipline.

Beyond economic relations: responding to the changing development project

Shifts within the development project of the 1980s have led to a greater role for NGOs in development efforts. For instance, Abu Sarker[5] notes that in the case of Bangladesh, reduction in public services and state spending was accompanied by increased support for NGOs by Bangladesh's external development partners. More generally, the downsizing of state-based functions of social welfare and development have resulted in the emergence of NGOs as prominent players in development efforts.[6] NGOs are also at the centre of the proliferation of a range of approaches including eco-, participatory, autonomous and sustainable development which are, in some respects, less directly informed by the drive for economic growth.[7] In other words, although development has always been multifaceted and while the economic remains important, these diverse shifts signal the dispersion and diversification of development efforts and programmes in recent decades.

Much of development studies is not well placed to adequately analyse the multifaceted and changing nature of development efforts. Despite the recent emergence of 'post-development' literature, which I will turn to shortly, much of critical development studies retains Marx's critical irruption into classical political economy as its legacy. Dependency theory and its contemporary variants focus on the exploitative and uneven relations set up in the world capitalist economy;[8] the historical-analytic approach of

Immanuel Wallerstein's world systems theory defines the boundaries of a historical system on the basis of the division of labour;[9] the regulation school focuses on 'regimes of accumulation' of economic products and accompanying 'modes of regulation';[10] and various other political economy of development approaches analyse commodity chains and consider the differential positions occupied by human subjects in global production and consumption networks.[11]

These approaches have much to offer in explicating the inequalities perpetuated through the world capitalist system as they are a well-developed and wide-ranging set of analytical tools for studying relations of production and their associated effects. However, despite the influence Marxist-derived approaches have exerted, it is untenable to assume that drawing on economic relations allows us to adequately deal with *all* relations of domination through the multifaceted development enterprise, or with development as a whole. Nor should the economic assume priority: as several critical scholars[12] have argued, the *economic* is a cultural element that is specific, in the first instance, to eighteenth and nineteenth century Western Europe. It has only subsequently been universalised, in part through Marxism and related critical approaches based in economic relations.[13] The requirement to move beyond approaches based in economic relations is rendered more pressing as development becomes increasingly dispersed beyond the economic sphere from the mid-1980s.

Philip McMichael's[14] effort is interesting in the context of these shifts for its acknowledgement of and attempts to deal with these shifts while broadly maintaining a political economy framework. McMichael argues that the reshuffle of development from the 1970s represents a shift from the 'development project' to the 'globalisation project': a shift from a nationally to a globally managed pursuit of economic growth. To come to terms with other aspects of the reconfiguration of development, and to identify possibilities for resistance to dominant economic forces, he frames an opposition between economic 'globalists' who embody a rational and neoliberal economistic ethos, and cultural 'localists' who advocate local knowledge, small-scale communities, and expressivism and self-empowerment.[15] For instance, he argues that globalisation (conceived primarily as an economic process) weakens nation states, but where this occurs, 'citizens have fresh opportunities to renew the political process ... [and generate] opposition'.[16] These 'responses to globalisation' include fundamentalism; new social movements such as environmentalism, feminism and the cosmopolitan localism exemplified in the Chiapas Indigenous movement; and the reinvigoration of civil society more generally. The importance of the new social movements is particularly manifest in the approaches adopted by NGOs.

Although McMichael's interpretation clearly recognises the need to account for the shifts from the 1970s into the 1980s, his separation of economic from non-economic relations and forces shares problems with more conventional economic approaches because it elides the way in which relations of power proceed through economic *and* non-economic relations. In other words, the investing of expressivist, culturalist and localist movements with the power to subvert dominant economism and development limits the analytical purchase we can bring to bear upon the reshuffle of the development project and the current conjuncture. In doing this it both limits interpretation of developmentalism as a culturally and historically contingent conceptualisation of social change and diverts attention from the ways in which the movements that have emerged with the reshuffle of development may themselves be part of an operation of power and governance. It also diverts attention from the likely linkages between the 'economic' and 'non-economic' in the new initiatives that emerge through the reconfiguring of development.

From approximately the mid-1980s, a new body of critical literature has emerged which is not constrained by this centring of economic relations. 'Post-development'[17] takes a radical stance by questioning the very category and project of development itself. This scholarship draws on the discursive turn in the social sciences as well as local, indigenous, and marginalised knowledges to challenge many of the received orthodoxies of other approaches. Contributors have thus analysed development not only as a form of economic exploitation, but also as environmentally maladaptive, as a discourse, a way of imagining the world, and violence against local and indigenous cultures. With this broad purview, post-development offers ways of mitigating the centring of economic relations which has tended to dominate development studies.

The development *dispositif*

Within post-development literature, one of the most promising avenues for coming to terms with the complex and multifaceted nature of development has been opened up by Arturo Escobar[18] and James Ferguson[19] through their introduction of Foucault's notion of *dispositif*, or apparatus. Foucault uses the term *dispositif* to refer to a 'thoroughly heterogeneous ensemble' of discursive and material elements.[20] A *dispositif* may consist of 'discourses, institutions, architectural forms, regulatory decisions, laws, administrative measures, scientific statements, philosophical, moral and philanthropic propositions' and so on.[21] The *dispositif* is not simply the collection of elements per se but also the 'system of relations ... established between these elements'.[22] The relationships between the various elements can be conceptualised in terms of relations of knowledge (discourse), power and subjectivity.[23]

In these relatively broad terms, the notion of the *dispositif* is appropriate for considering the postwar development project that emerges and operates as a complex ensemble of institutions, discourses, resource flows, programmes, projects and practices. Furthermore, because a heterogeneous collection of elements which acts on and emerges through the actions of a multitude of subjects clearly cannot operate entirely in concert, this conceptualisation avoids the tendency, indulged by some post-development writers, to view development and its effects as monolithic and uniform.[24] The heterogenous nature of the apparatus, and the idea that effects are not necessarily predictable, means that a wide range of both positive and negative outcomes can be generated through development without attributing these to a meta-subject or force, or requiring that we solely see imposition or interdiction at play. At the same time, though, such ensembles operate to achieve overall effects, thereby serving a dominant strategic function.[25] For example, Foucault states that in the case of the *dispositif* of madness in the nineteenth century, such a function was 'the assimilation of a floating population found to be burdensome for an essentially mercantilist economy'.[26] Hence while the various elements of the development *dispositif* clearly do not always operate in concert, they do have a relation to one another, they form an identifiable project, and they have an overall strategic effect, as Escobar[27] points out, of governing the Third World.

While Ferguson and Escobar introduce the *dispositif*, they do not offer a significant explication of the term, and their use of it can be taken further and deployed more carefully. For instance, while there is much to recommend Ferguson's grounded ethnographic approach to the development apparatus, he regularly refers to it as a 'conceptual apparatus', even indicating that this specification derives from Foucault.[28] However, Foucault clearly states that the *dispositif* is an ensemble of material and discursive elements.[29] The development *dispositif* may organise the way development scholars and practitioners *conceptualise* development, but this is something quite different from a conceptual apparatus. Moreover, the idea that any single dimension of knowledge, power or subjectivity (or any other set of relations such as the economic) should not be prioritised or given a central organising role is central to the analytic framework of the *dispositif* and efforts to avoid the problems of the approaches discussed above.

Although Escobar uses the term apparatus much less regularly, a similar problem is evident in the place he accords the apparatus in relation to developmentalism, or the discursive formation of development. He states that: 'The ensemble of forms found along these axes [of knowledge power and subjectivity] constitute development as a discursive formation, giving rise to an efficient apparatus that systematically relates forms of knowledge and techniques of power.'[30] While it is somewhat unclear what is giving rise to the 'efficient apparatus' in this statement, Escobar appears to be suggesting that the discursive formation gives rise to the *dispositif*, or that it at least has a prominent organising role. Such a reading is supported by the role he claims for discourse in an earlier article, where he states that the 'discourse of development ... was able to form systematically the objects of which it spoke, to group them and arrange them in certain ways, to give them a unity of their own'.[31] However, while in *The Archaeology of Knowledge* Foucault argued that discursive formations order the relationship of a range of material and discursive elements,[32] he also struggled to justify this prioritising of discourse before adjusting his methodology with works including *Discipline and Punish* and *The History of Sexuality*.[33] This later approach views relations of discourse and relations of power (both conceptualised as 'practice') as mutually conditioning. In short, it is not possible to prioritise the discursive dimension of development over the more concrete development apparatus. Thus while Escobar and Ferguson have introduced the notion of the *dispositif* it must be used more carefully to satisfactorily extend our analytical tools for understanding the shifting development project.

The notion of dispositif is not articulated closely in Foucault's work and problems in translation potentially cause confusion. Despite the emergence of the term 'apparatus' as the most common translation, translators have noted that there is no straightforward corresponding term in English.[34] This perhaps accounts for some mistranslations, most notably in *The History of Sexuality*[35] where *dispositif* has been translated as a 'construct' or 'deployment'.[36] In this situation Gilles Deleuze's[37] explication is useful as it as the only significant elaboration of the *dispositif*.

Deleuze conceptualises the *dispositif*, in the first instance, as a *concrete social apparatus* and a 'tangle, a multilinear ensemble'.[38] This formulation conveys the concern, shared by Foucault and Deleuze, that theory should be a tool to aid analysis rather than a reified entity or end in itself.[39] In more detail, Deleuze's account renders the multilinear ensemble as:

> composed of lines, each having a different nature. And the lines in the apparatus do not outline or surround systems which are each homogeneous in their own right, object, subject, language, and so on, but follow directions, trace balances which are always off balance, now drawing together and then distancing themselves from one another.... Visible objects, affirmations which can be formulated, forces exercised and subjects in position are like vectors and tensors.[40]

Thus an element of the *dispositif*, whether it be an institution, a particular programme, or a practice, is integral to the apparatus. An element emerges and becomes recognisable at the same time as it gains a level of density in the *dispositif*. Following their emergence, elements are always subject to renegotiation, displacement, or consolidation. While the *dispositif* is flexible and somewhat amorphous, it consists in, and is therefore identifiable when, we find 'strategies of relations of forces supporting and supported by, types of knowledge'.[41]

Deleuze explicates three dimensions – relations of knowledge, power and subjectivity – of the *dispositif*, which correspond to each of the three major aspects of Foucault's work. This is a heuristic rather than substantive differentiation since the dimensions of knowledge, power and subjectivity are recursive and formative of each other; they are 'variables which supplant one another'.[42] In other words, the dimensions of knowledge, power and subjectivity 'are irreducible, yet constantly imply one another'.[43] While a *dispositif* exhibits a certain level of coherence and density, the multiplicity of relations that make up the development ensemble are continually renegotiated and open to contestation, reaffirmation, or consolidation. In this sense, the *dispositif* can be viewed as a more or less durable shifting coagulation of heterogenous elements. Over the decades from the 1950s to the 1970s, the development *dispositif* both attains a level of density and exhibits a multiplicity of 'internal' shifts and minor reconfigurations. These include discourses about participation, rural versus urban development, community development and so on. However, the period from the late 1970s and into the 1980s sees a major reconfiguration of the development project, giving rise to interpretations such as McMichael's thesis about a shift from a development to a globalisation project.

The notion of *dispositif* provides a critical interpretive and analytical framework that moves beyond the problems of approaches based in economics and can accommodate the flux that characterises the current state of play in development efforts. It allows us to maintain the various elements of the reconfigured development project and the accompanying relations of knowledge, power and subjectivity in their appropriate dispersion. This means that an initiative need not be reduced to any particular set of relations. The *dispositif* also allows the drawing out of the interconnectedness among various sets of relations that emerge in 'new' initiatives in development such as autonomous development and the microcredit movement in order to consider how development reinvents itself. To develop and concretise this analytical framework I consider the relationship between liberalism and relations of power and governance, before turning to the rise of neoliberalism and NGOs. I then briefly discuss the notions of autonomy and empowerment that are prominent in NGO discourse before turning to the microcredit movement.

Governmentality, NGOs and neoliberalism in the development *dispositif*

A central theme in Foucault's work on power is the correlation between the rise of the self-regulating and self-producing subject of liberalism and the increasing penetration of the mechanisms of power and governance into both the social and individual body. With his neologism 'governmentality', Foucault disrupts conventional political theory by showing that while liberalism, as both a political theory and rationality of government, concerns itself with a self-determining and autonomous subject, it is actually under the cover of and through such a view and modality that contemporary power and governing proceeds.[44] The 'free subject' of liberalism is produced as s/he is acted upon and acts upon her- or himself without the need for the operation of power as imposition or interdiction. Hence the extension of a certain type of control and governing of human subjects is consistent with the principle of liberal political rationality that '"One always governs too much" – or, at any rate, one always must suspect that one governs too much'.[45]

For Foucault, governmentalisation occurs through the increasing involvement of the lives of individuals in the exercise of formal or state power.[46] Crucial to this process are broad social programmes and goals such as security, health, and economic development that can garner widespread support and also be mobilised to discipline individual subjects. Giovanna Procacci,[47] for instance, shows how the recasting of pauperism from a wealth–poverty opposition to the employment–unemployment couplet forms part of the governmentalisation of nineteenth century European society. This becomes necessary in the context of economic growth and development of political economy because the wretched peasant embodies the danger of subversion (since s/he challenges the injunction to wealth) and at the same time is a privileged object in so far as s/he is 'the ideal model for the expansion of needs'.[48] The key point is that with such shifts the surveillance, monitoring and disciplining of personal conduct comes to be possible and be effected through social integration in terms of a wider goal.[49] Governmentality is thus both an individualising and totalising form of power.[50] Crucial here is the role of the seemingly non-political role of technologies and expertise such as social work, teaching, and economic and town planning which, as a range of governmentality scholars[51] who extend upon Foucault's neologism have shown, link technologies of individuation with wider programmes. These technologies both incite subjects to act upon themselves, and thereby engage in self-production and regulation with certain effects, and connect subjects with wider programmes and goals including economic development.

From the late 1970s these 'non-political' technologies became reinvigorated through the rise of neoliberalism which 'reactivates liberal principles: scepticism over the capacities of political authorities to govern for the best ... [and] vigilance over the attempts of political authorities to seek to govern'.[52] In this schema, markets replace government planning, social service and welfare is discouraged, and economic entrepreneurship is promoted. As leading governmentality scholar Nikolas Rose[53] has shown, this neoliberal environment is fertile ground for a variant form of governmentalisation that does not require 'society' or the state for the governing of subjects through the choices of, among others, consumers, employees, managers and investors. Although the context is different, there are clear resonances with recent programmes of the World Bank and International Monetary Fund (IMF) and the decline of nation-state involvement in development efforts in the Third World. Thus while much governmentality literature is interested in operations of power which both integrate subjects into the modern state, we can also consider a more general formulation in which subjects become more involved in the operation of power through neoliberalism. This approach is not at odds with the governmentality literature because, as Miller and Rose note, the state does not equal or give rise to government, but rather is 'a particular form that government has taken, and one that does not exhaust the field of calculations and interventions that constitute it'.[54]

In the Third World as in the West, arguments about neoliberalism usually take a more traditional form with the rise of NGOs and civil society frequently posed as a counterpoint to both the new neoliberal orthodoxy (especially the tyranny of the market), and the corruption, inefficiency and mismanagement of the state. However, the relationship of NGOs to more 'official' elements of the development *dispositif* or to neoliberal governance is not easily characterised. On the one hand, NGOs appear to be opposed to neoliberalism and neoclassical economics in their emphasis on community, mobilisation of local people and opposition to IMF and World Bank programmes such as structural adjustment. Yet on the other hand and despite these obvious differences, NGOs, often with their roots in Western populisms, notions of civil society and local level organisation of citizens, eschew the involvement of state bureaucracies in the lives of 'local people' – a perspective which is broadly consistent with the aims of the structural adjustment policies of the IMF and World Bank. On this point Watts[55] notes that World Bank discourse has changed to emphasise the powers and capacities of ordinary people at the same time as there has been a hardening of development economics. Similarly, Doug Porter[56] detects a parallel between the metaphors of 'market' and 'community'. He notes that in the application of neoclassical economic rationality to public life, it is argued that these metaphors, if let alone, tend 'toward wise equilibria'.[57] In short, the political valence of the rise of NGOs is not readily identified in the neoliberal environment.

In this situation any effort to decide if the rise of NGOs and civil society challenges mainstream or official developmentalism would be without clear resolution. Moreover, it would mirror the traditional philosophical oppositions which obscure the operation of power and governance through seemingly non-political technologies as explicated by Foucault and other governmentality scholars. In other words, efforts which seek to dichotomise development actors and efforts in terms of an a priori assumption about their position in terms of operations of power and governance do not allow for adequate analysis. In place of such approaches, the view of development as a shifting ensemble of heterogenous elements consisting of a range of interrelationships allows that development initiatives be considered without overly predetermining or simplifying analysis. The *dispositif* thus guards against overly general interpretations of recent developments. Nevertheless, it is apparent from the above discussion that the rise of NGOs should not necessarily be read as emancipatory. To the contrary, the combination of the winding back of state involvement in development, the rise of neoliberalism and the status of NGOs as 'non-political' technologies, are bases for the emergence of a range of practices which enable a greater penetration of power into the Third World through the development *dispositif*. To explore this further I want to consider the popular NGO operative notions of autonomy and empowerment.

Beyond participation: autonomous development and empowerment

Notions of autonomy and empowerment are prominent in NGO discourse as a means for locating ethical practice.[58] For Raff Carmen, autonomous development contrasts with any 'interventionist project orchestrated from the outside', and instead promotes an approach which is 'rooted in autonomous human agency'.[59] From this perspective, the closely related ideas of community development and participation are critiqued to the extent that they integrate Third World subjects in interventionist projects. Hence Carmen outlines a critique of Robert Chambers' influential Rapid Rural Appraisal, or 'putting people first' methodology,[60] and the notion of participation in development efforts:

> If participation is to be a vehicle, a feel-good enhancer or a cost-cutting device – [sic] in a word, a means towards an end such as fitting projects to people or empowering people in the 'we must help them' or 'we must enable them' mode – let this be clear.
>
> If, on the other hand, participation is genuinely about power – about people's ownership and control – then participation is not the most obvious nor the first term which springs to mind.[61]

This leads Carmen to arrive at the idea of 'autonomous development' wherein 'autonomy' means that Third World subjects are quite capable of alleviating and eradicating poverty themselves, and refers to 'the development of their [the poor's] bargaining power to an extent that [interveners] cannot unilaterally impose their conditions and regulations upon the poor as passive recipients'.[62] In short, Carmen, and the movement of which he is part, advocates a shift to 'people's self-development: autonomous human agency and people's *power*'.[63]

While the critique of more conventional approaches to development is well taken, the ideas of people-power, empowerment and autonomous human agency also deserve to be scrutinised. Carmen's implicit understanding of power, which he does not elaborate, emerges as a common-sense one in which preconstituted individuals exercise free will as they direct their own actions. The version of subjectivity in operation here is that of the liberal free subject. However, through analysis of contemporary liberal governance in the West, governmentality literature has shown that subjects are constituted through processes of subjectification which are infused with operations of power, and that the directing of our own actions is bound with this governance. The (self-)positioning of our individual lives within the objectives set by reformers – whether activist or expert – in search of some social good links us 'to a subjection that is the more profound because it appears to emanate from our autonomous quest for ourselves, it appears as a matter of our freedom'.[64] It is in this context that Barbara Cruikshank argues that: 'we have wildly underestimated the extent to which we are already self-governing. Democratic government, even self-government, depends upon the ability of citizens to act upon their own subjectivity, to be governors of their selves'.[65] Cruikshank goes on to show how self-esteem, and also empowerment, serve as political technologies in this operation of government.[66]

In the Third World context, the political technology of empowerment is currently in the process of being developed. Mohammad Asinur Rahman, long-term practitioner and advocate of self-development, autonomy and empowerment, notes that 'the absence of an authentic people's point of view remains a serious limitation on how we define the dimensions of social development'.[67] This requires:

> a process of *empowering and enabling* the people to articulate and assert, by words and by deeds, their urges and thinking ... [as] one of the core dimensions of social development itself, for social development cannot have started if the people are unable to thus express and assert what social development means to them.[68]

While empowerment is always a complex and contradictory process, there are striking parallels with the production of the liberal subjects as analysed by governmentality scholars. Here development and empowerment are intimately bound, signalling that the latter is not an apolitical process but one linked with a particular project.

Rahman's version of empowerment is fundamentally about the production of self, and, in particular, that version of subjectivity promoted through the Western social sciences which enables subjects to generate and act upon their selves. It engenders 'the feeling of knowing from self-inquiry and reflection', is directed toward building the 'self-confidence of the disadvantaged', and is about:

> a process of 'awakening' or 'animation' ... [which] implies not merely learning, knowing and understanding but also experiencing and grasping one's own intellectual powers in the same process, experiencing, in other words, *self-discovery, including the discovery of oneself as a thinker and creator of knowledge.*[69]

Empowerment in development, along with the related notion of autonomy, is thus both about the construction and positioning of a particular type of self, and a linking of one's self to the question of social development. Hence, the application of the notions of autonomy and empowerment in the Third World context signal both the export of the technologies of subjectification of Western governmentality and the enrolment of Third World subjects in developmental projects through these technologies. Autonomy, empowerment and related notions thus deserve to be further scrutinised.

One way to redirect our discussion of these notions in order to begin to take account of subjectivity as a political terrain is to consider development efforts in general as processes in which people are both acted upon by others and act on themselves. In this schema, notions of autonomy and empowerment are not accorded a special status. In order to consider the power-effects of particular development practices within the framework of the *dispositif*, we can ask how particular practices, initiatives or projects on the one hand reinforce conventional developmentalist modalities, integrate subjects into the development *dispositif*, displace or write out other subjective modalities, or, on the other hand, disperse and proliferate modalities beyond developmentalism. This analysis requires the consideration of 'new' practices including microcredit both in terms of continuities and shifts from previous approaches, and simultaneously in terms of inter-relationships between relations of knowledge, power and subjectification.

As noted throughout this volume, the microcredit movement is a significant phenomenon in the scheme of contemporary development efforts. Microcredit programmes have attracted international interest, perhaps in part because of their focus on empowerment, to become a major movement in the quest for sustainable and equitable development. The Grameen Bank had 2.3 million borrowers as of August 1998,[70] and the Microcredit Summit Secretariat (MCS) reports that the Bangladesh Rural Advancement Committee serves one million families.[71] Wood and Sharif[72] note that the Grameen Bank model 'is developing "panacea" status' as most bilateral and multilateral lenders, including the World Bank, are eager to promote and fund microcredit programmes.[73] Microcredit has also been well received in mainstream development circles, with numerous quantitative studies revealing positive effects.[74] Despite this positive press, closer examination of microcredit demonstrates both its continuities and discontinuities with previous development efforts. In turn this points to subjectification as a key political terrain of the contemporary development *dispositif* and a neoliberal developmentalist governmentalisation of the Third World which links individual selves with international capital markets. I begin with the popular Grameen Bank because of the lead role it has had in influencing other microcredit programmes.

Microcredit: neoliberal developmentalism and governmentalisation

In recounting the story of the foundation of the Grameen Bank, founder and managing director Muhammad Yunus recalls his frustration with economic theory, which led him to 'run away from the textbooks ... to confront real life as it unfolded each day' in the villages around Chittagong University in Bangladesh.[75] The situation Yunus found in the villages led him to provide small collateral-free loans that he had no trouble in having repaid. Although Yunus initially had difficulty finding mainstream support for his venture, these early successes led to the formation of the Grameen Bank in 1983.[76] Grameen operates on very different principles from traditional banks: borrowers own 92 per cent of Bank shares, collateral is not required and loans are made exclusively to poor people, 94 per cent of whom are women.[77] As Yunus states, 'The less you have the higher priority you get in receiving loans from Grameen. If you have nothing, you get the highest priority'.[78] There is also a major contrast with traditional forms of lending for development. When Grameen loans are compared with those of organisations such as the World Bank and national foreign aid bodies, the difference in size of loans is striking, foreign development experts are absent and faith is placed less in technocratic programming and more in the resourcefulness of local people. Credit is also channelled directly to the local poor, thus avoiding the commonly cited problems of mismanagement and corruption. This shift from more traditional development approaches has no doubt contributed to the popularity of microcredit. Microcredit is also viewed as positive for other reasons: the provision of credit to those would not otherwise have been able to obtain it except perhaps through an exploitative relationship with a moneylender is readily seen as a step forward. Jessica Matthews goes so far as to comment that microcredit may have 'found a spark to revolutionary change'.[79]

However, if we return to Yunus' experience in the villages around Chittagong University in the mid-1970s which led to the formation of Grameen, his evaluation of the situation is striking for both its neoliberalism and economism, and thus its concurrence with emerging and established trends in the shifting development *dispositif*. The problems he encountered were viewed as eminently solvable with 'some individual initiative and determination' and 'working capital'.[80] Yunus states he 'ran away from the text-books', but the solution which was so self-evident to him falls entirely within the developmentalist framework. Notions of individual initiative, determination and provision of capital to improve people's situation and increase economic growth are a micro-version of the dominant economistic development approach, and resonate with aspects of modernisation theory which dominated in the 1950s and 1960s. Thus while it is possible to view microcredit as a radical departure from conventional development practice, it also exhibits significant continuities with the approach of previous decades and does not introduce a rupture or significant shift in the development *dispositif.*

This continuity in relations of discourse is paralleled by continuity in relations of power and governing. In illustrating a contrast with conventional banks, Yunus writes that:

> Grameen literally runs after poor women who are terribly alarmed at the very suggestion of borrowing money from the bank, do not have any business experience whatsoever, may never have touched paper money in their lives, and never dared to think about running a business of their own. Grameen tries to convince them that they can successfully run a business and make money.[81]

While the aim of this statement is to highlight the liberating role Grameen plays, it also illustrates continuities between Grameen operations and the early years of the World Bank's operation in which demand for loans had to be created.[82] As with the World Bank, local people need to be convinced of the need for Grameen involvement. This effort at enrolment of subjects in the developmentalist Grameen Bank project signals the operation of related processes of subjectification, discipline and governance through the linking of individual subjects with a broader economic programme.

The directions of subjectification promoted by Grameen and the wider microcredit movement, including their consistency with neoliberalism, are made explicit in various microcredit promotional publications. The focus on income generation and self-employment is a consistent theme in the microcredit approach, with the MCS noting that one of the characteristics of successful microcredit programmes is the provision of 'appropriate management expertise' to their 'microentrepreneurs'.[83] The result is that microcredit exhibits a consistency with the aims of mainstream neoliberal developmentalist institutions such as the World Bank, and promotes a valorisation of developmentalist subjectivities. President of the Bank James D. Wolfensohn stated approvingly in 1996 that:

> [M]icrocredit programs have brought the vibrancy of the market economy to the poorest villages and people of the world. This business approach to the alleviation of poverty has allowed millions of individuals to work their way out of poverty with dignity.[84]

While dignity is no doubt involved, it is defined as a particular modus vivendi embodied in the business approach to poverty. As Yunus states, the aim of Grameen lending is to make 'it easy for a poor "nobody" to take the leap to become an enterprising "somebody"'.[85] Here the entrepreneurial subjectivity is elevated above other subjective modalities that the targets of microcredit programmes may already be living or inclined to take up.

Yunus goes so far as to link credit with the discursive archetype of liberal Western subjectification, the notion of human rights. He states that 'credit is a human right ... If we can come up with a system which allows everybody access to credit while ensuring excellent repayment, I guarantee you poverty will not last long'.[86] He goes even further stating that:

> In the 'right' world, we have to instil in people's minds that everyone creates his or her own job. We can build institutions so that each person is supported and *empowered* to do this. The more self-employment becomes attractive, wide-ranging, and *self-fulfilling*, the more difficult it will be to attract people for wage jobs.[87]

While notions such as empowerment and self-fulfilment have widespread appeal, I have discussed how these notions are not apolitical but a terrain that is organised and managed. In the case of microcredit operations, self-fulfilment is simultaneously defined, produced and managed by institutions such as Grameen as successful entrepreneurialism and a developmentalist approach to wealth. An accompanying effect of this individualisation of poverty is its depoliticisation: as the poor are made responsible for their poverty, redistributive approaches to poverty alleviation tend to be ignored.[88]

The process of subjectification necessarily involves disciplinary operations. These operations, and indeed the disciplinary imperatives of Grameen, are less openly discussed in the literature than other aspects of microcredit. Discipline begins with the enrolment of microcredit members, and the requirement that prospective lenders form into a peer group or 'loan committee' of five.[89] The groups are designed to act as a 'monitoring, supervising and problem solving body',[90] and to provide social solidarity and a forum for discussion of social development issues. However, Aminur Rahman's[91] fieldwork shows that in recent practice the work group operates primarily as a means for recovering loan repayments. The processes for the formation of these groups and the initial lending processes are illustrative of the disciplinary operation.

A group receives formal recognition from Grameen, and thereby an opportunity to loan money, when all members learn and memorise the rules and regulations of the Bank, and when they pass an oral examination.[92] In these early stages, the role of the bank loan officer is to 'convince the borrower that she can use money to improve her life'.[93] Once groups are formed, between six and eight groups then create a loan centre.

> Women who belong to a new loan center take the responsibility of building a center-house or finding an available free space within their vicinity for the weekly meetings and loan operation. Fulfilment of these basic requirements by borrowers at a center makes them eligible for loans. The Bank grants credits to individual borrowers sequentially by establishing a unique time cycle. In the first sequence of the cycle

only two members from a group receive loans. The bank worker observes their loan repayment behaviours for at least two months and their satisfactory completion of the loan repayments entitles the next two in the group to receive loans. In this micro-credit program the individual is kept in line by a considerable amount of pressure from other members of the group.[94]

The formation of the loan committee and the deployment of its system of peer accountability represent a multistage disciplinary technique. The first stage, which involves an initial period of training and self-learning about Grameen rules and modes of operation, serves to enrol subjects into Grameen entrepreneurialism and associated subjective modalities. In the second stage, this first operation is linked to the simultaneous discipline of both individuals and peers. Here the linking of provision of a loan to one member with the behaviour of other members of the group, initially through the mechanism of a time delay, is a particularly innovative and important part of this technique since it establishes a direct relation between personal desire or need and the imperative to discipline others. Through the disciplinary technique of the loan committee, lenders are continually examined. This extends from the initial oral examination regarding rules and procedures of Grameen, to the supervision by the bank officer of the initial repayments, to the peer supervision enacted by members. It is in this disciplinary context that stringent loan conditions can be met and that the very poor are judged a good credit risk.[95]

Disciplinary rituals carried out at the loan centres complement the peer accountability engendered through the structure and operation of the loan committee. While the operation of power is more diffuse as microcredit recipients go about their daily lives, the loan centre is the site where the lines of force of the disciplinary technology of Grameen microcredit are gathered together and are most dense. Prior to the weekly meetings with the bank officer, recipients gather at the loan centre and assemble in a matrix (usually six by five) according to their loan committee groups.[96] When the Bank officer is present and all members are assembled, the members rise, salute, and recite the Grameen Bank credo: 'Discipline, Unity, Courage, and Hard Work' prior to physical exercises and collection of payments from members.[97] In his observation of Grameen loan centre operations, David Bornstein notes that the 'rules [of Grameen] act as a tight web ... ensuring that villagers are brought together frequently in a setting where they are forced to answer for their actions before all eyes'.[98] The closing of the meeting involves members reciting Grameen's 16 decisions that include injunctions such as:

- Prosperity we shall bring to our families.
- We shall grow vegetables all year round. We shall eat plenty of them and sell the surplus.

- We shall always keep our children and the environment clean.
- For higher income we shall collectively undertake bigger investments.
- If we come to know of any breach of discipline in any centre, we shall all go there and help restore discipline.[99]

The disciplinary imperative of Grameen operations extends beyond techniques of the loan committee and the operation of the centre meetings to account for the high percentage of women members. While Grameen's practice of targeting poor women is broadly seen as commendable by outside donors and lenders, closer scrutiny reveals a different story. Rahman[100] shows that while the official line is that targeting women provides faster improvements in family conditions and solidarity for women, the bank practice of actually excluding men from the programme and focusing on women has much more to do with the ease in disciplining the different genders. Through his fieldwork, Rahman found that men were regarded as arrogant and difficult to deal with by bank workers. As a result they tended to be discouraged or excluded, while women are accepted because they are more easily traced in the village and because they tend to be shy, passive and submissive. Furthermore, loans may in fact end up being provided *to men by women*, who are placed under pressure by male husbands and family members. As Rahman reports, women can thereby find themselves the target of increased pressure and violence as they negotiate *both* the requirements of Grameen and pressure from men.[101] Thus the disciplinary operation is also strongly gendered.[102]

This local operation of discipline also systematically integrates microcredit recipients into the financial and economic networks of the microcredit organisation and the development *dispositif* on a long-term basis. The MCS reports that one of the characteristics of successful microcredit programmes is 'the incentive of access to larger loans following successful repayment of first loans'.[103] The result is that people may be recipients of microcredit for many years. In reporting favourably on the operation of Grameen, Matthews states that after ten years of borrowing, 48 per cent of borrowers had crossed the poverty line.[104] Slightly more optimistic is Yunus' quoting of figures that after eight to ten years 57 per cent of Grameen borrowers had escaped poverty.[105] That it should take such a number of years to significantly improve the situation of approximately one half of Grameen Bank recipients signals the high repayment rates, lack of concessionality and linkage of local branches with the rest of the lending organisation and its broader imperatives. In the case of Grameen, branches borrow from headquarters at 12 per cent and lend at 20 per cent.[106] The margin is, of course, extracted from the recipients in the microcredit programmes. In the spirit of entrepreneurialism, this allows the branches to become profitable and Grameen to expand its operations.

Central to this integration of subjects into microcredit operations and wider financial and economic networks is the question of lender or microcredit institution sustainability,[107] including access to capital markets in place of reliance on donor capital. In this context, microcredit programmes are distinguished from 'the traditional moneylender's crippling rates of interest', while rates of interest determined by the global capital market are accorded a quasi-natural status, with the 'marriage of microcredit and commercial financial markets' high on the MCS agenda.[108] Where borrowing from commercial capital markets is currently practised for the provision of microcredit programmes, it is viewed favourably. Thus the MCS is able to approvingly note that 'the world's most sophisticated capital markets have actually been linked with the promise to pay of a woman microentrepreneur selling her wares on a street corner in La Paz'.[109] Beyond the acceptance of market rates as valid as part of the quest for lender sustainability, what can be overlooked is the fact that on-lending involves costs above the market rate. These costs must be ultimately extracted from the final borrowers in microcredit programmes as they are linked with commercial markets through disciplinary techniques.

When funds are provided on a concessional basis outside the market, the MCS sees these as a temporary measure in the microcredit institution's graduation to self-funding through commercial markets. Thus 'soft loans should be provided in an environment of market discipline', which includes 'clearly articulated and measurable performance measures'.[110] This graduation process, which is viewed as a key way in which microcredit programmes can be expanded to meet the MCS goal of providing microcredit to 100 million of the world's poorest families by 2005, signals the potential for a massive extension of the disciplinary techniques associated with joint-responsibility systems and the accompanying valorisation of developmentalist subjective modalities.[111] In short, it signals the possibility of a greater penetration of power into the social body of the Third World, and the closer integration of Third World subjects into the global development *dispositif* through the political technology of microcredit.

This linking of First World capital markets with the production and encouragement of the Third World entrepreneur in a neoliberal policy environment is a significant development in the individualising and totalising operation of power which Foucault terms governmentality. At the local level, microcredit programmes have the effect of promoting entrepreneurial subjective modalities over other ways of being and depoliticising poverty through an individualistic rather than redistributive approach to its alleviation. They do so by inscribing neoliberal developmentalism through innovative disciplinary techniques. The linking of these micro-programmes – operating at the level of individual selves – with world capital markets is an individualising–totalising operation par excellence. Just as the peasant was a privileged object of intervention in the expansion of nineteenth century European governmentalisation, the world's poor are currently targeted through popular and apparently apolitical microcredit programmes to act upon their selves in concert with wider developmental goals in a neoliberal and developmentalist governmentalisation of the Third World.

This is not to suggest that governmentalisation can be entirely effective, that people are not empowered by microcredit, or that microcredit cannot sometimes be of real assistance in improving people's lives. Rather, it is *precisely through* the empowering nature of microcredit that entrepreneurial subjectivities and approaches to poverty alleviation are valued and promoted over others and the operation of governmental discipline is extended. The point is not that microcredit should be viewed entirely in the negative, but that 'new' initiatives deserve to be scrutinised in terms of the political effects of their continuities and discontinuities with earlier approaches. While microcredit exhibits clear discontinuities with earlier and more conventional development practices, the deployment of neoliberalism and entrepreneurialism highlights that microcredit deserves not to be viewed as a complete break with the past but as a reconfiguring of development practice *and* its accompanying operations of power and governance.

Conclusions

In the context of shifts in the operation of development from the 1980s, the notion of *dispositif* emerges as a useful framework for considering both the ways development reinvents itself, and the relations of power which operate through these reinventions. The *dispositif* allows us to move beyond problems surrounding critical approaches based in economic relations and to more adequately analyse the reconfiguration of development through the rise of neoliberalism and NGOs. While McMichael's approach opposes the rationalism and economism of globalisation with the culturalism and localism of new social movements embodied in NGOs and civil society thereby eliding the ways in which these developments are part of the operation of power, the *dispositif* enables a less programmatic approach by conceptualising development as a shifting ensemble of elements which exhibits certain continuities and discontinuities with previous formations. Shifts in development are negotiated within, and therefore can be analysed in terms of, the framework of the earlier *dispositif* and, more broadly, developmentalism.

Using this conceptualisation demonstrates that the reconfiguration of development involves a shift in the operation of power that is linked with but not dependent upon economic relations. This shift involves a greater penetration of power into the Third World through development as the role of nation states in development efforts is wound back, along with increased pressure from institutions such as the World Bank for a neoliberal economic policy environment. This link with changes in economic relations cannot be separated from the rise of NGOs, increased emphasis on civil society and contemporary popular and alternative approaches that emphasise notions of autonomy and empowerment. Following the problematisation of the terrain of the self explicated by Foucault and other governmentality scholars, these developments cannot necessarily be viewed as emancipatory, but instead need to be considered in terms of the complex mix of effects they generate. These effects can just as readily include the reinforcing of conventional developmentalist modalities, the integration of subjects into the development *dispositif*, the displacement or writing out of other subjective modalities and a neoliberal governmentalisation of the Third World as they can include the easing of economic hardship and the dispersion and proliferation of subjective modalities beyond developmentalism.

Notes

1 See Abdullah, M. M. (1979) *Rural Development in Bangladesh: Problems and prospects* Dacca: Nurjahan Begum, Mohammadpur, pp. 48–59.
2 Sharif, I. (1997) 'Poverty and Finance in Bangladesh: A new policy agenda' in G. Wood and I. Sharif (eds) *Who Needs Credit?* London and New York: Zed Books, p. 61.
3 MCS, *The Microcredit Summit: February 2–4 1997, Declaration and plan of action* www.microcreditsummit.org/declaration.htm Microcredit Summit Secretariat, accessed 23 April 2001, Section: *Preamble*.
4 See Schuurman, F. J. (ed.) (1993) *Beyond the Impasse: New directions in development theory* London: Zed Books.
5 Sarker, A. E. (1996) *The Role of Non-governmental Organisations in Rural Development: The Bangladesh case* Clayton, Victoria: Monash Asia Institute, Centre of South Asian Studies, Monash University, p. 4.
6 See World Bank, *For Nongovernmental Organizations/Civil Society: Overview – NGO World Bank collaboration*, www.worldbank.org/ngos then select *Overview* hypertext: World Bank, accessed 3 April 2001.
7 For discussion of the increase and broadening in the role of NGOs see Fisher, J. (1998) *Nongovernments: NGOs and the political development of the Third World* West Hartford, CT: Kumarian.
8 See Hout, W. (1993) *Capitalism and the Third World: Development, dependence and the world system* Aldershot: Edward Elgar; and Sklair, L. (ed.) (1994) *Capitalism and Development* London and New York: Routledge.
9 See Wallerstein, I. (1979) *The Capitalist World-Economy* Cambridge: Cambridge University Press; Wallerstein, I. (1994) 'Development: Lodestar or illusion' in L. Sklair (ed.) *Capitalism and Development* London and New York: Routledge; and Wallerstein, I. (1994) 'World-systems Analysis' in D. Held, D. Hubert, D. Seymour, A. Giddens and J. Thompson (eds) *The Polity Reader in Social Theory* Cambridge: Polity.
10 See Lipietz, A. (1992) *Towards a New Economic Order: Postfordism, ecology and democracy* New York: Oxford University Press, pp. 6–8.
11 See Gereffo, G. (1994) 'Capital, Development and Global Commodity Chains' in L. Sklair (ed.) *Capitalism and Development* London and New York: Routledge; Hoogvelt, A. (1997) *Globalisation and the Postcolonial World: The new political economy of development* Basingstoke, UK: Macmillan; and McMichael, P. (1996) *Development and Social Change: A global perspective* Thousand Oaks, CA: Pine Forge Press.
12 See Baudrillard, J. (1975) *The Mirror of Production* St. Louis: Telos Press;

Dumont, L. (1977) *From Mandeville to Marx: The genesis and triumph of economic ideology* Chicago: Chicago University Press; and Polanyi, K. (1957 [1944]) *The Great Transformation: The political and economic origins of our time* Boston: Beacon Press.
13 Baudrillard, 1975, pp. 84–91.
14 McMichael, 1996.
15 Ibid., pp. 255–6.
16 Ibid., p. 211.
17 The approach has been named by, among others, Arturo Escobar (1992) 'Imagining a Post-Development Era? Critical thought, development and social movements' *Social Text*, 10 (2); Rahnema, M. and Bawtree, V. (eds) (1997) *The Post-Development Reader* London and New Jersey: Zed Books; and Watts, M. (1995) '"A New Deal in Emotions": Theory and practice and the crisis of development' in Crush, J. (ed.) *Power of Development* London and New York: Routledge. A selection of other contributions to post-development include: Alvares, C. (1992) *Science, Development and Violence* Delhi: Oxford University Press; Apffel-Marglin, F. and Marglin, S. (eds) (1990) *Dominating Knowledge: Development, culture and resistance* Oxford: Clarendon Press; Crush, J. (ed.) (1995) *Power of Development* London and New York: Routledge; Dallmayr, F. (1992) 'Modernisation and Postmodernisation: Whither India?' *Alternatives*, 17 (4); DuBois, M. (1991) 'The Governance of the Third World: A Foucauldian perspective on power relations in development' *Alternatives*, 16 (1); Escobar, A. (1984) 'Discourse and Power in Development: Michel Foucault and the relevance of his work to the Third World' *Alternatives*, 10 (3); Escobar, A. (1988) 'Power and Visibility: Development and the intervention and management of the Third World' *Cultural Anthropology*, 3 (4); Escobar, A. (1992) 'Planning' in W. Sachs (ed.) *The Development Dictionary: A guide to knowledge as power* London: Zed Books; Escobar, A. (1995) *Encountering Development: The making and unmaking of the Third World* Princeton, New Jersey: Princeton University Press; Esteva G. (1987) 'Regenerating People's Space' *Alternatives*, 12; Esteva, G. and Prakash, M. S. (1998) *Grassroots Post-Modernism* London and New York: Zed Books; Ferguson, J. (1990) *The Anti-Politics Machine: 'Development', depoliticization, and bureaucratic power in Lesotho* Cambridge: Cambridge University Press; Latouche, S. (1996) *The Westernisation of the World* Oxford: Polity; Lummis, C. D. (1991) 'Development Against Democracy' *Alternatives*, 16 (1); Nederveen-Pieterse, J. (1991) 'Dilemmas of Development Discourse: The crisis of developmentalism and the comparative method' *Development and Change*, 22 (1); Rist, G. (1997) *The History of Development: From Western origins to global faith* London and New York: Zed Books; Sachs, W. (ed.) (1992) *The Development Dictionary: A guide to knowledge as power* London: Zed Books, 1992.
18 Escobar, 1995.
19 Ferguson, 1990.
20 Foucault, M. (1980) 'The Confession of the Flesh' in C. Gordon (ed.) *Power/Knowledge: Selected interviews & other writings 1972–1977 by Michel Foucault* New York: Pantheon, p. 194.
21 Ibid.
22 Ibid.
23 Deleuze, G. (1992) 'What is a *dispositif?*' in T. J. Armstrong (ed.) *Michel Foucault: Philosopher* New York and London: Harvester Wheatsheaf.
24 See Esteva and Prakash (1998) and the critique of post-development by Corbridge, S. (1998) ' "Beneath the Pavement Only Soil": The poverty of post-development' *Journal of Development Studies*, 34 (6).
25 Foucault, 1980, p. 195.
26 Ibid.

27 Escobar, 1995.
28 Ferguson, 1990, pp. xv, 25, 276.
29 Foucault, 1980, p. 194.
30 Escobar, 1995, p. 10.
31 Escobar, 1984, p. 386.
32 Foucault, M. (1972) *The Archaeology of Knowledge & The Discourse on Language* New York: Pantheon Books, p. 72.
33 Dreyfus, H. L. and Rabinow, P. (1982) *Michel Foucault: Beyond structuralism and hermeneutics* Chicago: University of Chicago Press, pp. 105, 63–7.
34 For example, see the note by Armstrong in Deleuze, 1992, p. 159.
35 Foucault, M. (1981) *The History of Sexuality: An introduction* London: Penguin.
36 Halperin, D. M. (1995) *Saint Foucault: Towards a gay hagiography* New York and Oxford: Oxford University Press, note 6 on pp. 188–9.
37 Deleuze, 1992.
38 Deleuze, 1992, p. 159.
39 See Foucault, M. and Deleuze, G. (1977) 'Intellectuals and Power' in D. F. Bouchard (ed.) *Language, Counter-Memory, Practice: Selected essays and interviews by Michel Foucault* Ithaca, New York: Cornell University Press, p. 208.
40 Deleuze, 1992, p. 159.
41 Foucault, 1980, p. 196.
42 Deleuze, 1992, p. 159. Furthermore, this is not a list which claims to entirely map the social field because I am advancing a specific analytical tool rather than a general theory or method.
43 Deleuze, G. (1988) *Foucault* London: Athlone, p. 114.
44 Foucault, M. (1991) 'Governmentality' in G. Burchell, C. Gordon and P. Miller (eds) *The Foucault Effect: Studies in governmentality* London: Harvester Wheatsheaf; Foucault, M. (1997) 'Security, Territory, and Population' in P. Rabinow (ed.) *Michel Foucault: Ethics, the essential works I* London: Penguin; Foucault, M. (1997) 'The Birth of Biopolitics' in P. Rabinow (ed.) *Michel Foucault: Ethics, the essential works I* London: Penguin.
45 Foucault, 'The Birth of Biopolitics', 1997, p. 74.
46 Foucault, 'Security, Territory, and Population', 1997, p. 68.
47 Procacci, G. (1991) 'Social Economy and the Government of Poverty' in G. Burchell, C. Gordon and P. Miller *The Foucault Effect: Studies in Governmentality* London, Harvester Wheatsheaf, pp. 151–68.
48 Procacci, 1991, p. 155.
49 Cf. Miller, P. and Rose, N. (1990) 'Governing Economic Life' *Economy and Society*, 19 (1): 2 – regarding the aligning of economic, social and personal conduct with broader governmental objectives and goals.
50 Foucault, M. (1982) 'The subject and power' in H. L. Dreyfus and P. Rabinow *Michel Foucault: Beyond structuralism and hermeneutics* Chicago, University of Chicago Press, pp. 208–28, 213.
51 See, for example, Barry, A., Osborne, T. and Rose, N. (eds) (1996) *Foucault and Political Reason: Liberalism, neo-liberalism and rationalities of government* Chicago: University of Chicago Press; Rose, N. (1991) *Governing the Soul: The shaping of the private self* London and New York: Routledge; Rose, N. (1993) 'Government, Authority and Expertise in Advanced Liberalism' *Economy and Society*, 22 (3); Rose, N. and Miller, P. (1992) 'Political Power Beyond the State: Problematics of government' *British Journal of Sociology*, 43 (2).
52 Rose and Miller, 1992, p. 198.
53 Rose, 1993, 1991. Rose, N. (1996) 'The death of the social? Re-figuring the territory of government' *Economy and Society* 25 (3): 327–56.
54 Miller and Rose, 1990, p. 3.
55 Watts, 1995, p. 58.

56 Porter, D. (1995) 'Scenes From Childhood: The homesickness of development discourses' in J. Crush (ed.) *Power of Development* London and New York: Routledge, pp. 82–3.
57 Ibid.
58 My discussion here does not aim to be a comprehensive study of the NGO sector or the way it operates, but rather to tap into the key themes of autonomy and empowerment. For one example of the centrality of these themes in the popular rhetoric and practice of 'capacity-building' see Eade, D. (1997) *Capacity-Building: An approach to people-centred development* Oxford: Oxfam, UK and Ireland. For a more general entry into people-centred or self-development see *People-Centred Development Forum*, http://iisd1.iisd.ca/pcdf/ International Institute for Sustainable Development [1999], accessed 23 April 2001.
59 Carmen, R. (1996) *Autonomous Development, Humanizing the Landscape: An excursion into radical thinking and practice* London and New Jersey: Zed Books, pp. 6, 7.
60 Chambers, R. (1983) *Rural Development: Putting the last first* London and New York: Longman.
61 Carmen, 1996, p. 51.
62 Verhagen quoted in ibid., p. 52.
63 Ibid., p. 53. On self-development, see Rahman, M. A. (1993) *People's Self-Development: Perspectives on participatory action research* London and New Jersey: Zed Books.
64 Rose, 1991, p. 256.
65 Cruikshank, B. (1996) 'Revolutions Within: Self-government and self-esteem' in A. Barry, T. Osborne and N. Rose (eds) *Foucault and Political Reason: Liberalism, neo-liberalism and rationalities of government* Chicago: University of Chicago Press, p. 235.
66 Ibid., pp. 236, 238.
67 Rahman, 1993, p. 205.
68 Ibid., pp. 205, 206.
69 Ibid., pp. 206–7, my emphasis.
70 'Peoples Fund' *The Facts and Figures of Grameen Bank* www.peoplesfund.org/ Grameen Trust, accessed 23 April 2001.
71 MCS, Section: *The case for microcredit*, Subsection: *Programs grow to serve large numbers of very poor people*. Microcredit has also expanded outside Bangladesh: the Foundation for International Community Assistance has affiliated microfinance programmes in 14 countries that serve 70,000 borrowers. See Ibid.
72 Wood, G. and Sharif, I. (1997) 'Introduction' in G. Wood and I. Sharif (eds) *Who Needs Credit?* London and New York: Zed Books, p. 29.
73 Sharif, 1997, p. 62.
74 For example, see Khander, S., Samad, H. and Khan, Z. (1998) 'Income and Employment effects of Micro-Credit Programmes: Village-level evidence from Bangladesh' *Journal of Development Studies*, 35 (2).
75 Yunus, M. (1997) 'The Grameen Bank Story: Microlending for economic development' *Dollars and Sense*, July–August no. 212. Infotrac Database, A19807547, p. 3.
76 Ibid.
77 Ibid.
78 Ibid.
79 Matthews, J. (1994) 'Little World Banks' in K. Danaher (ed.) *50 Years is Enough: The case against the World Bank and the International Monetary Fund* Boston: South End Press, p. 185.
80 Yunus, 1997. In this document Yunus also states that 'Handouts take away initiatives from people. Human beings thrive on challenges not on palliatives'.

81 Ibid.
82 See Caufield, C. (1996) *Masters of Illusion: The World Bank and the poverty of nations* New York: Henry Holt and Company, pp. 53, 56; and Rich, B. (1994) *Mortgaging the Earth* Boston: Beacon Press, p. 68.
83 MCS, Section: *Microcredit: Empowering poor people to end their own poverty*, Subsection: *Beyond Microcredit: Other financial and business services.*
84 Quoted in Ibid., Section: *Poverty and the struggle to overcome it*, Subsection: *Foreign aid, public welfare programs and the poorest.*
85 Yunus, 1997.
86 Ibid.
87 Ibid., my emphasis.
88 See Wood and Sharif, 1997, pp. 35–6, especially for discussion of attempts by the World Bank and other donors to limit the mobilisation agendas of NGOs by pushing them into the narrower role of provision of microcredit.
89 Matthews, 1994, p. 184; Yunus, 1997.
90 Yunus, 1997.
91 Rahman, A. (1999) 'Micro-credit Initiatives for Equitable and Sustainable Development: Who pays?' *World Development*, 27 (1): 71.
92 Ibid., p. 71, note 7 on p. 81.
93 Matthews, 1994, p. 184.
94 Rahman, 1999, p. 71.
95 In Grameen operations, loan rates are 20 per cent, members are required to invest in income-generating productive activities within seven days of loan acceptance, and there is a mandatory savings requirement. See Matthews, 1994; Rahman, 1999, p. 75.
   The MCS confirms the linking of the poor as a good credit risk with disciplinary techniques such as loan committees by stating that 'Very poor people are a good credit risk, especially in the context of mutual-responsibility systems.' MCS, Section: *Microcredit: Empowering poor people to end their own poverty*, Subsection: *The case for microcredit.*
96 Bornstein, D. (1997) *The Price of a Dream: The story of the Grameen Bank and the idea that is helping the poor to change their lives* Chicago, IL: University of Chicago Press, p. 95.
97 Ibid., p. 93.
98 Ibid., p. 98.
99 Quoted in Ibid., p. 97.
100 Rahman, 1999, pp. 69–71.
101 Ibid., pp. 72–3. The fact that Grameen loans are not always or entirely used for income-generating or self-employment activities highlights the complex and contested nature of subjectification. My earlier comments about the directions of subjectification evident in microcredit and microfinance literature cannot be taken as evidence that developmentalist subjectivities *are* comprehensively produced. Instead, an analysis of subjectification through microcredit could only be approached effectively through extensive fieldwork.
102 For discussion of Grameen loan operations in relation to women's empowerment see Hashemi, S. M., Schuler, S. R. and Riley, A. P. (1996) 'Rural Credit Programs and Women's Empowerment in Bangladesh' *World Development*, 24 (4); and Papa, M. J., Auwal, M. A. and Singhal, A. (1995) 'Dialectic of Control and Emancipation in Organizing for Social Change: A multitheoretic study of the Grameen Bank of Bangladesh' *Communication Theory*, 5 (3).
103 MCS, Section: *Microcredit: Empowering poor people to end their own poverty*, Subsection: *Characteristics of successful microcredit programs for the poorest.*
104 Matthews, 1994, p. 184.

105 Yunus, M. (1998) 'Poverty Alleviation: Is economics any help? Lessons from the Grameen Bank experience' *Journal of International Affairs*, 52 (1): 59.
106 Matthews, 1994, p. 184.
107 See Wood and Sharif, 1997.
108 MCS, Section: *Meeting the financial needs of the movement*, Subsection: *Microcredit and the commercial financial markets.*
109 Ibid.
110 MCS, Section: *Meeting the financial needs of the movement*, Subsection: *Types of funding needed.*
111 The production of developmentalist and entrepreneurial subjectivities within the context of mutual-responsibility systems deserves further study. In particular, exploration of the ways in which pre-existing socio-cultural frameworks are blended with neoliberal individualism could improve our understanding of microcredit, and throw light on an important confluence in contemporary development efforts.

4 Social capital, microfinance, and the politics of development[1]

Katharine N. Rankin

In the past decade, a consensus has emerged among scholars and practitioners of development that "social capital" – popularly defined as local forms of association that express trust and norms of reciprocity – can contribute significantly to the alleviation of poverty worldwide.[2] Such claims about the promise of social capital rest largely on the discovery by Robert Putnam (1993), the term's most vociferous proponent, that dense associational networks within civil society correlate positively with indicators of political democracy and economic growth. Conversely, as Putnam (1995) argues with regard to the US polity, political malaise and economic stagnation can be traced to declining stocks of social capital in neighborhoods and communities. If we take the World Bank (2001) as a reliable authority on the matter, the task of development is to identify, use, invest in, and create an enabling environment for this particular form of capital.

In contrast to earlier "basic needs" (or welfare) approaches to poverty alleviation, the potential of social capital theory lies in its recognition of social networks and associational life as *resources* for fuelling development from the bottom-up. Indeed this recognition has inspired the World Bank and other mainstream development agencies to endorse some innovative, once marginal, approaches to development, such as the now popular "microfinance" models through which the poor receive credit on the basis of their membership in self-regulating "solidarity" groups. Given the propensity of microfinance programs to target their services to women, current trends favoring the mobilization of social capital within communities also appear to have finally responded to decades of advocacy for gender equality by feminist economists and development practitioners.

This chapter first considers the genealogy of social capital employed by the World Bank and mainstream development agencies, in which social capital is construed within the liberal tradition as the cultural properties, such as trust, norms, and networks, that enhance efficiency by facilitating cooperation.[3] This theoretical orientation conflates development with economic growth and embraces the rational, utility-maximizing individual as the locus of progressive change. I then examine the claims of social capital theory and their practical manifestation in microfinance programs against the grain of three alternative approaches: (1) Marxian interpretations of social embeddedness (*à la* Pierre Bourdieu), (2) neo-Foucauldian "governmentality" studies that give a political–economic perspective on the recent "career" of social capital,[4] and (3) a feminist ethnographic study of a local cultural economy in Nepal, where planners are aggressively promoting microfinance models.

The microfinance sector offers an instructive context for exploring the different programmatic implications of liberal and Marxian theories of social capital. Paradoxically, both perspectives find expression within the dominant "Grameen model" now endorsed by most of the mainstream development agencies. Based on the pioneering innovations of the Grameen Bank in Bangladesh, the model evokes union and feminist traditions in its formulation of the "solidarity groups" through which women receive credit collateralized by "group guarantee" rather than by tangible assets. This rhetoric of "solidarity" implies that women who participate in group lending will identify collectively to resist their common oppression, much as a Marxian approach to social capital might prescribe. Yet in practice, the financial imperatives for sustainability often lead microfinance programs to engage the collective only in the most instrumental manner – reducing administrative costs and motivating repayment – at the expense of the more time-consuming processes of consciousness-raising and empowerment. Mere participation in the group borrowing process is often considered a proxy for empowerment, and assumed to generate ample quantities of social capital (in the liberal sense of the term).

Ethnographic research I have conducted on the cultural politics of social change in a Nepalese merchant community identifies some of the many barriers to women's solidarity in the South Asian context. This research points to the instrumental role of associational life and collective norms and values in *producing* and *maintaining* existing gender (and other social) hierarchies. On the basis of this research, I caution that in the absence of a structural analysis of social capital, microfinance and similar development strategies could end up only *exacerbating*, rather than challenging, existing social hierarchies. A structural analysis draws attention to the ideological as well as material dimensions of social change. I thus conclude with some guidelines for designing microfinance programs – and in general practicing a kind of development – that could engage women's solidarity to challenge existing patterns of subordination rooted in dominant gender ideologies.

The claims of social capital theory in development discourse

Development discourse has generally evoked social capital in the sense popularized by sociologist Robert Putnam, as "features of social organization, such as trust, norms, and networks, that can improve the efficiency of society by facilitating coordinated actions" (1993: 167).[5] When people engage in networks and forms of association, the argument goes, they develop a framework of common values and beliefs that can become a "moral resource" (Putnam, 1993: 169) or the "glue that holds a community together" (Potapchuk *et al.*, 1997). The trust that emerges from common understanding will in turn generate norms of reciprocity that can help confront the "tragedy of the commons," whereby individual opportunism leaves common property resources under-cultivated (Putnam, 1993: 172). Shared values endow society with a "logic of collective action" (Olson, 1965) by instilling in individuals a sense of stewardship for the common good and by ensuring social sanction against defection from the collective interest (Putnam, 1993, 1995; Potapchuck *et al.*, 1997; Wilson, 1997). Trust and norms of reciprocity, in other words, enhance "participants' taste for collective benefits" (Putnam, 1995: 67).

On the face of it, the conclusion that social networks enhance social opportunity is relatively uncontroversial and has animated public intellectual life for centuries.[6] Almost everyone knows from experience how important networks are to success – in business, in the job market, in the arts, in academia, in human well-being itself. Yet never before have social networks and associational life been featured so prominently among the leading development institutions as *prescriptions* for sustainable development and economic growth. In particular, the World Bank has in recent years advocated social capital as a key ingredient for development. According to the Bank's website,

> Social capital refers to the institutions, relationships, and norms that shape the quality and quantity of a society's social interactions. Increasing evidence shows that social cohesion is critical for societies to prosper economically and for development to be sustainable. Social capital is not just the sum of the institutions which underpin a society – it is the glue that holds them together.
>
> (World Bank, 2001)

This formulation draws on Putnam's research in Italy and North America, which demonstrates that at aggregate levels, indicators of social capital (such as membership in civic associations) correlate positively with indicators of political democracy and economic growth (such as voting rates and per capita income). Among economists in particular, social capital has been embraced as something of a "magic bullet" with the power to correct state and market failure (Edwards, n.d.). This view underlies the recent worldwide, nearly evangelical, faith in non-governmental organizations (NGOs) and non-profits – rooted in civil society and mobilizing social capital – as the most appropriate institutions to carry out development. It also rests fundamentally on liberal rational choice theory, which interprets the development process to be driven foremost by the decisions of equally endowed, self-maximizing individuals subscribing to principles of economic rationality (Risman and Ferree, 1995; Nelson, 1996).

Recent sociological research has challenged the deterministic relationship Putnam draws between social capital and development, thus expanding theories of social capital to encompass the "downside" of social capital (Portes and Landolt, 1996), as well as the much-overlooked role of macro-economic and political processes in structuring degrees of civic engagement (Skocpol, 1996; Tarrow, 1996; Foley and Edwards, 1997; Gertler, 2000). These debates have forced significant analytical clarity upon social capital theory by raising questions about which kinds of networks are desirable, and in which contexts. World Bank economist Michael Woolcock (1998) has perhaps pushed these analytical distinctions furthest to develop a typology of different types of social capital and their likely outcomes. At the micro-level, he accounts for both intra-community ties ("bonding" social capital, or "integration") and extra-community networks ("bridging" social capital, or "linkage"). Social opportunity requires high levels of both integration and linkage. Woolcock's typology also encompasses the macro-political framework – cross-cut as well by horizontal and vertical dimensions – that itself can facilitate or impede the capacity of communities to mobilize social networks.[7] State institutions can have more or less institutional capacity ("organizational integrity") and more or less responsiveness to civil society ("synergy"). High levels of both are needed for states to achieve the cooperation, accountability and flexibility characteristic of successful "developmental states" (the classic examples being Japan, South Korea and Singapore; Evans, 1995).

Woolcock's multi-scalar typology finds some expression in the World Bank's analytical framework, which distinguishes between "horizontal" and "vertical" forms of association. In the Bank's definition of social capital, due attention is also given to the "enabling social and political environment" that must support efforts of social groups to act in their own self-interest if social capital is to achieve its developmental potential. Crucially, the Bank's representation of the "enabling environment" encompasses not just the state and broader civil society, as in Woolcock's formulation, but also the market and the corporate sector. Community welfare can be maximized when these three pillars of social capital – states, businesses, and civil society – mutually reinforce one another's objectives: "economic and social development thrive when representatives of the state, the corporate sector, and civil society create forums in and through which they can identify and pursue common goals" (Evans, 1995).

Such assertions notwithstanding, further exploration of the Bank's web-based resources reveal far more about what civil society can do for states and markets than what either states or markets can do for enhancing social capital within civil society. For example, we learn that social networks among the poor could facilitate the deepening of formal markets; social networks among the elite could enhance the vitality of the corporate sector; social capital could benefit firms by reducing transaction costs; and "pre-existing" social capital within civil society could facilitate efforts to "privatize state-owned industries in a social environment where the rule of law is weak" (World Bank, 2001). When more specific reference is made to the relevance of social capital for development work, that is, the onus appears to fall on civil society to generate the social capital for sustainable economic growth and widespread participation in political democracy. In this instance, too, the socio-structural perspectives of Woolcock and others appear to have been overlooked entirely. Some examples of the "Sources of Social Capital" specified on the Bank's website illustrate how in practice the World Bank engages social capital in the most narrow sense, as membership in associations:

> *Families*: As the main source of economic and social welfare for its members, the family is the first building block in the generation of social capital for the larger society.
> *Communities*: Social interactions among neighbors, friends and groups generate social capital and the ability to work together for a common good. This is especially important among the poor as social capital can be used as a substitute for human and physical capital.
> *Ethnicity*: Ethnic relations come up frequently in discussions of social capital. Whether it is immigration, microenterprise development, tribal nepotism or racial conflict, ethnic ties are a clear example of how actors who share common values and culture can band together for mutual benefit.
> *Gender*: Social networks of impoverished women ... are necessary for women to obtain income and other necessities.
> (World Bank, 2001)

Several assumptions about the way social capital is construed to inform development practice become apparent here. First, social capital (even ethnic ties in the context of racial conflict) has inherently benign qualities; families and communities are assumed to be the harmonious institutional frameworks within which the benefits of social ties and networks are enjoyed. This formulation overlooks the possibility that associational life might instill not cooperation but conflict – an oversight that decades of feminist-economic research on the household should by now have purged from even the most mainstream development institutions.[8] It also restricts the scale of analysis to individual tastes, preferences, and behaviors, and remains squarely within the liberal theoretical tradition. From this point of view, the task of development practice is to craft more associative subjects by creating opportunities for membership in various forms of associational life.

The social struggle in social capital

A different view of social capital – one that does not find expression in development policy circles – can be found in the work of Marxian anthropologist Pierre Bourdieu. In *Outline of a Theory of Practice* (1977), where Bourdieu first develops a framework for studying social and cultural forms of capital (to which he collectively refers as "symbolic capital"), the analysis focuses squarely on social structure. Individuals do not generate social capital and are not the primary unit of analysis. Rather, social capital inheres in the social structure and must be conferred value by a society consenting to its cultural logic. Within this logic, differently positioned individuals experience associational life differently; some benefit at the expense of others. The benefits and costs of participation are distributed unequally. One does not acquire or squander social capital on the basis of individual choice; rather, one accrues obligation and opportunity to participate in social networks by virtue of one's social position.[9]

For Bourdieu, social networks operate as one among many cultural dimensions of profit and exchange. He thus rejects a narrow understanding of economism as economic practice, and argues instead for:

> extend[ing] economic calculation to *all* the goods, material and symbolic ... that present themselves as *rare* and worthy of being sought after in any particular social formation – which may be fair words or smiles, handshakes or shrugs, compliments or attention, challenges or insults, powers or pleasures, gossip or scientific information, distinction or distinctions.
>
> (1977: 177–8)

In an "economics of practice," then, associational life and social networks are forms of "symbolic capital" – "the sum of cultural recognition that an individual could acquire through skillful manipulation of the system of social symbols."[10] Like Putnam (and liberal formulations of social capital in development discourse), Bourdieu recognizes the mutual embeddedness of economic and social life. Both strains of social capital theory challenge the artificial divide between culture and economy by bringing the former under the scrutiny of economic categories. In Bourdieu's Marxian approach to cultural politics, however, associational life appears not as benign and harmonious but as inherently conflictual and contradictory.[11]

For Bourdieu, expanding an understanding of capital to encompass symbolic forms (including shared cultural norms and social networks) facilitates an analysis of the exploitative dimensions of culture and social practice. His notion of the "economics of practice" is intended to clarify the *ideological* dimensions of social capital and the modes of domination inherent in some forms of reciprocity and association. First, a theory of the economics of practice highlights the role not only of individual self-interest, but also of *class* interest in the logic (or ideology) of reciprocity. Among equals, gifting and acts of generosity provide an economic guarantee because they oblige a return. Among those of unequal status, however, gifting and other modes of reciprocity generate affective bonds that obfuscate the hierarchical nature of social relationships. In Nepal, the affection and kindness high-caste patrons may lavish on their low-caste inferiors, for instance, serves as a palliative for the abuses of caste distinctions. Of gifting practices within patronage relationships, Bourdieu (1977: 195) writes:

> Goods are for giving. The rich man is "rich so as to be able to give to the poor," say the Kabyles. This is an exemplary disclaimer: because giving is also a way of possessing (a gift which is not matched by a counter-gift creates a lasting bond, restricting the debtor's freedom and forcing him to adopt a peaceful, cooperative attitude); because in the absence of any juridical guarantee, or any coercive force, one of the few ways of "holding" someone is to *keep up* a lasting asymmetrical relationship such as indebtedness, and because the only recognized, legitimate form of possession is that achieved by dispossessing oneself – i.e. obligation, gratitude, prestige, or personal loyalty. Wealth, the ultimate basis of power, can exert power, and exert it durably, only in the form of symbolic capital.

Bourdieu thus urges us to recognize a second ideological function of social capital: that gestures of giving and kindness can in fact function as a form of domination, a "symbolic violence" with the pernicious effect of binding the oppressed to their oppressors through feelings of trust and obligation:

> the best way in which the master can serve his own interests is to work away, day in, day out, with constant care and attention, weaving the ethical and affective, as well as economic, bonds which durably tie his *khammes* [bonded laborer – or low caste client in the Nepal context] ... to him ... In a society in which overt violence ... meets with collective reprobation ... symbolic violence, the gentle, invisible form of violence, which is never recognized as such, and is not so much undergone as chosen, the violence of credit, confidence, obligation, personal loyalty, hospitality, gratitude, piety – in short, all the virtues honoured by the code of honour – cannot fail to be seen as the *most economical mode of domination*
>
> (1977: 190, 192; emphasis added)

Third, to the extent that such forms of social bonding and associational life generate common values or a moral community, we may begin to question how such values operate as forms of power within culture. For

Bourdieu, morality falls within the realm of "doxa" – "that which is accepted as a natural and self-evident part of the social order and is not open to questioning or contestation" (Agarwal, 1994: 58). When social hierarchy assumes a moral force in society, ideological constructions and perceptions of the subordinate can converge, as revealed in the domain of practice Bourdieu calls "habitus." Social change thus requires the awakening of "political consciousness," through which subordinate groups recognize the established order as an arbitrary human construction and fashion alternative futures.

Feminist research on the politics of consciousness has developed a far more complex understanding of women's relationship to hegemonic patriarchal structures than that offered by Bourdieu's typology of "doxa," "habitus," and "political consciousness." For example, research in the Asian and Middle Eastern contexts suggests that women recognize (even covertly resist) male domination as ideology, but also comply in strategic ways that ensure their own and their children's security.[12] The key point for our purpose is to acknowledge that common moral frameworks are not *in themselves* desirable planning objectives, so long as they serve to entrench dominant cultural ideologies and undermine the potential for critical awareness on the part of the oppressed. To the extent that development programs nourish local forms of association underpinned by common moral frameworks, they risk exacerbating already existing lines of hierarchy, coercion and exclusion. The task for development from this point of view is to foster forms of associational life among the oppressed that transform individual recognition of oppression into more collective, overt forms of consciousness and resistance (Agarwal, 1994).

Social capital as a governmental strategy

Given the pragmatic insights for planning practice that can be derived from Bourdieu's social capital framework, we may wonder why the latter does not receive due attention in the World Bank's website on social capital (and in development discourse more generally). Why does development discourse defend a benign role for social capital to the point of effacing the qualitative distinctions even its own theorists (e.g. Michael Woolcock, 1994) have drawn between different types of associational life? Why do mainstream development institutions now promote microfinance as a programmatic strategy that mobilizes local social capital, when until just two decades ago such small-scale forms of petty capitalism might have been viewed as anachronistic "vestiges of 'traditional' society, with no place in modern, 'developed' societies" (Walters, forthcoming)? And, in so doing, why do they target poor women as entrepreneurial agents of local economic development, when until recently conventional wisdom dictated that credit and other capital inputs be extended to small farmer households via their male heads?

To answer these questions we must keep in mind the global political–economic conjuncture within which social capital has emerged as the favored theoretical framework for understanding and alleviating poverty – and within which microfinance for women has emerged a favored model of development. Foremost, we must not forget that the recent "career" of social capital (to borrow an expression from Mayer (2001)) coincides with the conclusion of the Cold War, dubbed sympathetically by another social capital theorist, Francis Fukuyama, as the "end of history" itself (Goonewardena, 2000).[13] Or that these events also paved the way for other, somewhat lesser endings, including state-centered planning and the comprehensive welfare state. Unmoored from state institutions, development planners with the best of intentions must now turn to civil society to do their good work – buttressed by policies and programs intended to devolve capacity to the local level. Much has been said about the opportunities this political economic conjuncture presents for grassroots mobilization, local self-reliance, participatory processes, and development informed by local knowledge (e.g. Mayer, 1994). Without disputing the potential for such progressive outcomes, I wish to emphasize the extraordinary omission in most of the social capital literature of the implications of this conjuncture for the cherished local capacities, on the one hand, or for the emergence of social capital as a politically expedient concept for those setting the terms of the new world order, on the other.[14]

Regarding the latter, the social capital framework enables the architects of neoliberal economic policy to cast the reconfiguration of state–society relations in progressive terms – local capacity building, local self-reliance, net social benefits from reduced transaction costs, and increased returns to human capital. As such, social capital can be expected to fill the vacuum left by the restructuring of the welfare state in countries around the world. By some accounts, state restructuring can actually *facilitate* the accumulation of social capital within civil society; Fukuyama (1996: 17) writes that:

> societies that rely on a powerful and all-encompassing state to promote economic development run a double risk. Not only will state-supported companies be less efficient and risk breaking national budgets in the short run, but the very intervention of the state may weaken the society's underlying propensity for spontaneous sociability in the long run.

Social capital thus offers a "governmental strategy" for shifting the onus of development from the state to civil society and to third-sector agencies working on its behalf.[15]

By focusing on the poor as agents of their own survival, the framework obscures the structural sources of inequality *produced* by the present political–economic conjuncture. Research on the impacts of structural adjustment programs, for example, has by now amply documented that women bear a disproportionate share of the social costs of state restructuring; in particular, women's unpaid domestic labor absorbs much of the shock to poor households from cuts in subsidies for healthcare and agricultural inputs (Benería, 1992; Sparr, 1994; Bakker, 1996; Tsikata and Kerr, 2001). Feminist economists have argued that structural adjustment policies themselves reveal a gender bias in their assumption that households can infinitely bear the devolution of maintenance and caring activities from the public to the private sector (Elson, 1991; Benería, 1995; Cagatay et al., 1995; Bakker, 1996). To the extent that women successfully "build social capital" through collective responses to inflation and cuts to public social protections (e.g. Lind, 1992), their labor underwrites the transition in macroeconomic policy from the Keynesian welfare state to the neoliberal "workfare" state (Jessop, 1994). Through social capital, cultural values – and the subjectivities of women – thus become instrumental to strategies of governance. Culture, rather than programs of the state, becomes the medium through which the actions of individual women may be connected up with imperatives of government (Rankin, 2001a).

By focusing on the benign qualities of social capital, mainstream development discourse offers a clear economic, and even moral, justification for reducing the state's role in the provision of basic social protections. Needless to say, representations of social capital as potentially (or inherently) conflictual and contradictory – not to mention as implicated in maintaining dominant social and political ideologies, as Bourdieu argues – could readily upset the governmental function of the term noted here. First, a more conflictual view of social capital would too easily undermine the claims now circulating in mainstream development discourse about capacities for local self-reliance. Second, such a formulation would draw analytical attention to forms of associational life that do not presently appear on the social capital radar screen – namely, social movements to protest the social costs of economic restructuring and the devolution of social protections (Mayer, 2001). Mainstream development discourse has too great a political investment in *diverting* attention from the ways in which political economy structures associational life to admit into its analytical frame Marxian and other socio-structural perspectives on social capital.

The social capital in microfinance

In light of the governmental function of the term noted here, we can further note that the "capital" in social capital is not innocent. By announcing its semantic proximity to markets it constructs a "zone beyond politics," subject only to "natural" laws of economic rationality and requiring no lines of political accountability (Walters, forthcoming). As such, it also provides some ready answers to the architects of the new world order, who wish not only to manage the social costs of neoliberalism, but also to extend market rationality to regions formerly governed by centralized states or beyond the reach of global capitalism. In this regard, consider the recent flourishing of microfinance as a development strategy. While the *idea* of rotating credit groups is as old as commerce itself (and anthropologists and other social scientists have been documenting such informal lending arrangements since they first became interested in cultural "others" (e.g. Geertz, 1962; Mintz, 1961), its rise to mainstream prominence as a development strategy, like social capital, coincides with the recent resurgence of neoliberal economic ideology. Microfinance programs proliferated rapidly in the 1990s with the restructuring of previously nationalized banking systems and the devolution of rural credit delivery to a new set of financial institutions specializing in banking with the poor. They also mark an important shift in approaches to poverty alleviation, from state-subsidized universal access to credit for male-headed subsistence family farms (through "small farmer" credit programs) to third-sector microfinance institutions targeting poor, rural women as entrepreneurial agents.[16]

The "feminization of development" entailed in microfinance is now commonly justified through efficiency and empowerment arguments that draw on the principles of social capital theory. Women in many rural agrarian societies typically lack the collateral, literacy, numeracy, and freedom of mobility necessary to compete for credit from conventional institutional sources. At the same time, women spend disproportionately more of their incomes on household welfare than men and typically exhibit higher repayment and lower default rates (Kabeer, 1994). Thus extending women credit for small-scale enterprise will likely have beneficial outcomes for all household members, poor communities, and lenders themselves (Morduch, 2000). The dominant model of microfinance – the group lending model pioneered by the Grameen Bank in Bangladesh – socializes the costs of lending to poor women by providing them access to credit on the basis of "social collateral" obtained through membership in borrower groups. Here social capital helps correct for imperfect information about borrowers lacking in formal credit and employment histories and substitutes for collateral by ensuring against default through social sanction and peer enforcement. As the World Bank social capital web page puts it, "poor but closely-knit communities pledge their social capital in lieu of the material assets that commercial banks require as collateral" (World Bank, 2001).

For poor women, the theory goes, participation yields not only an economic payoff in increased access to financial services, but also an empowerment payoff in new forms of bridging and linking social capital that emerge from participation in networks of borrower groups (Servon, 1998). As one scholar recently put it in a study of the Grameen Bank in Bangladesh, borrowers' interaction at "center meetings" (during which borrower groups convene to repay their loans) "facilitates [their] ability to establish and strengthen networks outside their kinship groups and living quarters" (Lawrance, 1998: 2). Donors thus consider microfinance to be a "win–win" approach to development because investors can mobilize bonding social capital to enhance the financial viability of banking with poor women; and poor women gain access to both social and financial resources that allow them to help themselves through the market mechanism (Mayoux, 1995; Fernando, 1997; Morduch, 2000; Rankin, 2001a).

Even as microfinance advocates draw on liberal theories of social capital to promote this approach to poverty alleviation, they also evoke feminist and union traditions when they coin the expression "solidarity groups" for the women's borrower groups. The implication here is that women's associations through microfinance generate not just social and economic capital, but also collective consciousness of, and resistance to, oppression. Evoking "solidarity" imputes to microfinance programs (and the social capital they generate) a capacity to mobilize women for transforming gender ideology. It also echoes the programmatic implications of a Marxian understanding of social capital (*à la* Bourdieu), which emphasizes the role of ideology and consciousness in social change. Gramscian, Habermasian and Frerian traditions have, for over half a century, been working out the long-term communicative and institutional processes through which such collective consciousness can arise – and could provide ample fodder for fashioning microfinance programs. Yet in practice, microfinance models advocated by mainstream donors, such as the World Bank, respond more to lenders' concerns with financial sustainability and profit than to established traditions of fostering radical collective action.

For example, the present "microfinance orthodoxy" lies now in a "minimalist" or "credit-only" approach to poverty lending, as pioneered by the Grameen Bank (Rhyne and Maria Otero, 1994). This approach must be viewed in contradistinction to "social services" approaches through which, in South Asia, small-farmer credit programs had been integrated with a range of community development initiatives. Responding to macro-regulatory imperatives for market-driven development, the minimalist approach pares down microfinance to the strictly financial dimensions of poverty alleviation (credit, savings, and increasingly insurance and other financial instruments). In this context, solidarity groups function foremost to provide lenders a mechanism for "slash[ing] administrative costs," "motivating repayment," and "introducing financial discipline through peer pressure" (Yaron, 1991). Faced with management structures that award remuneration and status on the basis of outreach and repayment rates, moreover, staff have little incentive to attend to the difficult task of fostering an institutional climate for building collective consciousness (Ackerly, 1997; Goetz, 1997; Rankin, 2001b). Under these circumstances, the health of the financial system, rather than the welfare of the population, becomes the core objective of microfinance.

Cultural articulations: social capital and solidarity in the Nepalese context

In the absence of an institutional focus on gender transformation, the "solidarity group" model thus takes as given that which must instead be *established* – the conditions of possibility for those in subordinate positions to identify collectively in opposition to forces of domination. To assess the potential for such transformatory outcomes, even the basic assumption that existing stocks of bonding social capital provide a cultural rationality for women to join together in groups must be examined in relation to local cultural economies. What opportunities and constraints exist within culture for women to mobilize social capital for emancipatory ends? What are the progressive and regressive tendencies of social capital itself? Do liberal or Marxian theories best capture the role of social capital in social life? To examine questions of cultural articulation, I turn now to ethnographic research in a Newar merchant community characterized by extraordinarily dense forms of associational life.[17] Among the scores of ethnic groups within Nepal, the Newars are known for their highly active religious and cultural associations (*guthis*), their highly structured kin and caste relations, and the dense networks of obligation and reciprocity engendered by both. Historically, Newars have been among the most active of Nepalese ethnic groups in commercial enterprise and long-distance trading, and are known for their permissive cultural ideologies regarding women's involvement in commerce.

Conventional representations of Newars' propensity for festival, feasting, and religious devotion often overlook the ideological function of associational life in maintaining social hierarchy and inequality. Like liberal theories of social capital, the representations focus on the role caste, kin, and religious associations have played for centuries in supporting socioeconomic development – in the Newar case, developing and preserving the spectacular medieval temples and townscapes, as well as an insular, highly ritualized cultural tradition amidst the flux of a thriving trans-Himalayan trade. Planners often evoke the Newar *guthi* associations, which not only regulate participation in religious and social life but also often distribute "micro-credit" to their members on a rotating basis, as a cultural referent for microfinance and the solidarity group concept (e.g. Dhakhwa, 1995).

As caste-based associations, however, *guthis* also have hierarchical and coercive dimensions that can perhaps be best grasped with reference to Bourdieu's perspective on social capital. For example, within *guthis* members often describe the norms of association entailed in mandatory membership as exacting onerous, if not unbearable, costs in terms of time, labor, and money. These costs accrue most notably through the feasting obligations that punctuate all life cycle rituals, ancestor worship, festivals, and other occasions for propitiating the deities. Members endure these obligations, often at the expense of basic material comforts, only to escape the even more burdensome social sanctions against nonconformity – tantamount, in some cases, to excommunication from Newar social life. One might say that in the Newar "economics of practice" finance capital gets transmuted into social capital through investments in *guthi* membership and religious piety. Profits transformed into social investments establish a sound reputation critical for survival in Newar social and economic life. The honor that accrues from fulfilling social obligations is thus one's best economic guarantee, the shame in forsaking them one's surest demise.

The flip side to the intense solidarity among *guthi* members is a vigorous exclusion of outsiders, most notably lower castes and women. *Guthis* thus serve a crucial role in regulating social hierarchy by establishing and maintaining shared moral frameworks justifying segregation. To the extent that bonding social capital does exist in Newar society, it exhibits many of the "dark sides" of social capital now routinely noted in the literature. Generating social capital through the onerous *guthi* obligations preserves ancient cultural traditions, but also entails significant costs that can undermine both commercial initiative (by diverting financial capital) and social transformation (by monitoring existing lines of in/exclusion). These findings caution against the tendency within liberal social capital theory of imputing to "primitive" societies a logic of solidarity that has been "lost" in capitalist contexts where individual self-interest prevails. Following Bourdieu, they suggest a more analogous relationship between capitalist and non-capitalist societies with respect to the role of social *and* material capital: in both contexts an ethic of social hierarchy and individual gain structures practice not just in the market, but also in the domain of social investment (Rankin, 1996). In both, norms of reciprocity and common moral frameworks offer an ideological justification for uneven accumulation. Development planners must therefore recognize that idealistic recourse to traditional forms of social capital offers no necessary defence against naked self-interest and may in fact exacerbate existing sources of inequality.

The Newar case also illustrates how, from the perspective of women, relying on honor and reputation to build networks and establish social trust, as advocated by Putnam, can be problematic. Maintaining *guthi* and other social obligations is considered a matter of household honor, to be endured despite extraordinary costs. In addition to transmuting finance capital into social capital, the Newar "honor economy" also expresses – indeed produces – Newar gender ideology. Put starkly, men's honor depends crucially on relationships with women, who not only perform the onerous domestic labor entailed in keeping up social obligations, but also must exhibit qualities of moral, sexual, and social propriety. While for men honor functions as a possession (one either has it or one does not), for women, honor operates as something more like a character trait that reflects not only on themselves, but also on their household or patriline (Liechty, 1995). A woman's honor is gauged primarily through sexuality and ritual pollution (as opposed to integrity in maintaining social investments); if not properly managed, women's sexuality and regular episodes of ritual pollution can compromise the pedigree of an entire household or lineage.

Here again, we see how common moral frameworks can *limit* the scope for associational life to generate transformatory consciousness and action. It is with recourse to the morality of honor that women self-regulate in matters of dress, extra-household mobility, and social exchange. In addition, caste and ethnicity are obvious examples of the kinds of social differences that structurally preclude women in certain locations from viewing their interests in solidarity with women in others. Even within Newar caste groups, structural antagonisms prevail. Within joint family households, for instance, women's personal strategies for accruing material resources and political power often entail efforts to control the labor of junior women, especially recently married daughters-in-law. For their part, daughters-in-law in joint family households have a vested interest in conflict with their mothers-in-law as a means for promoting the eventual break-up of the extended family and establishing themselves as the senior woman in a new nuclear household. Such antagonisms extend across households over time as they go through cycles of expansion through marriage alliances and contraction through the splitting of joint families (Rankin, 2001b).

In microcredit programs, "solidarity" groups are expected to mobilize existing networks, trust, and norms of reciprocity in order to perform not only the *financial* tasks of selecting borrowers, evaluating proposals, and monitoring repayment, but also the *socially transformatory* task of challenging gender ideology. In light of the hierarchical and coercive frameworks within which social capital can operate, however, one might wonder whether the solidarity groups could in fact entrench, rather than challenge, some already existing modes of subordination. Given the limitations of bonding social capital briefly explored here, what evidence exists that microfinance programs create new linking forms of social capital that are beneficial to women's empowerment?

Ethnographic research in South Asia on the articulation of microfinance programs with a wider cultural context offers considerable cause for skepticism. For example, women have been shown to self-select for group members with significant assets – such as husbands with income – thus concentrating microfinance services among those with access to other forms of capital and excluding "the poorest of the poor" (Ackerly, 1997; Fernando, 1997). Groups also tend to self-select for members with identical caste and ethnic identities, mitigating possibilities for gender solidarity across other socio-cultural difference (Rankin, 2000). Moreover, women often borrow from local moneylenders and other sources in order to meet the rigorous weekly repayment schedules – thus recycling their debt and entrenching the very class-based hierarchies that microfinance programs are intended to address (Rahman, 1999). When group members do vigorously monitor one another's consumption and repayment patterns in accordance with program incentive structures, they can generate an environment of hostility and coercion that in practice atomizes rather than unites them (Ackerly, 1997; Fernando, 1997). Finally, in spite of expectations about the capacity of microfinance programs to transform existing gender ideologies, in at least two respects, they seem to have the effect of entrenching, not challenging, the gender division of labor and power. Women receive the credit, but it is often their husbands who actually control its investment and the income generated by it (Goetz and Gupta, 1996). And, to the extent that women do initiate income-generating activity, they are often encouraged to take up enterprises, such as sweater-knitting, that do not disrupt practices of isolation and seclusion within their households (Mayoux, 1995; Ehlers and Main, 1998; Goetz and Gupta, 1996).

Social capital and the cultural politics of social change

The trends cited above can be traced in large part to the interpretation of social norms and networks that underlies the Grameen model of microfinance now widely promoted by mainstream development agencies. Drawing on liberal theories of social capital, these interpretations expect that opportunities for association afforded women through "solidarity groups" will foster the social networks and common moral frameworks necessary for cooperation and collective action. This idea has indeed introduced a remarkable financial innovation in rural credit delivery – namely that social collectivity can substitute for collateral in underwriting loans to poor women. But in evoking radical traditions of organizing and resistance (*à la* "solidarity"), the dominant microfinance model implicitly (and sometimes explicitly) makes claims about the potential for social networks to empower women and transform social relations.

Without wishing to refute such radical *potential*, this chapter has argued that the first step to its realization must be to introduce into the analytical frame of social capital theory the Marxian perspectives of Pierre Bourdieu. This framework clarifies the coercive and exploitative dimensions of social capital (as one among many goods in an "economics of practice"), and its role in maintaining social hierarchies. Corroborated here by ethnographic research from Nepal, it demonstrates the ways in which common moral frameworks generated by social norms and networks can be implicated in cultural ideologies that justify and perpetuate inequality. In this view, promoting social capital through networks and norms of reciprocity may in fact leave people – even the oppressed – free to carry on oppressive relations. The crucial task for development vis-à-vis the poor and disadvantaged is thus to bring them to *collective* consciousness of their subordinate location so that they are able overtly to challenge the social structure. The latter interpretation of social capital has not adequately informed development approach and has been largely absent from representations of social capital theory in development discourse. I have argued that this omission must be understood in relation to the "governmental" role played by social capital, in providing a moral justification for economic restructuring and the devolution of social protections from the state to civil society. As a programmatic manifestation of liberal theories of social capital, microfinance demonstrates a clear gender dimension to this governmental function: here the transition from state-led to market-led approaches to poverty alleviation has been anchored in women's capacity to leverage social capital on behalf of the financial sustainability of formal lending institutions.

Ethnographic research on the "economics of practice" in a Newar merchant community has suggested that development interventions seeking to indiscriminately promote social capital risk entrenching the hegemony of dominant interests. This research suggests that, at a minimum, practitioners and policy makers must develop typologies for distinguishing between regressive and progressive forms of associational life. This goal requires a socio-structural approach that both investigates individuals' locations within social structures (as does Bourdieu's) and locates structures within a broader macroeconomic context (here Woolcock's typology is instructive). It also requires an analysis of the dialectical relationship between the material and ideological dimensions of social change (Agarwal, 1994). Credit programs that leave ideological structures intact, for example, cannot in themselves catalyze social change. Even in the context of expanding women's access to credit, the ethnographic evidence now shows that without due attention to the cultural politics of social change, microfinance programs may in fact serve to defend existing hierarchies along the lines of class, caste, and gender.

Programmatically, then, several procedural conclusions emerge. As the microfinance example demonstrates, the mere formation of solidarity groups does not guarantee progressive outcomes and may in fact perpetuate existing social hierarchies. Solidarity among women can, however, serve as a powerful tool for progressive social change, as long as it fosters critiques of dominant cultural ideologies. In the context of microfinance programs, planners might introduce strategies for "conscientization" about the broader macro-regulatory context and for reframing individual resistance to local gender ideologies as more collective, overt forms of action. For example, training in numeracy and basic banking principles can assume a political function as aspects of popular economics education that seeks to foster a collective critical awareness of power relations and policy affecting women's lives.[18]

More generally, once development planners understand the ideological dimension of social change, then the crucial issue shifts from the search for *the* authoritative development model, to concerns about the locus and mechanism of social criticism. The latter priority demands that planners play a role in creating the social spaces and institutional means for collective reflection on individual experiences of subordination and powerlessness. A first step is to construct development institutions with organizational cultures, management styles, incentive structures, and staffing policies that can respond to women's strategic interests in challenging oppression. Such procedural considerations could facilitate the design of programs that encourage women (and others in subordinate social locations) to negotiate their differences and recognize shared aspects of their subordination. This kind of social network – a solidarity grounded in women's own analysis of dominant cultural and political ideologies – can provide the surest foundation for "development," in collective strategies for challenging the social basis of inequality.

Notes

1 Research for this chapter was conducted under the auspices of a Fulbright-Hays Research Grant. I am grateful to the two anonymous reviewers, Chris Cavanagh, Amrita Daniere, Kanishka Goonewardena, Margit Mayer, and Norma Rantisi for their comments on an earlier draft of this paper, and to Diana Strassman for her kind assistance in navigating the review process. Earlier versions of the chapter were presented at the 1999 Annual Conference of the International Association of Feminist Economics (Ottawa, Canada) and the 2001 Annual Conference of the Association of Amercian Collegiate Schools of Planning (Cleveland, Ohio).
2 A World Bank web page, now an international clearinghouse for the latest research and theories on the promises of social capital, announces at the outset that "social capital is critical for poverty alleviation and sustainable human and economic development" (World Bank, 2001).
3 I use "liberal" here in the sense of political liberalism, whose essence "lies in its recognition of individual desiring as the basic fact of modern civil association" (Minogue, 1994). The liberal emphasis on rational choice presumes all individual behavior to be rationally calculated to advance the actor's material interests.
4 I have borrowed this expression from Margrit Mayer (2001); see also Jane Jenson (1998).
5 The ideas underlying social capital – concerned with the capacity of community members to cooperate for mutual benefit – have been circulating within political theory for well over a century (Lemann, 1996). Yet never before have they been taken up so enthusiastically in mainstream policy circles. Putnam's "Bowling Alone" and *Making Democracy Work* in particular have had an extraordinary impact, far beyond most academic writing (Edwards n.d.).
6 The genealogy of the term can perhaps be traced most directly to French envoy Alexis de Tocqueville who observed in eighteenth-century America a "propensity for individuals to join together to address mutual needs and pursue common interests" (Wilson, 1997: 746).
7 Putnam himself distinguishes between horizontal and vertical forms of social capital, but in the absence of an analysis of the macro-regulatory context.
8 For a summary of this research see Kabeer (1994: 95–135).

Social capital and microfinance 107

9 On Bourdieu's structural interpretation of social capital, see also Foley and Edwards (1999) and Woolcock (1998); these sources do not, however, elaborate the broader "economics of practice" crucial for understanding Bourdieu's specifically Marxian view of the socio-structural determinants of individuals' access to social capital.
10 See Honneth (1995: 187). Bourdieu adopted the term "social capital" in his later work, *Distinction* (1984), to denote specifically that part of "symbolic capital" relating to social location.
11 Indeed, what is *missing* in Bourdieu's understanding of economism is an analysis of disinterested, cooperative, or soladaristic action (Ortner, 1994). For the purposes here of examining the engagement of social capital theory in development discourse, however, Bourdieu's emphasis on the conflictual and contradictory dimensions of social life offers an important challenge to the dominant liberal tradition.
12 See, for example, Ong (1997), Kandyoti (1991), and Rankin (2001b); needless to say, this formulation applies with equal force to Anglo-middle-class women negotiating patriarchal institutions in Western contexts.
13 See Goonewardena's "The Future of Planning at the End of History" (2000) for an excellent discussion of Fukuyama's conservative prophecy and its implications for planning theory and practice.
14 For some exceptions in this regard see Foley and Edwards (1997), Skocpol (1998), and Walters (forthcoming). For a discussion of the analogously ideological function of social capital in the North as well as in the South see Mayer and Rankin (forthcoming).
15 Here I am drawing on Foucauldian "governmentality" studies which provide a method for understanding the dynamic of state power and the "capillary" ways it operates through civil society as a disciplinary force (see Foucault, 1991; Gordon, 1991; and Miller and Rose, 1990 for summaries of this method). Social capital (and microfinance) can thus be viewed as "governmental strategies" that help establish the *idea* of self-regulating markets as a legitimate and ethical objective of government (Rankin, 2001a).
16 Small-farmer credit programs and other forms of "poverty lending" by the state have their own set of problems, which are beyond the scope of this paper.
17 This research was conducted over the course of several visits to Nepal: over an 18-month period in 1993–1995, a six-week period in 1996, and a four-week period in 2000, under the auspices of a Fulbright-Hays Research Grant, a Cornell University Mario Einaudi Center for International Studies Summer Fellowship, and a Social Sciences and Humanities Research Council (Canada) Assistance for New Researchers Grant respectively. Within the merchant community of Sankhu, I engaged ethnographic techniques of open-ended, unstructured interviews, focus groups, and participant observation on the general topic of the cultural politics of markets. Informants were sampled selectively to ensure a diverse range of responses by caste, gender, class, age, and neighborhood. Observations and interview content were recorded in field notebooks to be later catalogued by key words and concepts; interviews were conducted in Nepali (in which I have been conversant since 1986 over the course of prior study, research, and employment in Nepal). Forty lengthy unstructured interviews were recorded on audio cassette, transcribed and translated for in depth narrative analysis. These observations were supplemented by a 150-household survey dealing with labor and investment practices and, for historical perspective, archival research on the economic history of the town. To research financial policy, I conducted 35 in-depth, structured interviews with planners in the central bank, managers of financial institutions and representatives of donor agencies, focusing on the relationship between

economic liberalization and preferential credit schemes. In November 1994 and May 2000 I also visited project sites of two "Grameen replications" in southern Nepal. Findings from this research are also documented in Rankin (1996, 2000, 2001a, b), as well as in a dissertation on *The Cultural Politics of Markets: Economic Liberalization and the Challenge for Social Planning in Nepal* (Cornell University, 1999).

18 One intermediary organization supporting such overtly political practices – Alternative Women in Development – works with microfinance programs to help them "ground women's self-employment efforts in the broader context of women's collective empowerment, community development, and human rights" (Alt-WID, 2001).

References

Ackerly, B. (1997) "What's in a Design? The Effects of NGO Programme Delivery Choices on Women's Empowerment in Bangladesh" in Goetz, A. M. (ed.) *Getting the Institutions Right for Women in Development*, New York: Zed Books, pp. 140–60.

Agarwal, B. (1994) *A Field of One's Own: Gender and Land Rights in South Asia*, Cambridge: Cambridge University Press.

Alt-WID "Microenterprise: A Solution to Women's Poverty?" Online, available at http://www.geocities.com/altwid_ny/ (accessed 2 February 2001).

Bakker, I. (1996) "The Gendered Foundations of Restructuring in Canada" in Bakker, I. (ed.) *Rethinking Restructuring: Gender and Change in Canada*, Toronto: University of Toronto Press, pp. 3–12.

Benería, L. (1992) "The Mexican Debt Crisis: Restructuring the Economy and the Household" in Benería, L. and Feldman, S. (eds) *Unequal Burden: Economic Crises, Persistent Poverty, and Women's Work*, Boulder, CO: Westview Press, pp. 83–104.

—— (1995) "Toward a Greater Integration of Gender in Economics" *World Development* 23 (11): 1839–50.

Bourdieu, P. (1977) *Outline of a Theory of Practice*. Cambridge: Cambridge University Press.

—— (1984) *Distinction: A Social Critique of the Judgement of Taste*, Cambridge, MA: Harvard University Press.

Cagatay, N., Elson, D. and Grown, C. (1995) "Introduction." *World Development* 23 (11): 1827–36.

Dhakhwa, U. (1995) "Developing a Finance System which Serves the Majority" paper prepared for the National Seminar on Rural Finance, Kathmandu.

Edwards, M. (n.d.) "Enthusiasts, Technicians and Sceptics: The World Bank, Civil Society and Social Capital." Online, available at www.worldbank.org/poverty/scapital/library/Edwards.pdf. (accessed 7 August 2001).

Ehlers, T. B. and Main, K. (1998) "Women and the False Promise of Microenterprise" *Gender and Society* 12 (4): 1–13.

Elson, D. (1991) "Male Bias in the Development Process: An Overview" in Elson, D. (ed.) *Male Bias in the Development Process*, Manchester: Manchester University Press, pp. 1–28.

Evans, P. (1995) *Embedded Autonomy*, Princeton, NJ: Princeton University Press.

Fernando, J. L. (1997) "Nongovernmental Organizations, Micro-credit, and

Empowerment of Women" *The Annals of the American Academy of Political and Social Science* 554: 150–77.

Foley, M. W. and Edwards, B. (1997) "Escape from Politics? Social Theory and the Social Capital Debate" *American Behavioral Scientist* 40 (5): 550–61.

—— (1999) "Is it Time to Disinvest in Social Capital?" *Journal of Public Policy* 19 (2): 141–73.

Foucault, M. (1991) "Governmentality" in Burchell, G., Gordon, C. and Miller, P. (eds) *The Foucault Effect: Studies in Governmentality*, Chicago: University of Chicago Press, pp. 87–104.

Fukuyama, F. (1996) "Trust: Social Capital and the Global Economy." *Current* 379: 12–18.

Geertz, C. (1962) "The Rotating Credit Association: A 'Middle Rung' in Development" *Economic Development and Cultural Change* 10 (3): 241–63.

Gertler, M. (2000) "Social Capital" in Johnson, R. J., Gergory, D., Pratt, G. and Edwards, M. (eds) *The Dictionary of Human Geography*, Oxford: Blackwell, p. 747.

Goetz, A. M. (1997) "Local Heroes: Patterns of Fieldworker Discretion in Implementing GAD Policy in Bangladesh" in Goetz, A. M. (ed.) *Getting the Institutions Right for Women in Development*, New York: Zed Books, pp. 161–75.

Goetz, A. M. and Gupta, R. S. (1996) "Who Takes Credit? Gender, Power, and Control over Loan Use in Rural Credit Programs in Bangladesh" *World Development* 24 (1): 45–63.

Goonewardena, K. (2000) "The Future of Planning at the End of History" University of Toronto, unpublished manuscript.

Gordon, C. (1991) "Governmental rationality: An introduction" in Burchell, G., Gordon, C. and Miller, P. (eds) *The Foucault Effect: Studies in Governmentality*, Chicago, IL: University of Chicago Press, pp. 1–52.

Honneth, A. (1995) "The Fragmented World of Symbolic Forms: Reflections on Pierre Bourdieu's Sociology of Culture" in Wright, C. W. (ed.) *The Fragmented World of the Social: Essays in Social and Political Philosophy*, Albany: State University of New York, pp. 184–201.

Jenson, J. (1998) "Mapping Social Cohesion: The State of Canadian Research" Canadian Policy Research Network (CPRN) Study NO. Fl03, Ottawa, Canada.

Jessop, B. (1994) "Post-Fordism and the State" in Amin, A. (ed.) *Post-Fordism: A Reader*, Cambridge, MA: Blackwell, pp. 251–79.

Kabeer, N. (1994) *Reversed Realities: Gender Hierarchies in Development Thought*, New York: Verso.

Kandyoti, D. (1991). "Islam and Patriarchy: A Comparative Perspective" in Keddie, N. R. and Baron, B. (eds) *Women in Middle Eastern History: Shifting Boundaries in Sex and Gender*, New Haven, CT: Yale University, pp. 23–42.

Lawrance, L. Y. (1998) "Building Social Capital from the Center: A Village-Level Investigation of the Grameen Bank" Programme for Research on Poverty Alleviation, Working Paper #22, Grameen Trust, Dhaka, Bangladesh.

Lemann, N. (1996) "Kicking in Groups" *The Atlantic Monthly* April: 3–14.

Liechty, M. (1995) "Fashioning Modernity in Kathmandu: Mass Media, Consumer Culture, and the Middle Class in Nepal" PhD dissertation, University of Pennsylvania.

Lind, A. (1992) "Power, Gender and Development: Popular Women's Organizations and the Politics of Needs in Ecuador" in Escobar, A. and Alvarez, S. E.

(eds) *The Making of Social Movements in Latin America*, Boulder, CO: Westview Press, pp. 134–49.

Mayer, M. (1994) "Post-Fordist City Politics" in Amin, A. (ed.) *Post-Fordism: A Reader*, Cambridge, MA: Blackwell, pp. 316–37.

—— (2001) "Transformations in Urban Struggles: From 'Social Movement' to 'Social Capital'?" Paper presented at the June 2001 conference of the Research Committee on Urban and Regional Development of the International Sociological Association, "Social Inequality, Redistributive Justice and the City" Amsterdam.

—— and Rankin, K. N. (forthcoming) "Social Capital and (Community) Development: A North/South Perspective" *Antipode*.

Mayoux, L. (1995) "From Vicious to Virtuous Circles? Gender and Micro-enterprise Development" UN Research Institute for Social Development, Occasional Paper no. 3.

Miller, P. and Rose, N. N. (1990) "Governing economic life" *Economy and Society* 19 (1): 1–27.

Minogue, K. R. (1994) "Liberalism" in Outhwaite, W. and Bottomore, T. (eds) *The Blackwell Dictionary of Twentieth-Century Social Thought*, Cambridge, MA: Blackwell, pp. 333–6.

Mintz, S. (1961) "Pratik: Hatian Personal Economic Relationships" in Garfield, V. E. (ed.) *Symposium: Patterns of Land Utilization and other Papers*, pp. 54–63, proceedings of the 1961 Annual Meeting of the American Ethnological Association (AES). Washington, DC: AES.

Morduch, J. (2000) "The Microfinance Schism" *World Development* 28 (4): 617–29.

Nelson, J. (1996) *Feminism, Objectivity and Economics*, New York: Routledge.

Olson, M. (1965) *The Logic of Collective Action; Public Goods and the Theory of Groups*, Cambridge, MA: Harvard University.

Ong, A. (1997) *Spirits of Resistance and Capitalist Discipline: Factory Women in Malaysia*, Albany: State University of New York Press.

Ortner, S. B. (1994 [1984]) "Theory in Anthropology since the Sixties" in Dirks, N. B., Eley, G. and Ortner, S. B. (eds) *Culture/Power/History: A Reader in Contemporary Social Theory*, Princeton, NJ: Princeton University, pp. 372–411.

Portes, A. and Landolt, P. (1996) "The Downside of Social Capital" *The American Prospect* 7 (26): 18–23.

Potapchuk, W., Crocker, J. and Schechter, W. (1997) "Building Community with Social Capital: Chits and Chums or Chats with Change" *National Civic Review* 82 (2): 129–40.

Putnam, R. (1993) *Making Democracy Work: Civic Traditions in Modern Italy*, Princeton, NJ: Princeton University Press.

—— (1995) "Bowling Alone: America's Declining Social Capital" *Journal of Democracy* 3, January: 65–78.

Rahman, A. (1999) "Micro-credit Initiatives for Equitable and Sustainable Development: Who Pays?" *World Development* 27 (1): 67–82.

Rankin, K. N. (1996) "Planning for Equity: Ethical Principles from Newar Representations of Finance" *Studies in Nepali History and Society* 1 (2): 395–421.

—— (2000) "Social Capital and the Foundations of Democratic Public Culture: Contributions from Critical Ethnography of Nepal" paper prepared for the 6th Annual Conference of the University of Toronto-York University Joint Centre for Asia Pacific Studies, "Democracy and Identity Conflicts in Asia: The Politics of Cultural Difference in an Age of Globalization" 4–5 December 2000.

—— (2001a) "Governing Development: Neoliberalism, Microcredit, and Rational Economic Woman" *Economy and Society* 30 (1): 18–37.

—— (2001b) "Planning and the Politics of Markets: Some Lessons from Financial Regulation in Nepal" *International Planning Studies* 6 (1): 89–102.

Rhyne, E. and Otero, M. (1994) "Financial Services for Micro-enterprises: Principles and Institutions" in Otero, M. and Rhyne, E. (eds) *The New World of Microenterprise Finance: Building Healthy Institutions for the Poor*, London: Intermediate Technology Publications, pp. 5–31.

Risman, B. and Ferree, M. M. (1995) "Making Gender Visible" *American Sociological Review* 60 (5): 775–83.

Servon, L. J. (1998) "Credit and Social Capital: The Community Development Potential of U.S. Microenterprise Programs" *Housing Policy Debate* 9 (1): 115–49.

Skocpol, T. (1996) "Unraveling from Above" *The American Prospect* 7 (25): 115–50.

Sparr, P. (1994) "What is Structural Adjustment?" in Sparr, P. (ed.) *Mortgaging Women's Lives: Feminist Critiques of Structural Adjustment*, New York: Zed Books, 1994, pp. 1–39.

Tarrow, S. (1996) "Making Social Science Work Across Space and Time: A Critical Reflection on Robert Putnam's *Making Democracy Work*" *American Political Science Review* 90 (2): 389–97.

Tsikata, D. and Kerr, J. (2001) "Introduction" in Kerr, J. and Tsikata, D. (eds) *Demanding Dignity: Women Confronting Economic Reforms in Africa*, Ottawa: The North-South Institute.

Walters, W. (forthcoming) "Social Capital and Political Sociology: Re-imagining Politics?" *Sociology*.

Williams, R. (1977) *Marxism and Literature*, Oxford: Oxford University Press.

Wilson, P. A. (1997) "Building Social Capital: A Learning Agenda for the Twenty-first Century" *Urban Studies* 34 (5–6): 745–60.

Woolcock, M. (1998) "Social Capital and Economic Development: Toward a Theoretical Synthesis and Policy Framework" *Theory and Society* 27: 151–208.

World Bank (1999) "What is Social Capital?" Online, available at http://www.worldbank.org/poverty/scapital/whatsc.htm. November 11 (accessed 3 September 2001).

—— (2000) "Sources of Social Capital" Online, available at http://www.worldbank.org/poverty/scapital/sources/index.htm. October 5 (accessed 3 September 2001).

—— (2001) "Social Capital for Development" Online, available at http://www.worldbank.org/poverty/scapital/ August 7 (accessed 3 September 2001).

Yaron, J. (1991) *Successful Rural Financial Institutions*, Washington, DC: World Bank.

5 Rebuilding social capital in post-conflict regions

Women's village banking in Ayacucho, Peru and in Highland Guatemala

Denise Humphreys Bebbington and Arelis Gómez

Introduction

Programs to provide financial services to the very poor, and in particular to women, have become a widely accepted approach to alleviating poverty in both developing and developed countries. Research on these programs has tended either to focus on credit technologies and methodologies that allow microfinance institutions to expand financial services to the poor while achieving financial sustainability, or on the employment and income generation impacts of credit. Likewise evaluations of microfinance programs have emphasized questions of financial sustainability, efficiency, scale of operations and changes in income at the household level. Often overlooked in these studies and evaluations are the dynamics of the social and associational arrangements used by microfinance programs to promote group solidarity and cooperation as a means to overcome the high cost of lending to clients with little or no assets.

Yet for such mechanisms to function properly, and to avoid opportunistic and self-defeating behavior, borrowing groups need to quickly and firmly establish an atmosphere of mutual trust and cooperation. In some situations such group cohesiveness is more easily accomplished than in other situations – levels of education and poverty notwithstanding. What then are the factors that enable group members to more readily trust one another and so to assume risks together? Is there a relationship between social cohesiveness in groups and financial success?

Working in situations of both ongoing and post-conflict present special challenges to efforts to build (or rebuild) such trust. Violence and uncertainty undermine trust and confidence, making cooperation all the more difficult. Humanitarian assistance programs can compound the problem with paternalistic approaches, turning once vibrant citizens into passive beneficiaries.

Building mutual trust and *confianza* has been framed as the challenge of building social capital (Putnam 1993; Coleman 1988). In this chapter we will use examples from two village banking programs, in post-conflict

Ayacucho, Peru (with FINCA Peru) and in Highland Guatemala (with the NGO FAFIDESS),[1] to illustrate how the provision of financial services contributed to the rebuilding of such social capital. The experiences of group managed lending schemes, such as the village banks promoted by FINCA International (the Foundation for Community Assistance), and traditional rotating savings and credit associations known as ROSCAs, suggest that there is indeed an important relationship between the social dynamic of the group and favorable financial outcomes. Our findings indicate that the more members trust each other, the better able they are to engage in mutual risk-taking and reap the benefits.

Lending, saving, and social capital

Community lending and savings schemes over time

Community-based lending and savings schemes are not new. Nor were they invented in the latest development fad of microfinance, with some researchers suggesting that variants of group lending and savings schemes may extend back over 400 years (Ardener 1995). Thus rotating savings and credit associations, or ROSCAs, have provided and continue to provide useful alternative financial services to participants without any external promotion, and remnant practices of ROSCAs can be found around the world. From West Africa where they are called *esusu*, with *esu* being the word used for contributions (Ardener 1964), to Indonesia where members organize into rotating credit societies known as the *arisan* or into savings and loan groups known as *simpan pinjam* (Hospes 1995: 130-3) and the Caribbean (Besson 1995: 263-4) where they are known as *san* in the Dominican Republic, boxes in Martinique, and *pardners* in rural Jamaica, community members have organized themselves on principles of fairness, reciprocity and mutual trust, to save and lend. In Latin America ROSCAs are common and continue to be a popular alternative among office workers to raise capital for special needs. In Bolivia they are known as *pasanaco*, and in Peru as *panderos*. In Guatemala, there is the *cuchuval* (in Quiché *cuchu* means meeting or group and *val* means to rise up) and as *tanda, cundina, quinela* – among the more frequent names given to ROSCAs – in Mexico (Vélez-Ibañez 1983: 16–17). According to Ardener (1964: 217), who conducted an extensive comparative survey of ROSCAs, the benefits of pooling resources are clear: "The most obvious function of these associations is that they assist in small-scale capital formation, or more simply, they create savings. Members could save their contributions themselves at home and accumulate their own funds, but this would withdraw money from circulation: in a rotating credit association, capital need never be idle."

Village banking and social capital

Village banking methodology

A wide variety of microfinance programs employ methodologies with features similar to traditional ROSCAs. One methodology that has been particularly successful with capitalizing poor women is the village banking methodology promoted by the Foundation for Community Assistance (FINCA International). The methodology, based upon principles of self-help and self-management, primarily targets poor women in urban and semi-urban settings.[2] Members are at once owners, administrators and clients of their banks. In contrast to other microfinance programs, the village banking model[3] emphasizes personal savings and provides a series of scaled up loans over a three year period to encourage small scale capital accumulation. In this model, 20 to 30 women organize themselves into village banks. Participants are self-selected and may often be friends, neighbors, or relatives and programs often have selection criteria which might include: preference for mothers with children, permanent residence in the community, reputation for honesty, and hard work. They must also agree to save on a weekly basis and to use the loan for some type of economic activity of their own. An orientation period (pre-bank phase) allows women to learn about the methodology, to establish their internal rules and to elect leaders who will be responsible for administering the bank during the first cycle. FINCA assigns a promoter to the bank to provide guidance and support over the life of the bank.

The FINCA program consists of loan periods, or "cycles," lasting 16 weeks.[4] Loans are distributed by FINCA to the "external account" of each bank at the beginning of the cycle and members make loan repayments (to the external account) and savings deposits (which form part of the internal account) at weekly meetings. At the end of each cycle all loans must be repaid to the bank and any outstanding debts cleared. The bank then repays its loan to FINCA and is ready to receive a fresh loan for the new cycle. Interest rates charged by the NGO to village banks range from between 2.5 to 4 percent.

As in traditional ROSCAs, village banks use social capital as collateral to make credit available to participants who have little or no physical assets to pledge. Another characteristic that village banks share with ROSCAs is that the group's financial resources are always invested. In both the Guatemalan and Ayacucho programs, the village banks begin lending with US$50. At the end of the ninth cycle (after three years) members will have the capacity to work with loans of US$300 and have achieved accumulated savings of US$300. By then women are considered ready to graduate. However in practice members prefer to continue working with the NGO and generally the NGOs are in no hurry to see their better clients go elsewhere.

There are important features of the village banking model that depart significantly from other microfinance and government sponsored credit programs for the poor. Because the credit is not single purpose, women are allowed to use the loans according to their best prospects. The informal training which is provided over the cycles does not attempt to teach specific business or technical skills; rather it focuses on helping women administer their bank while building confidence in their capacities to save, borrow, and invest. By not specifying uses of credit up front, village banking embraces diversification and leaves the decision of how to use the resources to the borrower. It allows the borrower to initiate a start up business, a feature microfinance programs rarely permit. While interest rates have been a point of debate – village bank rates tend to be higher than other microfinance programs – they are market based. Also significant is the flexibility banks exercise to take advantage of peak money making periods (which is further described in the Ayacucho case), allowing members to change activities according to best prospects and to lower borrowing levels during economic downturns. Banks can also distribute advantages and disadvantages by having a mix of members with differing types of economic activities and differing levels of profitability. As long as members meet their obligations this varying level of income generating capacity does not appear to lessen the cohesiveness of the banks. Clearly, however, for the village bank and its members to thrive a surplus must be made.

Confianza and mutual risk-taking

Village banks, like most other formal and informal financial mechanisms, work on trust. If trust fails among the members of the group, the bank falls into disagreement and disarray. Members withdraw their savings, may choose to drop out and eventually the bank ceases to function. Yet in the literature on solidarity lending programs there is little mention of the role of mutual trust, reputation and other forms of social capital. Instead greater importance is given to the social pressure function of the group as the motivation for repayment.

Studies of microfinance programs employing solidarity group methodology note that research on intra-group dynamics is scarce and that more work needs to be done in this area (Hulme and Moseley, 1996). While pressure from the group may certainly play a role in repayment, the experiences of village banking programs in Peru, Guatemala and elsewhere suggest that negative factors (i.e. the threat of sanctions) are not the social glue that creates a cohesive, successful bank. Sanctions might keep a member from defaulting but what is it that gives members the courage to trust each other, to take risks together? How is it that these women with little previous formal organizational experience and no previous credit experience manage to cooperate and save amounts of money that have previously eluded them as individuals?

Putnam (1993) has argued that overcoming problems of collective action and self-defeating opportunism is easier when a community has a tradition of collective practice or social capital[5] in the form of norms of reciprocity and networks of civic engagement. The willingness to cooperate is bolstered by such traditions and he uses the example of ROSCAs as the principal analogy on which he builds his theoretical argument.

In village banks as in ROSCAs, trust plays an enormously important role in keeping things efficient, in reducing transaction costs, in smoothing relations, in making everyday things work. If we accept that mutual trust is a key ingredient to a village bank's operation then we must ask how is this trust established among members? What factors might enhance or impede the creation of trust among members? And importantly for post-conflict societies, how can trust and confidence be restored? We will borrow from the current discussion of social capital and attempt to link some aspects of this discussion in order to understand the internal dynamics of village banks we have seen in Ayacucho, Peru and Highland Guatemala.[6]

In the village banks of both Ayacucho and Highland Guatemala the establishment of *confianza* has been critical to the success of the banks. We prefer to use the term *confianza* rather than trust, as Vélez-Ibañez does (1983: 11) because *confianza* refers not only to the notion of trusting one another but also to the relationship of generosity, intimacy, and personal interest in one another. And because community banks often include members who are unknown to one another, *confianza* also encompasses the notion of a *willingness* to establish such generosity and intimacy.

Vélez-Ibañez describes how *confianza en confianza* (trusting in mutual trust) among members of Mexican ROSCAs allows trust to be extended outside members' circle of friends, building an ever larger virtuous circle: "Mutual trust in others eventually reinforces trust in the trust-worthiness of self. To trust others who are not known eventually reinforces trust in still others who are yet to be known" (1983: 137–8).

Like the ROSCAs described by Vélez-Ibañez, village banks develop rules, parameters and rituals to operationalize *confianza*. These serve to reduce the effects of uncertainty and help bind persons to certain behaviors and relationships. We might hypothesize then that communities with larger stocks of social capital would find a comfortable synergy with the methodology of village banking – which requires a high degree of trust and collaboration. Conversely, communities with less social capital would have greater difficulty in establishing trust and thus the banks would have greater difficulty in maintaining internal cohesion and financial health. These banks would suffer lower savings rates, and higher rates of default, drop-out and even embezzlement.

Social capital then is an important asset, like financial capital or human capital (Woolcock 1998 and Bebbington 1999), and can accumulate as banks move through the loan periods. In the beginning members of a

Rebuilding social capital 117

bank may exhibit a disposition towards extending *confianza* to one another and according to how the bank functions, this initial social capital can be strengthened or weakened. However it requires time and a certain amount of collective history before the group can solidify these norms of trust and cooperation. *Confianza* may initially be extended but it is only solidified based on action. Conversely *confianza* in the banks can be destroyed by a number of events leading to conflict, among them: lack of transparency in the bank's transactions, failure by members to keep their commitments, failure of the bank's officers to enforce the rules, and failure to develop procedures for providing fair access for all members to the bank's resources.

The role of the financial intermediary, usually a non-governmental organization, is critically important in setting the atmosphere for trust, transparency, and collaboration. Where social capital already exists, and the disposition to trust and cooperate is greater, NGO promotional work is easier. Conversely, in situations of violent conflict, economic chaos, discrimination, and entrenched corruption, it is that much harder to build social capital. The NGO then must work quickly to establish an atmosphere of honesty and transparency, to promote client confidence and trust in the organization by assisting bank members to create clear rules and procedures to govern the bank.[7] These rules and procedures help to operationalize *confianza*.

Village banks begin lending and saving with low levels of *confianza* – enough to be able to distribute loans and collect savings, and begin the process of mutual risk-taking. If each member repays her loan on time, trust and confidence is strengthened and in the next round the group feels empowered to risk a bit more. Thus *confianza* and mutual risk-taking are synergistic. With each successful cycle of lending and repayment, the stock of social capital grows.

Conversely, if lending activities begin too quickly, before bank members have had the chance to develop a sense of trust and responsibility towards one another, the cohesiveness of the bank is at risk and conflict will likely ensue. Thus the initial pre-lending period where members have the opportunity to learn the methodology, to establish their internal code of conduct and to begin to work together is important. Equally important, risk-taking can only be carried out at a pace and level within the expectations of members. In the early phases of a village bank when loan amounts and savings are modest, members are willing to risk their resources with others. As the bank advances through the loan periods, loan amounts increase, savings grow and reputations become increasingly important in order to access greater amounts of capital. As both loan amounts and savings increase, the risk to members increases and thus internal rules and systems of the bank become increasingly important in resolving potential conflicts. Weekly meetings require more discussion on the merit and viability of proposals. Struggling members may seek advice from their fellow bankers – and for the most part bank members demonstrate enormous solidarity. By the fourth or fifth loan period (between one and one-and-a-half years) the loan amounts and personal savings can reach significant levels.[8] It is here that a sense of fairness and transparency must be vigorously exercised to maintain internal cohesion, for there is always a greater demand for credit than there are resources to fund initiatives. Thus to encourage greater savings and risk-taking, a greater stock of social capital is required.

Up to now we have referred to social capital to describe practices and relationships existing within the banks, however there is another level of social capital that merits further examination and it involves the relationship between the village banks and the intermediary financial service provider. The quality of financial intermediation provided by NGOs to village banks is a significant factor in banks' success. On the one hand, NGOs that are internally cohesive, well-managed with committed staff, themselves will more likely produce village banks of like quality. The greater the NGO's stock of social capital (networks and relationships) the better the organization can link its clients to other actors, private and public, expanding their social networks in ways that are useful for production and marketing initiatives.

The history of credit programs in most Latin American countries is a tale of broken promises. State sponsored financial institutions and promotional loan schemes intended to help the poor rarely fulfilled their mandates and with the economic crises of the 1980s they weakened significantly only to be closed a decade later. To further complicate matters and weaken public trust in the notion of credit, private banks and private investment companies have lured the unaware into depositing their savings in mismanaged and sometimes fraudulent schemes. Moreover, NGO credit programs have contributed to confusion about credit by offering loans that in essence were little more than grants to clients with little capacity to borrow and pay. Given the NGO's reticence to enforce repayment, borrowers would take advantage of this weakness, participants would more often than not default on their loans and these credit programs became known as working a "*fondo perdido*" (i.e. as a lost fund). In other instances, NGO clients would claim that project resources were charity from external sources and thus did not feel compelled to repay their loans.

This has generated not only suspicion and mistrust among the poor seeking credit but also a general mistrust of the capacity and seriousness of NGOs to offer financial services to the poor.[9] These missteps have a high cost for both clients and NGOs providing financial services. When an NGO credit program collapses, in the short run it may mean the end of a project. However, the undermining of mutual trust and cooperation has more damaging, longer term implications. NGOs ought therefore to invest significant time and resources in creating rules and procedures that enhance notions of reliability and confidence. NGOs must not only carefully select and trust their clients, they must also convince their clients that they too are trustworthy. The rules they establish must be seen as fair by their clients and more importantly they must enforce them.

By virtue of their social isolation, poor women are difficult clients to recruit. Cultural and social factors may aggravate their isolation (Yunus 1999). Situations of conflict pose special problems, particularly when the result is a larger number of war widows as in Highland Guatemala and Ayacucho. In FINCA Peru, the program methodology created simple rituals, on the one hand to give the program a distinct identity from other credit programs, and on the other hand to foster a spirit of camaraderie and solidarity. Encouraging members to articulate their personal hardships and dreams is at the center of FINCA's social empowerment strategy for women. The weekly meetings often include discussions that resemble something more like a group therapy session than a bank meeting. Beyond the emotional appeal of this approach, it helps isolated women extend their social networks with important impacts.

NGOs that are both knowledgeable of the region and sensitive to their clients' needs will be better able to look for synergism that will enhance benefits to their clients. They will understand the dimensions of the client's poverty and vulnerability, what Rahman and Hossain (1992 quoted in Hulme and Moseley 1996: 118) refer to as the "downward mobility pressures" caused by larger structural factors, family crises, natural disasters, and life cycle events that affect their clients. NGOs sensitive to the social and cultural needs and practices of their clients are likely to develop more appropriate development strategies and interventions. Carroll's study of successful NGOs[10] in Latin America (1992: 150–1) argues that the best organizations have the flexibility to experiment and change paths if necessary, and have mastered the art of responding and leading, listening and teaching.

The capacity to innovate and rethink strategies is an important quality for NGOs providing financial services and in the cases of Peru and Guatemala both FINCA and FAFIDESS have experimented with and made modifications to the village banking methodology. In FINCA Peru, senior management used its knowledge of local conditions and strong relationships with the banks to develop and perfect innovations. This willingness to modify the methodology permitted FINCA to tailor its program to client needs. Hulme and Moseley (1996) similarly note the importance of experimentation and methodological refinement in providing microfinance services. They also note that successful models provide a starting point for experimentation not emulation.

Turning social capital into financial capital

The case of FINCA Peru in Ayacucho

Regional context and program origins

Ayacucho lies within the heart of the "Trapezio Andino," a group of five departments in Peru's Southern Sierra considered to be among the poorest in Peru. The City of Ayacucho is perched atop a high valley floor (about 2,600 meters above sea level) and remains rather isolated, though only some 500 kilometers from Lima. Rich in history and culture, Ayacucho became known internationally as the birthplace of the Shining Path (Sendero Luminoso) one of Latin America's most violent terrorist movements. In 1980, the Shining Path began an armed struggle that effectively shut off Ayacucho from the rest of Peru for the next 13 years. The effects of the war have been devastating economically, socially, and culturally. Thousands were killed and forced to flee from villages to the cities of Ayacucho, Huanta and Lima leaving behind land, homes, and livelihoods. It is estimated that more than 30,000 rural families were displaced internally in the Department of Ayacucho and another 25,000 families left the Sierra to resettle in Lima (FINCA Peru Project Document 1993).

Post-conflict Ayacucho remains economically depressed and socio-culturally disarticulated from 14 years of war, isolation, and abandonment. There is little public investment and much private investment is linked to the profits of narcotics trafficking. Tourism is recovering slowly, though physical infrastructure remains inadequate. The agricultural sector remains depressed and lacking other alternatives many Ayacuchanos head to the coast as permanent or temporary migrants. Informal traders and service providers abound in Ayacucho's markets. As elsewhere in Peru, women have become pivotal income earners for their families by becoming active participants in the informal sector.

Ayacucho lags far behind the national averages for social indicators: illiteracy and infant mortality rates remain high. The average life expectancy for this largely Quechua-speaking population is significantly below the national average. The number of families headed by women continues to rise, and these families are typically among the poorest of the poor. Popular organizations remain weak, a lasting effect of the protracted and violent nature of the civil war. Many peasant leaders were either killed by the Shining Path or by the military, or forced to flee. Humanitarian assistance programs have tended to be paternalistic.

FINCA Peru began lending and savings operations in mid-1993. Some years earlier, a trial program of ten village banks was launched with $10,000 of private funds under another NGO. This successful experience served as a precursor to the creation of a fully-fledged FINCA program in Ayacucho supported by North American donor agencies. The role of charismatic leadership is often critical in the start up phase of an NGO's operations (Carroll 1992) and the influence of the co-directors – both Quechua-speaking Ayacuchanos with extensive experience in non-formal educational programs and credit cooperatives in the Andes – in shaping the program's culturally sensitive approach to its poor, mostly indigenous clients cannot be overlooked. Their familiarity with post-conflict Ayacucho along with their high degree of commitment has given the program a unique (but often criticized) personalized touch evidenced in their detailed knowledge of each village bank.[11]

Linking social capital and financial capital: program methods

AYACUCHO METHODOLOGY

The selection of members is critical to the success of the village banks. As far as possible the program encourages each bank to recruit its own members, stressing the importance of selecting members with reputations for honesty and hard work. Prospective members without references are accepted but screened by program management to determine their seriousness and eligibility according to program criteria. When 25 to 30 women come together to create a bank, they begin an orientation – or pre-bank – phase that generally lasts four weeks but can be extended if necessary. The pre-bank phase also serves to screen out those individuals only interested in receiving loans and unwilling to participate in the tasks of administering the bank.

Because a large number of women participating in the program have weak literacy and mathematical skills, and may only speak Quechua, the pre-bank phase is tailored to provide a slow, supportive entry into village banking. Members begin by saving together while simultaneously setting their bank's rules and procedures, learning techniques to administer the bank, and selecting bank officers for the first loan period. The Ayacucho program stresses that all bank members must serve in positions of leadership over the nine cycles of the bank. While some positions require strong literacy and numeric skills, other positions do not. Still, women are encouraged to improve these skills, and the author's interviews with members indicate that indeed participation in the program leads women to increase these skills.

The pre-bank phase is also critical in cementing trust among members and building confidence in the bank's rules and procedures. While FINCA promoters help to guide members in developing their internal code, ultimately the members decide the sanctions to apply and how they will be enforced when members fail to meet obligations. In addition, members of the bank must demonstrate an understanding of the fundamentals of how a village bank operates. Once this initial phase is mastered then attempts to build the virtuous circle of trusting and lending begins.

An important feature of the village banking methodology is the weekly meeting whereby members conduct bank business, talk about their business activity, and exchange information. Often these meetings are seen as being costly for bank members yet this view seems to miss what women participants' value about village banking. While women may first be attracted to village banking by the possibility of acceding to loans, other factors lead them to continue in the program. The social function of the bank is enormously important for women. Carrying out tasks as a group is important to participants and the friendship and solidarity shared by members is noteworthy. Members remark that joining the program has brought them a new family. Meanwhile, saving and lending as a group also produces tangible benefits for members. As one participant noted: "to save as part of a group is very different, there's more discipline. I could not have saved this money on my own" (personal communication).

Ritual is woven into the weekly meetings to reinforce the rules and procedures and thus build trust and confidence in the banks. One of the more compelling rituals is the personal testimony where a woman will stand in front of fellow members and recount a personally difficult moment, an obstacle overcome, a failure, a fear. In the early cycles, weekly meetings use personal testimonies to help women break through their isolation and fear. Speaking aloud about failures and hopes seems to have both a cathartic and motivational effect for members. Women tell of never having managed money before in their lives, their fear of being cheated in the marketplace, their joy in learning to read alongside their youngest child. By sharing their stories, bonds of respect, trust, and solidarity are strengthened which will serve the group in more difficult moments.

Likewise, the Ayacucho program encourages each bank to recognize important achievements by organizing simple celebrations. The close of cycle is another important ritual which brings members together at the end of a loan period to clear debts, take stock of progress, elect new leaders, and prepare for the next round of loans. As the bank's accounts are kept on a large sheet of paper for all to review, each member can visually check her progress and ask questions. Frank and honest discussions about problems are encouraged, and members are expected to come forth with their own solutions. If necessary, the group assumes payment of any outstanding loans. The close of cycle might also serve as an opportunity for socializing, for recognizing both individual and group achievements, and for reflecting upon the difficulties overcome. A financially successful cycle builds confidence and increases trust among the members – a stock of capital that they take into the next round of lending and risk-taking.

In a twist of the original methodology, FINCA Peru has experimented with several important innovations which permit increased and more rapid capitalization of the banks and its members. An *Extraordinary External Account* was created allowing more advanced banks to access extra capital with longer loan periods for members who demonstrate capacity to invest and pay. These loans are generally made during key periods of the year for economic activity, especially around fiestas and holidays. The interest rate charged (usually 1 percent higher than the *External Account* loan) is returned to FINCA Peru and for especially large loans members are required to provide an additional guarantee.

Examining impacts

Notwithstanding the impressive array of impacts produced by the program, we will limit the following discussion to certain particularly important impacts: (a) small scale capital accumulation, (b) the expansion of women's economic activity, and (c) women's self-confidence and empowerment.

SAVINGS

By July 1997, some four years after FINCA opened village banks in Ayacucho, the combined savings of active and graduated members (a total of 3,660 members in 168 banks) exceeded US$1 million. No other NGO credit program had ever achieved such a feat before in Peru, and it was accomplished by providing services to very poor and inexperienced borrowers. More recent figures reveal that the entire FINCA Peru program (with the Lima and Huancavelica programs included) has achieved a savings rate of 122 percent. That is, for every dollar loaned, US$1.22 is saved – the highest savings rate of all FINCA village banking programs worldwide. (Gómez 1999)

FINCA's mandatory savings requirement of 20 percent of the loan amount is frequently surpassed in the Ayacucho banks where members regularly make extra voluntary contributions to increase their savings. In what has become a sort of savings competition between banks, and at times between individuals within banks, it is not uncommon for members to accumulate US$1,000 to $3,000 by the second and third year. Indeed the women associate their level of progress with the amount accumulated in savings, not the size of their loan.[12]

Poorer members with little formal education are some of the most successful savers. This reflects: personal determination to save, the lack of trusted alternative mechanisms to keep personal savings, the flexibility offered by the village banks to withdraw savings during emergencies, and the return members receive for savings kept in their village bank. Because the Ayacucho banks manage the *Internal Account* (consisting of savings) so that money is never idle, the dividends members receive are considered more attractive than alternatives.

The Ayacucho program documents note the promotional nature of its strategy – to move women out of poverty through self-employment. In practice, however, the program's emphasis on savings actually reflects a more defensive strategy which helps members to deal with uncertainty and problems of liquidity caused by fluctuations in income. Initially access to credit might be the incentive to join. However, over time members cite the ability to save as the feature they like best about village banking – in direct contrast to what most financial services NGOs believe their clients want.

WOMEN'S ECONOMIC ACTIVITIES

Despite their residence in the cities of Ayacucho and Huanta, bank members continue to rely on their strong rural ties as the basis for their economic activity (Alvarado and Ugaz 1998). This is seen in both their choice of business activity and their strategy of diversification. According to a survey of village bank members in Ayacucho conducted by Pait in 1996 (p. 64) the majority of participants (from 76 to 85 percent) were involved in a diverse range of trading activities which involved the buying and selling of agricultural products and other goods (grains, vegetables, assorted household and personal care products). Much of this activity had links to rural communities in the Department of Ayacucho.

In personal interviews members stressed the importance of diversifying their sources of income as a means to avoid risk. Of the members surveyed some 60 percent had other economic activities to complement a main activity (30 percent reported several activities of equal importance carried out simultaneously). This diversification of business income did not fall off as members gained in lending experience; instead diversification appeared to increase indicating that members had become adept at identifying opportunity (Pait 1996: 64–6).

FINCA also encouraged members to experiment with new, more profitable economic activities if they encountered problems, as was the case with members involved in clothes making and handicraft production. Within the banks, members with more dynamic business activities would help by offering to share information about profitable products and markets. Over 82 percent of members surveyed used the loan to invest in their own economic activity (one third of the women interviewed were widowed, separated, or single mothers), 8 percent said their spouse administered the loan, the remaining 10 percent said that the loan was either jointly administered with a spouse or another family member (Paint 1996: 42).

Participation in a village bank has also permitted women to collaborate in similar economic activities. First, because members were more familiar with the amount of capital needed, they were better able to coordinate decisions about loan amounts. Second, because they shared information about markets and products they took advantage of economies of scale by organizing collective purchases to obtain better prices. This type of collaboration was best seen among women involved in the harvesting and marketing of cochineal.

WOMEN'S SELF-CONFIDENCE AND EMPOWERMENT

The personal testimonies of members illustrate the degree to which the program has transformed them as individuals, boosting their confidence in their capabilities to achieve personal goals. Members refer to their experience with village banking as a personal awakening. The powerful experience with savings has produced a strong sense of personal pride and in turn loyalty to their bank and to FINCA and this is reflected in their hesitancy to leave the program.[13] Furthermore, the opportunities for learning money management, leadership and speaking skills, and the recognition and support from other women in the banks are a source of great satisfaction for members. In personal interviews members referred to their scant experience with money before joining the program and their new capacity to make financial decisions based on solid criteria. For married women, their increased contributions to the family's income (averaging roughly 60 percent of the total family income) permitted them greater say in the financial decisions in the family (Pait 1996).

However this newly discovered economic power has shifted roles within families often resulting in increased conflict within the family, particularly with spouses, but also with children and other family members. In some situations, women were pressured by their spouses to turn over their loans – and in some instances their entire savings – resulting in great anguish for both the member and the bank as illustrated in one case where a member who managed to save nearly US$3,000 was threatened by her husband into turning over her savings (personal communication).

Nor has success with lending and saving in their bank led members to approach formal financial institutions. To the contrary, members show little interest in leaving FINCA noting that FINCA enjoys their confidence and respect. This confidence however is not yet extended to the private banks operating in Ayacucho. If we see member graduation to the formal financial sector as part of economic empowerment then the program has not met such a goal. On the other hand members' new managerial capacity to make decisions regarding the bank's internal account, resources that can sometimes be in the range of US$10,000 to $15,000, is a skill women will take with them whatever they do, wherever they go.

The case of FAFIDESS in Guatemala

Regional context and program origins

About 50 percent of the Guatemalan population speaks one or more indigenous languages (Davis 1997). Though a largely rural, highland population it is also rapidly urbanizing, a phenomenon that has been aggravated by lack of access to resources (land, water, credit) to support rural livelihoods and the prolonged period of violence. Indigenous peoples are among the poorest, the most exploited, and the most discriminated against sector of Guatemalan society. Despite legislative attempts to protect the civil rights of the indigenous population, institutionalized discrimination remains firmly embedded in Guatemalan society (United Nations 1989). Yet despite a concerted campaign by successive military dictatorships (1978–1986) to alternatively eliminate and control popular organization (in particular the rural cooperative movement), local organizations persist. From organizing potable water projects to collectively organizing production activities, the resilience of rural communities is remarkable.

Acute concentration of wealth exacerbated social tensions, fueling violent responses from insurgent movements and counter-attacks by paramilitary organizations during the 1980s and 1990s. Civil strife has taken an enormous toll on society. During the height of violence it was estimated that one in five Guatemalans had been internally displaced by counter-insurgency operations. Over 50,000 were estimated to have been killed. Another 50,000 poor indigenous fled for their lives to neighboring Mexico.

Linking social capital and financial capital: program methods

The methodology used by FAFIDESS largely follows the original FINCA model. The program started in 1984 when John Hatch, founder of FINCA International, used donations from Rotary Club International to create the first village banks in Guatemala. FAFIDESS was then created by the local chapter of the Rotary Club. Typically, FAFIDESS village banks are associations of 20 to 50 women who join together to save and guarantee each other's loans. Loan amounts begin at US$100 and scale up according to savings levels. Members are required to save 20 percent of the loan amount to be deposited along the loan payments in equal installments. Loan periods range from 16-week to 20-week cycles depending on the maturity of the group.

Members of the group are self-selected but must know each other, reside in the same area, and be willing to guarantee each other's loans. They must also attend weekly or bi-weekly meetings. Groups go through a training/orientation period of four weeks during which they define the rules to govern their activities and train members in bank operations. The group selects an Administrative Committee comprised of a president, vice-president, treasurer and secretary to administer the bank operations. A promoter from FAFIDESS attends and supervises the meetings.

After nine cycles of operations, banks that meet defined performance criteria (mostly tied to repayment records, savings rates, management, and internal cohesion) graduate to "Silver" status and eventually "Gold" status. With each level, banks enjoy larger loan sizes, greater autonomy in the management of their loan portfolio, and work towards formalizing their banks as organizations (legal status mostly as development associations).

Examining impacts

SOCIAL CAPITAL/FINANCIAL CAPITAL

As of June of 1998 FAFIDESS had 163 active banks, 3,856 members, and a loan portfolio of nearly US$1 million. An evaluation of the quality of FAFIDESS banks based on: (1) level of organization; (2) cohesion; (3) savings/internal capitalization; (4) management; and (5) portfolio performance, revealed a high level of quality (Gómez 1999). All banks included in the survey were either rated as excellent or very good and were characterized by clear governance rules and regulations. The bank reflected high levels of internal cohesion/stability with an overall drop-out rate of only 9.8 percent in contrast with the 25 percent drop-out rates found in most microfinance programs. The persistency rate, defined as the number of founding members still remaining in the program after three years, was also very high (61 percent). The strong social capital indicators of these banks (internal cohesion, administration, and organization) resulted in a high level of savings and strong portfolio quality.

The savings or capitalization levels were rated excellent for 67 percent and very good for 33 percent, while portfolio quality was rated excellent for 88 percent of the surveyed banks. Bank savings as a percentage of the loan portfolio ranged from 42 percent among the youngest banks to 86 percent among the oldest – even though the mandatory savings rate is only 20 percent. Because *confianza* among members of the banks, and between members and program management, is high, savings rates are high. Similarly, because members place great value in their banks, repayments rates are high (100 percent for the surveyed banks). Also, because *confianza* is high the members are more willing to engage in ever increasing mutual risk-taking as reflected in the ever increasing amounts of money borrowed over time. While the starting loan amount for the surveyed groups was Q300 (less than US$40), the average loan increased up to Q6,000 after one year, Q12,000 after two years, and to Q14,000 after three years.

Conclusions

While we have focused on two successful savings and lending programs, we readily acknowledge the limitations of such methodologies. Proponents of microfinance often make lofty claims about what credit programs can achieve, ignoring indications that some participants clearly do not fare well and abandon the bank. Nor does access to credit necessarily foster increased economic and social empowerment – especially when credit programs, eager to grow, sacrifice the quality of their programs. It is also questionable whether access to credit and increased income will necessarily lead to greater empowerment of women participants if members of the household resist any shift of power. Indeed, Pait's survey of banks in Ayacucho found situations where a woman's participation in the village banking program led to greater conflict within her household as family members (generally husbands, but often sons) resisted her growing financial independence. Still, for the majority of women participants in the cases discussed here make a strong argument that it is possible for credit to contribute to empowerment, including the expansion of women's social and economic networks. The authors have had many opportunities to hear women members reflect on the profound impact of their participation in a village bank on their lives and the well-being of their families.

Why women stay in village banks

While the primary reason women join village banks is to gain access to loans, over time as banks mature and personal savings are accumulated, the reasons women cite for persisting in a bank, change. The social functions of the bank become increasingly important to members, and members also appreciate the quality of the reliability of the financial services their bank offers. Women with three or more years in the program indicate that they value the ability to save most, followed by the opportunity to meet and talk with other women, and only thirdly mention access to credit in the reasons why they continue to participate. As in ROSCAs (Ardener 1995), the group's social functions are important and attract continued participation.

The importance of social networks

Participation in village banking also increases members' social capital by expanding their social networks both within the banks and beyond. The bonds of friendship and solidarity among members foster mutual help and also lead members to share information which is useful in identifying new markets or suppliers, and determining potential business opportunities. In FAFIDESS, some groups have institutionalized collective activities by developing manuals and procedures for their operations. Members have also joined to pursue collective business opportunities. In one of the Ayacucho banks members formed subgroups based on economic factors – the purchase of cochineal, the sale of bricks, the sale of vegetables, etc. Because their activities required that they travel throughout the Department of Ayacucho to sell and purchase goods, the smaller groups served as a means to share information about markets and prices and as a means to obtain better prices. FINCA staff, both management and promoters, helped these networks extend further by linking banks and individual members to other private actors. For example FINCA helped members working in the harvest and purchase of cochineal to obtain profitable contracts with a national textile firm.

The atmosphere of trust and reliability thus spills over into activities outside the bank. These same social networks have supported members in difficult social situations, such as domestic abuse, death, or sickness. Some banks have institutionalized this support by establishing emergency funds usually fed by a percentage of the profits or fund raising activities. In the case of FAFIDESS, for an additional cost of $2 per loan, the program offers insurance in case of death or terminal illness of a member that covers the debt plus funeral expenses. By 2001, some 15 members had benefited from this facility.

While the success of village banking in Ayacucho reflects the internal social capital mobilized by the banks in benefit of their members, this experiment in trust and mutual risk-taking could not have been accomplished without the presence and continuous support of a sensitive financial intermediary and the charismatic leadership which extended its own relationships and social networks to benefit women who were considered too poor to be viable. "Despite being a program that serves persons of very little income, it gives the impression of having greater perspective for achieving sustainability than many traditional credit programs supporting micro and small enterprises" (Pait 1996).

One area for further research is how members' social networks and relationships constitute social wealth (favors, social credits) that might be used sometime in the future. At least in the examples from these banks, it implies that the women involved view wealth not only as the accumulation of individual assets but also the building a sort of social wealth. Here they view the relationships created and built in the banks as a sort of wealth, a form of insurance and also as a group identity that is valuable as well.

If this is the case then microfinance strategies that only emphasize individual asset accumulation may not respond to the different notions of wealth among women in contexts such as those of Ayacucho and Highland Guatemala. Moreover they may fail to foster the sorts of synergies between the formation of social wealth and individual assets that has occurred in these banks.

Looking for synergy

The two programs reveal the powerful relationship between *confianza*, group cohesiveness, and favorable economic outcomes. While neither program purposefully set out to build social capital among their clients, both programs tacitly understood the power of collective identity and action. Each program shared similar challenges: working with a poor, largely indigenous clientele with little or no experience using credit, and living in communities whose poverty and isolation was exacerbated by prolonged political violence and economic decline.

As with traditional savings and credit associations, participants found that they could use their relationships in order to overcome their lack of physical guarantees. By trusting each other and following a mutually agreed upon code of conduct, members were able to gain access to an increasing pool of resources. A virtuous circle was created whereby trust was lent so that the group could engage in mutual risk-taking. With each successful repayment of loans, trust and confidence in the bank increased which in turn led to a new round of risk-taking. With each successive cycle, the internal cohesion of the bank was strengthened. The banks also helped women to expand their social networks which could be used to benefit their economic activities.

The lessons learned from these programs give us insights about providing financial services in post-conflict situations. Perhaps the most important is how the process of building and strengthening social capital is related to financial success. Financial service intermediaries ought recognize and articulate the importance of building and strengthening social capital in their overall program goals (and not consider it as an indirect benefit of their programs). These organizations will therefore need to develop strategies and methods to build trust, confidence, and discipline within their programs. The primary focus of interventions in post-conflict societies, then, should be the restoration of social capital in order to create a basis for sustainable financial services and ultimately a platform from which other types of investment (financial and non-financial) can flourish.

Notes

1 Fundacion de Asesoria Financiera a Instituciones de Desarrollo.
2 FINCA notes that its methodology is most successful with "*la mujer urbano-marginal*" but in fact both the Ayacucho and Guatemalan programs include an interesting mix of participants who are urban and rural based. In Ayacucho, members live in the cities of Ayacucho and Huanta but are culturally and economically based in rural communities. In Guatemala, FAFIDESS organizes banks in rural areas.
3 There are now many variations to the original methodology as a number of NGOs such as CARE, Freedom from Hunger, Save the Children, and Catholic Relief Services among others have established their own programs.
4 In the original FINCA International methodology the program lasted nine cycles or three years at which time members were to graduate. Members and banks are now allowed to continue indefinitely.
5 Anthony Bebbington (1999: 2035–6) warns that "social capital belongs to that alarmingly long list of terms in development that are notoriously difficult to define."
6 Both authors have been involved with the Ayacucho program since its initia-

tion in 1993, Gómez as a former technical director for FINCA International and Humphreys Bebbington as representative for the Inter-American Foundation. Gómez has worked as a technical consultant and evaluator of village banking and microfinance programs around the world for nearly 20 years.
7 Ostrom (1990) similarly emphasizes the importance of clear rules for effective collective action.
8 This loan cycle is considered a critical point for weaker banks when desertion rates can suddenly rise. Members usually have accumulated enough funds that they feel the risk becomes too great to continue further.
9 Based upon the authors' substantial experience with NGO projects in Latin America.
10 Carroll (1992) refers to NGOs as GSOs or grassroots support organizations.
11 The president of FINCA Peru, Aquiles Lanao, has had a long association with the credit cooperative movement in Peru, and his collaboration with John Hatch (founder of FINCA International) in an early but failed version of village banking in Bolivia in the early 1980s, provided an important experience with the methodology. Morena Lanao, the Director of the Ayacucho program, and a former school teacher, developed pedagogical approaches for members with little or no reading and mathematical skills which promoters could incorporate into the meetings.
12 Authors' interviews with member of village banks in Ayacucho.
13 There is much debate about the topic of "graduation" in village banking. At the end of three years, members are expected to be ready to graduate to formal financial programs but this is rarely the case. Indeed in Ayacucho, members often chose to "recycle" themselves into a new village bank bringing their accumulated capital along with them.

Bibliography

Alvarado, J. and Ugaz, F. (1998) *Retos del financiamiento rural*, Lima: CEPES CIPCA, CES Solidaridad.

Ardener, S. (1964) "The Comparative Study of Rotating Credit Associations," *Man* 94 (2): 202–28.

Ardener, S. (1995) "Women Making Money Go Round: ROSCAs Revisited," in S. Ardener and S. Burdman (eds) *Money Go-rounds. The Importance of ROSCAs for Women*, London: Berg.

Bebbington, A (1999) "Capital and Capabilities: A Framework for Analyzing Peasant Viability, Rural Livelihoods and Poverty," *World Development* 27 (12): 2021–44.

Besson, J. (1995) "Women's Use of ROSCAs in the Caribbean," in S. Ardener and S. Burdman (eds) *Money Go-rounds. The Importance of ROSCAs for Women*, London: Berg.

Carroll, T. (1992) *Intermediary NGOs*, West Hartford, CT: Kumarian Press.

Coleman, J. (1988) "Social Capital in the Creation of Human Capital," *American Journal of Sociology* (94): 95–210.

Davis, S. H. (1997) *La tierra de nuestros antepasados: estudio de la herenciay la tenencia de la tierra en el altiplano de Guatemala* (trans. C. M. Cruz Valladeres) Centre de Investigaciones Regionales de Mesoamerica (CIRMA) and Plumsock Mesoamerican Studies La Antigua Guatemala and South Woodstock, UT.

Gómez, A. (1999) "Evaluación de la metodología de bancos comunales de mujeres rurales en Guatemala," a study prepared for the Inter-American Development Bank, Washington, DC.

FINCA Peru Project Documents 1993.

Hospes, O. (1995) "ROSCAs in Indonesia," in S. Ardener and S. Burdman (eds) *Money Go-rounds. The Importance of ROSCAs for Women*, London: Berg.

Hulme, D. and Moseley, P. (1996) *Finance Against Poverty*, Vol. 1, London: Routledge.

Karlan, D. (2001) "Social Capital and Group Banking," Paper presented at the 2001 LACEA PEG/NIP Conference at MIT.

Ostrom, E. (1990) *Governing the Commons*, Cambridge: Cambridge University Press.

Pait, S. (1996) "Estudio especial de seguimiento de microempresarias del programa de FINCA Peru en la region de Ayacucho," Lima: SASE.

Putnam, R. (1993) *Making Democracy Work*, Princeton: Princeton University Press.

United Nations (1989) Declaration on the Rights of Indigenous Peoples, UN Documents, E/CN.4.1995/2, New York.

Vélez-Ibañez, C. (1983) *Bonds of Mutual Trust*, New Brunswick: Rutgers University Press.

Woolcock, M. (1998) "Social Capital and Economic Development: Toward a Theoretical Synthesis and Policy Framework," *Theory and Society* 27 (2): 151–208.

Yunus, M. (1999) *Banker to the Poor*, New York: Public Affairs.

6 "Banking on culture"
Microcredit as incentive for cultural conservation in Mali

Tara F. Deubel

Throughout Africa, cultural conservation has become a pressing issue in response to the increased marketing of African cultural heritage as a lucrative global commodity. Countries such as Mali are experiencing unprecedented loss of their material cultural heritage in a global economy that places a high value on what is perceived as "authentic" African art in Western consumer nations. Western-style museums that are commonly state-run and located in large cities have encountered serious challenges in the African context, notably a lack of funding to maintain permanent collections or acquire national pieces that sell for much higher prices abroad. African community museums have met with similar obstacles in securing funds to protect their local cultural resources. As a result, African communities are seeking new measures to safeguard their material culture. Established in 1997, the *CultureBank* in Fombori, Mali serves as both a museum and lending institution that provides access to microcredit. Cultural objects placed in a community museum serve as collateral for small loans, thus enabling participants to gain financial benefits while retaining their cultural heritage *in situ*.

Not surprisingly, the *CultureBank* model has been well-received by both the Malian government and international organizations such as the World Bank which recently funded the establishment of two new *CultureBank*s in central Mali under the auspices of a Malian NGO.[1] In creating a private community museum that does not rely on government funds, the *CultureBank* alleviates financial pressure on Mali's Ministry of Culture to support local museums and develops the country's tourist industry by attracting visitors. In addition, the novel integration of a microcredit component appeals to donors interested in funding market-based development initiatives in Africa. The central questions posed in this chapter are whether the *CultureBank* model has been successful in integrating the goals of microfinance and cultural conservation, in increasing income generation among participants, especially women, and in curbing the loss of valuable cultural objects from the local community.[2] The discussion also examines how this institution serves as a site of cultural reproduction in which Dogon cultural identity is both reinforced and reinvented. Before explaining the impetus and program design of the *CultureBank*, a review of literature on microfinance, cultural heritage loss in Mali, and the Dogon population will provide the context in which this project took shape.

Measuring the impacts of microfinance as a development strategy

The microfinance industry has grown tremendously since its inception in the mid-1970s with the well-known Grameen Bank in Bangladesh and has since become a common development strategy for financially sustainable poverty reduction throughout the developing world. Since microfinance institutions (MFIs) worldwide generally lend to low-income clients who lack major assets, they tend to rely heavily on forms of joint liability to manage the financial risk of lending without collateral. In this model, a group of borrowers is collectively held responsible for a common loan and the social pressure exerted by the group helps ensure repayment.[3] Other collateral alternatives include compulsory savings programs that require clients to hold a certain percentage of the loan in savings, pledging assets worth less than half the loan value, or personal guarantees that oblige family members or friends to repay the loan in the case of default.

Although there is general consensus on "best practices" and program design of MFIs, little is known about their household level impacts (Mosley and Hulme 1998). Most studies of MFIs have focused on their financial sustainability citing loan repayment rates as evidence for program success; however, this indicator may merely demonstrate participants' ability to repay loans without taking into account the impact of lending on the enterprise itself (Buckley 1997). Furthermore, while microfinance programs have proven effective in a variety of settings, several studies argue that they fail to benefit the most impoverished populations and, in some cases, may further disadvantage participants, notably women who face increased social pressure to take loans and become trapped in a cycle of debt liability (Mosley and Hume 1998; Rahman 1999).

Despite the lack of impact assessments, some general conclusions can be drawn from previous studies. Khandker's (1998) work on MFIs in Bangladesh revealed that better credit availability does not necessarily ensure growth of income or employment in the rural informal sector. Ledgerwood (1995) reports that microcredit does not usually result in significant net gains in employment, but does lead to increased use of family labor, and while there is no solid evidence of business growth due to microlending, credit has enabled enterprises to survive in times of crisis. In terms of measuring positive impacts on family health, nutrition, and education, evidence is "negligible" at best.

Some impact studies also reveal important gender differences; for instance, women are more likely than men to invest income from loan-assisted activities in improving family welfare. In the Grameen Bank example, female participants have contributed profits to household income, expenditures for basic needs, employment opportunities, and nutritional intake (Webster and Fidler 1996:22).

The trend toward microfinance programs in the developing world has rapidly spread throughout the African continent in the past two decades, but the results of these interventions have also been mixed. In a study of MFIs in Kenya, Malawi, and Ghana, Buckley (1997) questions whether microfinance addresses the actual problems of African microentrepreneurs or merely offers the "illusion of a quick fix" (p. 1081) since less than 10 percent of respondents who had received formal credit in his study were able to demonstrate *any* type of change in technique or technology since they received their first loan. Several "non-finance" factors may explain the limitations of microfinance in Africa. For one, African microentrepreneurs are often involved in a variety of impermanent enterprises rather than a single occupation and resources tend to be spread thinly among competing activities. The pressure of extended family and kinship networks is another salient factor in draining entrepreneur resources.

Recognizing some of the same constraints to client impact, World Bank studies of informal sectors in West Africa emphasize the positive impacts of microfinance interventions. Defined as "very small enterprises that use low-technology modes of production and management," informal sectors in West Africa are very large and rapidly growing (Webster and Fidler 1996:5). They account for roughly one-third to one-half of GDP and one-third to three-quarters of total employment in West Africa. The majority of informal activity is associated with agriculture in rural areas although migration is spurring more rapid growth in urban areas as well. Key constraints in informal sector economies include saturated and stagnant markets, lack of access to credit and savings, weak technical skills, inadequate information, and poorly developed infrastructure. Women, particularly the poorest, are major participants in informal sectors, as is the case throughout Mali.

Low-income African entrepreneurs rely mainly on family and friends, commercial moneylenders and trade creditors, and *tontines* (rotating community savings groups) for savings and credit. While more entrepreneurs are able to access financial services from donor-supported NGOs and credit unions due to the growth of microfinance, virtually none interact with formal banks. Based on an examination of nine MFIs judged most effective in West Africa, Webster identifies their major strength to be outreach to some of the most inaccessible populations in the world and high quality services. Weaknesses include an uneven ratio of loan revenues to bank expenses (30–40 percent of expenses are met by revenues on average), difficulties in increasing the number of loans made due to a lack of start-up capital, and a lower financial sustainability rating than that of the best microfinance programs worldwide (ibid.:72). Due to the shortfall of village banks in meeting their operating costs, government and donor subsidies remain critical to the continued success of most African programs.

The *CultureBank* provides an example of microfinance innovation in the West African context by including cultural conservation as one of its primary objectives. This case highlights the potential of MFIs to combine the goals of other types of local institutions, in this instance a community museum and center for artisan training, community literacy, and cultural events. By applying a microcredit model, the *CultureBank* provides capital for participants to invest in small enterprise, promotes the conservation of Dogon cultural heritage and increases social capital by fostering contact between participants and joint involvement in income-generating activities as discussed below.

In evaluating program success, most MFIs only measure changes in income and neglect other crucial indicators of the impacts of microcredit on poverty. In their critique of MFI assessments, Johnson and Rogaly (1997) identify three sources of poverty: lack of income, vulnerability to income fluctuations, and powerlessness, defined as few choices and little control. In combining the goals of cultural conservation and poverty reduction, the *CultureBank* provides a crucial opportunity for community empowerment. By choosing to keep cultural heirlooms in a community museum in exchange for microcredit, participants are able to increase their control over their cultural heritage and their choices in how to conserve it in a financially beneficial manner. Although the microcredit component offers an important monetary incentive for the project, this system adds a significant non-monetary value to the program's structure. To understand how this method of conservation addresses a wider problem throughout Mali, it is necessary to first examine the reasons for cultural heritage loss.

Mali's cultural heritage crisis

The hallmark of the *CultureBank*'s institutional design is its use of cultural objects as loan collateral. The impetus for this stems from local concern with the ongoing expropriation of Malian art that is steadily emptying the country of its prized cultural heritage. While Mali has been particularly devastated by cultural heritage loss in recent decades, the international trade in African art is not a recent phenomenon. At the start of the colonial era in the late-nineteenth century, European collectors began to amass large quantities of African sculpture during early explorations and "collecting missions" through colonial territories. As Samuel Sidibé, Director of the National Museum of Mali, has noted: "The plundering of the African past gained legitimacy under the colonial practice of collecting missions" (Sidibé 1996:8). These missions served to furnish ethnographic collections at Western cultural institutions created expressly to house "primitive arts" of non-Western countries. The startling new artistic forms that entered the European art scene from Africa provided fresh inspiration for modern artists, such as Picasso and Braque among others, whose Cubist forms suggest direct links to features of African masks and sculptures (Hughes 1981).

Renowned for its incredible wealth in art and antiquities, Mali has long attracted collectors and pillagers alike to its cultural treasure troves. In reference to the massive flow of Malian art to Western countries during the past 60 years, journalist Michel Brent remarked that, "Not since the wholesale rape of Egypt's archaeological treasures in the first half of the nineteenth century has a country been so methodically stripped of its national heritage" (Brent 1994:26). The Niger River Valley is a rich archaeological site that has been targeted for pillage since archaeologists began to uncover ancient terracotta statues there in 1941 (Sidibé 1993). Dogon art has also held particular allure for Western collectors due to its unique stylistic appeal, rich cosmological symbolism, and ritual significance that has been well-studied by anthropologists and art historians (Ezra 1988; Griaule 1963; Imperato 1978; Laude 1973; Leloup 1994; Van Beek 1988, 2001).

The expansion of the tourist industry in Mali in recent decades and the rising value of African art in the international market are key factors driving cultural heritage loss throughout the country. In a nation beset by severe economic constraints, Malians often resort to selling pillaged artifacts and family heirlooms to antique dealers, art collectors, and tourists as a strategy of income generation and subsistence in an environment confronted by the adverse effects of desertification, climate change, frequent drought, and food insecurity.[4] African antique dealers often hire young Malian men to scour sites for antiques that they resell in urban centers such as Mopti and Bamako or overseas through a dense network of art traffickers that operate between West Africa, Europe, and North America (cf. Steiner 1994). From these vendors, the pieces move into private homes and collections, museums, and galleries across the globe.

The ramifications of the international trade in African material culture have been especially grave for the Dogon of Mali. Dogon art, a veritable "must have" for any serious African art collector, is especially desirable in this illicit trade due to the exorbitant prices it fetches in the international market.[5] Many Dogon villages have been almost entirely stripped of important cultural and historical items such as wooden statues, masks, and carved granary doors due to voracious Western demands for Dogon art. Dogon villages situated along the Bandiagara Escarpment in northern Mali are especially popular destinations for Western tourists. The growth of a tourist economy and the influx of foreign consumers have swayed many Dogon people to sell cultural objects in exchange for hard currency.[6]

The cultural heritage crisis in Mali has been the focus of several international, national, and binational measures, beginning with the *UNESCO Convention on the Means of Prohibiting and Preventing the Illicit Import, Export, and Transfer of Ownership of Cultural Property* (1970). This convention established "a framework for international cooperation to reduce the incentive of pillage by restricting the illicit movement of archaeological and ethnographic material across international boundaries" (Kouroupas 1995:32). An important element of this convention is the idea of cultural heritage as a "human right" that must be protected alongside other political rights. With the exception of five countries (United States of America, Canada, Australia, Argentina, and Italy) however, the majority of Western nations that import African art are not signatories to the UNESCO Convention (Brent 1994).

Under the Konaré administration, the Malian government passed important national legislation in 1985 and 1986 banning the exportation of antiquities. In 1993, Konaré, an archaeologist by training, also initiated a binational accord between the US Department of State and the Malian government that imposed a ban on American importation of a wide class of Malian antiquities from the Niger delta and Bandiagara region in particular. The ban requires US customs officials "to seize prohibited objects at the border and permits their recovery if they have illegally entered the country" (Shapiro 1995:42). However, these attempts to curtail rampant art trafficking have met with limited success. Although legislation has focused domestic and international attention on the current situation in Mali, it has not proven an efficacious deterrent to African exporters and their Western clients due to the lack of viable enforcement measures. Informal market networks have undermined any attempts to halt this lucrative enterprise; national treasures continue to move through these channels, continually depriving Mali of its cultural patrimony.

The Dogon of Mali

Historical and archaeological evidence as well as Dogon oral tradition suggest that the Dogon moved from the Mande area of the Mali Empire (present-day southwestern Mali and northeastern Guinea) to the rocky, remote Bandiagara Escarpment in the fifteenth century to escape widespread Islamization in the region, slave raids, and invasions from neighboring ethnic groups such as the Mossi, Songhay and Fulani (Leloup 1994). Displacing the earlier Tellem civilization that inhabited the cliffs from the eleventh to the fifteenth century, the Dogon established villages of 500 to 1,000 people along the cliffs (some up to 2,000 feet high) that stretch 125 miles from northeast to southwest parallel to the Niger River in northern Mali. The availability of water at the plateau rim and in the Séno plain favored Dogon settlement in the area by enabling the continuation of agriculture. The current Dogon population of the Bandiagara cliff numbers close to 300,000 (ibid.). About 700 villages remain in the cliff region today, most with fewer than 500 inhabitants (Ezra 1988).

A compelling reason why the Dogon have garnered so much attention from the outside world is that they have created some of the most remarkable forms of art found in West Africa. For the Dogon, as for many African peoples, art is not conceived as a separate realm of activity; it imbues all aspects of life. In fact, there is no word in the Dogon language that corresponds with the Western notion of "art." Dogon art serves functional as well as ritual purposes. In Dogon architectural forms such as men's meeting houses (*togu na*) and granary doors, incorporate cosmological symbols into the design. Doors, for instance, often feature breasts (a fertility symbol), animals, and mythological ancestor figures. The doors serve to keep children, thieves, and wandering animals out of the grain supply and are believed to offer supernatural protection.

The highly visible presence of art and ritual in Dogon society has long attracted Westerners to the area beginning with the seminal work of French anthropologist Marcel Griaule and his research team from *l'Institut d'Ethnologie* at the University of Paris who worked intermittently in the region from 1931–1956 and published widely on the Dogon. Since the 1980s in particular, "Dogon country" has hosted increasingly large numbers of foreign tourists who contribute to the degradation and disappearance of Dogon cultural heritage. The eagerness with which villagers sell items such as statues, masks, doors, and *togu na* pillars to tourists and antique dealers relentlessly combing the area for new merchandise is a stark index of the economic impoverishment of the Dogon region and the desperate need for sources of cash income.

The Dogon economy is based on subsistence agriculture (principally millet, sorghum, and fonio), animal husbandry, small commerce, and tourist revenues. Farming is a difficult undertaking due to the lack of permanent water sources on the cliffs, minimal amount of rainfall (between 20 to 28 inches per year), and poor soil quality on the sandy plain. Within the constraints of this economic system, Dogon communities have utilized certain customary credit arrangements to cope with recurring insufficiencies of both food and money. Some strategies cited by Fombori residents included repaying informal debt with in-kind field labor, loans in the form of grain or domestic animals, rotating credit associations (*tontines*), and loans from local merchants or family members engaged in labor migration. Customary credit arrangements are generally used to meet basic subsistence needs and not to expand or create small enterprise. Until the opening of the *CultureBank* and another local microcredit program sponsored by a Canadian NGO (USC Canada) in 1997, Fombori residents had virtually no access to formal credit. The advent of a formalized credit system in the village has enabled villagers to borrow money for the purposes of commerce expansion.

A local response to cultural heritage loss: the Dogon *CultureBank* of Fombori

Nestled at the base of the northeastern Bandiagara cliffs, Fombori is a small village in the greater Mopti region. The current population of approximately 1,080 people is distributed among 42 extended family households. All inhabitants are of Dogon ethnicity and speak the Jam-Si dialect of Dogon language. According to oral history, the first Dogon settlement in Fombori occurred in 1438. The principal livelihoods are small-scale subsistence agriculture and animal husbandry. Most residents also engage in small commerce activities at a nearby weekly market that typically include grain sales for women and livestock sales for men. Other occupations include vegetable gardening, cotton spinning, and specialty skills such as carpentry, masonry, blacksmithing, and pottery.

Over time the majority of Fombori's inhabitants have ceased practicing Dogon religious traditions in favor of Islam, which is now the dominant religion. Due to this shift, objects associated with Dogon rituals and ceremonies are not as highly valued as they were in the past. The burgeoning market for material culture has prompted many people to sell family heirlooms in recent years to supplement their meager cash earnings. In seeking to address the growing loss of the community's material cultural heritage, the Fombori community conceived of a novel response in establishing a *CultureBank* that utilizes culture as a resource for development.

The importance of material and non-material culture to development has long been underestimated. Rather than alleviating poverty, the ongoing loss of material culture in Africa has been a source of further impoverishment as it diminishes cultural resources over the long term. The role of material culture is especially important in many African societies that rely primarily on oral traditions rather than written history for their cultural memory. In both oral and written cultures, cultural objects embody histories and knowledge passed on through generations. When combined with myriad catalysts of environmental and social change in Mali, including climate fluctuations and desertification, urban migration, and the increasing dominance of Islam over indigenous African religions, the phenomenon of material culture loss has led to further dissipation of Malian cultural memory and epistemological frameworks that are indispensable for the social well-being and coherent development of African societies. The impetus to establish the *CultureBank* originated with the Women's Association of Fombori. The association opened an artisan center in 1992 that offered lodging for visitors and provided a limited means by which women could earn income. From this original idea evolved the concept of creating a small museum in Fombori in which community members could conserve and display Dogon material culture and generate income from visitors. Through donor assistance and a community contribution of labor and building materials, the Dogon

Museum of Fombori was constructed in 1995, although most villagers were reluctant to lend their objects to the museum, and the collection remained small. The tourist orientation of the museum was not effective since Fombori is not situated on a main tourist route and revenues from admission fees were minimal at best.

In 1997 the community of Fombori devised a plan to make the museum financially viable and to stimulate community interest in the project. Community members opted to combine the museum's central goal of cultural conservation with a microcredit initiative aimed at increasing villagers' access to credit for income-generating activities. The term "*CultureBank*" was coined to convey the new mission and activities of the institution (Crosby 1998). Formally inaugurated in 1997, the institution began providing loans with a small initial fund (approximately US$400) granted by USAID Mali and USC Canada and additional funds contributed later by the West African Museums Project based in Dakar, Senegal. Since 1999, the *CultureBank* has operated as a financially sustainable institution by generating funds exclusively from loan interest and revenues from tourism without outside donor assistance. A board of directors consisting of 11 volunteer members from Fombori meets on a monthly basis to oversee all management activities. The *CultureBank*'s part-time staff consists of a coordinator who manages the collection and leads tours, a loan manager, and a security guard.

The *CultureBank* program design: harnessing cultural collateral

The *CultureBank*'s program design reflects its dual goals of providing access to capital and conserving local cultural heritage. In exchange for each object placed in the museum, participants gain eligibility for a small business loan over a four to six month period at 3 percent interest per month. The amount of the loan is determined by the verifiable historical value of the piece that is assessed by the loan manager according to a questionnaire formula. Upon timely repayment, borrowers may opt to renew their loan for an equal or greater amount, thereby gaining access to a steady stream of additional income. This system enables participants to access increasingly large business loans over time in contrast with the finite, short-term profits gained by selling objects. Individuals retain ownership of their objects throughout the process. In the case of loan default, objects remain in the museum's permanent collection but cannot be sold or exchanged at any time.

From 1997 to 2002, the bank made 451 total loans (average size of US$22) with objects as collateral to 70 borrowers (60 percent women) at 3 percent interest per month. The rate of reimbursement has averaged 94 percent over the life of the project, and women consistently reimburse at a higher rate than men (97 percent compared to 90 percent). The average overdue loan is roughly double the size of the average loan in general, which suggests that loans of higher value are less likely to be repaid on time. The bank is currently operating on a total budget of approximately US$5,000. In total, the *CultureBank* has provided US$14,279 worth of loan funds to the community since 1997.

Beginning in 2000, the bank also provided loans without requiring objects as collateral as an experiment. Fifty-five "non-collaterized" loans worth a total of US$4,217 were made to 26 individual borrowers (77 percent male and 23 percent female) for a period of eight months at 3 percent interest per month. The majority of these borrowers were local merchants who obtained loan approval as a result of their local business reputations. The average loan size was US$77 and the reimbursement rate averaged 85 percent. This lower rate can be attributed to the higher loan values and the absence of collateral. The large overdue amount has decreased the total capital available for new loans and created a serious problem for the bank.[7] For the purposes of this study, borrowers with non-collateralized loans were not included in the sample.

In addition to providing microcredit, the *CultureBank* has amassed an impressive museum collection and has sponsored various community activities including Jam-Si literacy classes, artisan and conservation workshops, historical research and documentation, theater performances, and community festivals. These activities have had numerous positive economic, social, and cultural impacts on the community of Fombori and the surrounding area and have established a vital presence for the institution as a center for information exchange and skill development.

A modest building situated at the foot of the cliff and surrounded by a spacious courtyard, the Dogon Museum of Fombori (or "House of Dogon Heritage" as it is called in Jam-Si) houses a diverse collection of 440 objects from 13 surrounding villages. Pieces are displayed in three main galleries organized around common themes: (1) objects of general historical significance that reflect information on the culture and history of the Dogon and Tellem peoples (including archaeological artifacts and ritual statues); (2) objects related to women's roles in Dogon culture (e.g. pots, calabashes, household objects, jewelry, cloth, and decorative items), and (3) objects related to men's roles (e.g. weaponry, musical instruments, horse equipment, and masks). Certain objects in the collection belong to several individuals in the community and have been used to obtain collective group loans. For example, members of the women's association who obtained a collective loan using a fertility statue as collateral take turns using the full amount of credit from their loan in much the same way that traditional *tontines*, or rotating credit associations, operate. Collectively-owned objects are eligible for loans of greater value.

Participants in the sample population lent an average of two objects per person to the museum. Most people leave their objects in the museum after reimbursing loans for safekeeping even if they do not opt to renew their loan. The collection operates as a "living museum" in that people are welcome and encouraged to temporarily remove their objects for personal or ceremonial use. For instance, during a summer festival, community members borrowed various drums and musical instruments from the collection and returned them after use. In this way, the pieces do not become static entities in the museum but retain their currency in the cultural life of the community.

Over 2,000 people have visited the *CultureBank* museum since its opening in 1997, including several delegations from other regions of Mali interested in establishing similar institutions. Visitors provide additional income for the *CultureBank* by paying a nominal admission fee of US$1.50, which includes a guided tour of the museum collection and nearby Tellem cliff dwellings. Another important source of tourist income derives from the sale of items in a boutique where visitors can purchase locally-produced artisan goods at fixed prices. These items are sold on a consignment basis, and the bank charges a 10 percent commission that is used to fund community activities. None of the antique pieces can be purchased from the collection under any circumstances.

A unique variation on the microcredit model, the *CultureBank* successfully utilizes cultural objects as a new form of loan collateral. This example indicates that experimentation with alternative ways of collateralizing

Table 6.1 Type of objects in *CultureBank* collection

Type of object	Number	Percent of collection
Jewelry	195	44
Gourds	57	13
Household objects	40	9
Horse equipment	32	7
Cloth	22	5
Wooden statues	22	5
Weaponry	16	4
Ritual objects	14	3
Togu na pillars[a]	10	2
Musical instruments	9	2
Archaeological Artifacts	7	2
Pottery	7	2
Masks	5	1
Games	3	1
Weaving loom	1	0.5
Total	440	100

a A *togu na* is a traditional meeting house for men. It is a common feature in Dogon villages and usually consists of an open-air hangar supported by eight or more pillars made of stone or wood. The pillars often bear carved figures and symbols.

loans can lead to innovation in the local manifestations of formal credit arrangements. In examining the *CultureBank*'s use of material culture in microlending, an important question arises: what is the *value* of cultural heritage? In both symbolic and purely economic terms, this question is problematic. Ascribing market value to African art objects is a highly variable process that fluctuates considerably depending on the time and place of the sale. Some crucial factors that contribute to determinations of value are esthetic preference, availability or scarcity, provenance and authenticity (Stanley 1987). African art also rises in value as objects change hands several times in the successive transactions that move art from African sources to Western art dealers (Steiner 1995).

Beyond economic value, however, one must consider both the social aspects of material culture and the ways in which cultural values are constructed through the manipulation of goods in the material world (cf. Appadurai 1986; Douglas and Isherwood 1979; Kopytoff 1986). In the case of African art, the social life of objects undergoes a profound shift as they move from their original context in which they serve utilitarian and ritual functions in the community into markets as commodities that come to embody a new set of social relations, "in which the group identities of producers are tokens for the status politics of consumers" (Appadurai 1986:47).

In the *CultureBank* model, the market value of objects is not taken into consideration and thus loses relevance since the institutional objective is to prevent these goods from venturing into the market. In Greenberg's (forthcoming) definition of collateral, it must be at once valuable, durable, and transferable. He notes, "Collateral is only valuable if it is of interest to the lender. It is only worth what he says it is worth ... [which] may be a small fraction of its value to the borrower" (p. 5). The *CultureBank* departs from this definition because the objects accepted as loan guarantees are valuable due to their interest to the entire community as part of a collective conception of Dogon cultural heritage. There are no restrictions placed on the type of objects that can be used to obtain loans. Most of the items are older family heirlooms, but there are also newer pieces, such as sculptures created by a local artist. The presence of these objects is also revealing in that community members are not merely trying to save precious antiques (that would have a higher market value) but also recognize the value in conserving artwork of the present generation.

Advancing a different perspective on collateral, McNaughton, an art historian, insists on the need to recognize the cultural collateral of art:

> Artworks possess a special collateral that comes from the grandeur of cultural expression, so what is lost to Mali and Malians [when art is exported from the country] is a cultural resource worth at least as much money, because cultural resources are building blocks for many

of the finest ideas in a society. Artworks are among the world's most evocative and affecting objects. That power is nourished and amplified when it acts in networks of indigenous cause and effect. Thus, many consider it most lamentable when large numbers of a nation's antiquities are bought into foreign networks of commoditization that emphasize only material beauty, rarity, and age.

(McNaughton 1995:25–6)

Once in market circulation, art objects cease to enrich the life of communities from which they part irretrievably. Exchange networks diminish the inherent cultural value of goods that are transformed into vehicles for economic profit. By safeguarding cultural objects in a local museum, *CultureBank* participants are able to harness the cultural collateral of their heirlooms and maintain it for posterity. The museum thus becomes a site of cultural reproduction in which younger generations gain exposure to the histories, social memory, and material existence of past generations. The objects collected comprise more than an esthetic display; they reveal the stories of Dogon cultural identity and the ways in which Dogon people have marked this identity over time through their styles of dress, tool production, musical expression, and spiritual devotion, among others. By choosing to represent their heritage in a museum environment, Fombori residents are reproducing their culture in a way that allows them to remain in control of how the story is told. This public representation serves first their own need to conserve Dogon identity in face of rapid change and second educates outside visitors who come in search of an "authentic" experience of rural Dogon life.

Socioeconomic impacts

The sample population for this study consisted of 30 participants from Fombori, stratified by gender according to the total borrower population (60 percent women and 40 percent men). The age range is 22 to 80 with a mean age of 50. Respondents all share several characteristics: married status (with an average of 6.3 children), Muslim faith, Dogon ethnicity, and Jam-Si as their first language. The level of schooling ranges from zero to five years with an overall average of less than one year of formal education. The principal occupation is agriculture (mainly millet and sorghum), followed by commerce (90 percent) and animal husbandry (40 percent). The mean amount of annual household expenses is US$168. Respondents borrowed an average total amount of US$196 from the *CultureBank* from 1997 to 2002.

Of the 30 participants in the survey, all reported using loan funds to increase pre-existing small commerce activities or to initiate new ones at the weekly market in the town of Douentza. For women the most common

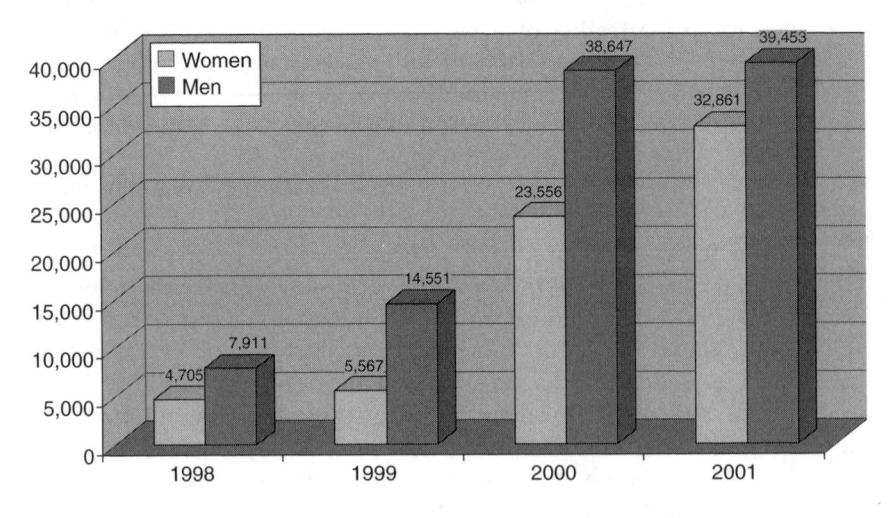

Figure 6.1 Average annual loan amount for sample population disaggregated by gender (in FCFA).

activity is buying and reselling millet grain and other food products while men engage primarily in the livestock trade. Most (97 percent) had never received formal loan assistance before the *CultureBank*.

Some important trends emerged from quantitative data analysis. The average annual amount of loans obtained from the *CultureBank* with objects as collateral has consistently increased from 1997 to 2002, with the largest increase of 165 percent occurring between 2000 and 2001. While women represent the majority of borrowers (60 percent) and reimburse loans at a higher rate than men (97 percent compared to 90 percent), they have less total loan funds at their disposal than men. Women's average annual income from commerce activities is also 67 percent lower than men's after loan assistance. These factors indicate that benefits from *CultureBank* loan assistance are not equitable for men and women despite the institution's commitment to provide a majority of loans to female clients.

Despite this gender gap in lending practices, the *CultureBank* has supported the expansion of women's local enterprises. The President of the Women's Association of Fombori commented on the benefits of the project for women, who comprise the majority of beneficiaries:

> Before the *CultureBank*, it was very hard for women to get loans for their commerce. Now we are able to use the objects we have inherited from our mothers and grandmothers to obtain loans. This is very important for us because not only are we protecting our inheritance,

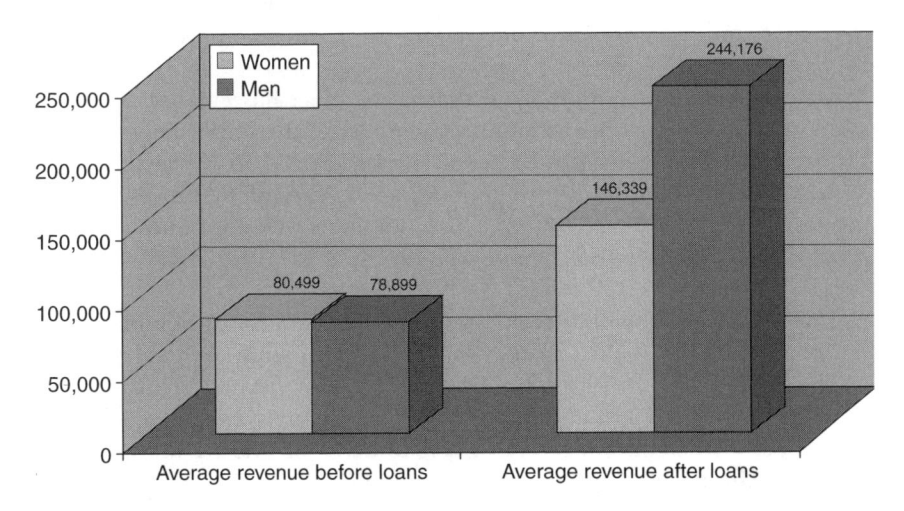

Figure 6.2 Average annual revenue from income-generating activities before and after loans (in FCFA).

but we are able to sell more items in the weekly market and earn extra income to support our families. I think the project has really helped village women in particular.

CultureBank loans have thus increased the economic autonomy of village women by providing them valuable access to microcredit to expand and initiate local commerce. However, economic benefits for women could be improved by increasing the loan amounts to match amounts received by men. This would decrease the current disparity that exists between male and female borrowers.

Results of statistical analysis demonstrate that participants have significantly increased their annual profits from income-generating activities after *CultureBank* loan assistance. Second, the total amount of loan funds borrowed correlates strongly with participants' annual average revenue from small commerce.[8] These findings affirm that the *CultureBank* has provided positive economic benefits to the target population by creating access to microcredit for income-generating activities and increasing their profitability.

Beyond economic benefits, the *CultureBank*'s main social and cultural impacts include fostering awareness of Dogon history and cultural heritage, promoting the conservation of cultural resources in the community, and increasing social capital among participants. All respondents reported that the *CultureBank* has benefited the community. The most frequent responses highlighted the retention of cultural objects in the local community (50 percent), the provision of microcredit loans (47 percent), and conservation of Dogon heritage (40 percent) as the primary benefits.

Many respondents emphasized that the project has created a greater awareness on the part of community members of the importance of local history and cultural heritage. Several cited the need to conserve Dogon heritage for present and future generations, as exemplified in the following quote by a 60-year-old sculptor from Fombori who continues to sculpt ritual statues that he recalls from his youth:

> We must keep the objects that we have inherited for our children and grandchildren. That way they will be able to study our culture and learn how our ancestors lived before us. Our heritage is something that we must respect and guard well. Today people are engaged in the religion of Islam, but it's not good to abandon the traditions of the past. The future happiness of our people will be determined by the strength of our connection to the past.

By establishing a community museum where people can view cultural objects and learn about the history, significance, and utility of the objects, the *CultureBank* has sparked interest in local history and intergenerational dialogue as village elders share their knowledge with younger members of the community who will be responsible for passing on the stories in the future. Many elders commented that members of the younger generation have less appreciation for history and that they are often the ones who sell Dogon objects to antique dealers to make money. Therefore, they saw the *CultureBank* as a positive step in teaching young people more about their history and encouraging them to value their cultural heritage. As an elder Islamic leader commented, "The *CultureBank* is a good way for visitors and especially children in the village to learn about Dogon culture."

Second, through efforts to educate the community about the importance of conserving archaeological sites and cultural objects, the *CultureBank* staff has promoted the goals of cultural conservation and discouraged the sale of material culture and artifacts. By making cultural heritage a visible and celebrated part of community life, the Dogon *CultureBank* of Fombori has reinforced its value as a local resource. Community members have identified the need to protect their objects along with the cultural information and social memory they contain.

A third critical outcome of the project is an increase in social capital among participants. A key concept in the dominant microlending model is the utilization of the social capital generated by groups of borrowers to ensure the program's success. Social capital refers to relationships and networks developed among groups of people that comprise a vital part of livelihood strategies in both urban and rural settings. In the microfinance sector, "the formation of social capital ... is affected by enlarging the political or economic resources of the informal groups of poor households and microfinance institutions that contribute to social cohesion" (Quinones and Seibel 2001:195).

Results of qualitative analysis support the argument that social capital has expanded in Fombori due to the increased contact among community members through *CultureBank* activities. Due to the geographic isolation of Dogon villages, it is common that residents of villages in close proximity may rarely see one another. The *CultureBank* has attracted people from surrounding villages and helped establish new social networks. Through joint income-generating activities, participants have collaborated to expand business enterprises and to initiate new ones. Literacy classes, workshops, and other community-wide activities, have also allowed community members to benefit from frequent contact with residents of Fombori and its environs.

CultureBank lessons for microcredit and cultural conservation

Clifford (1988) states that, "The relations of power whereby one portion of humanity can select, value, and collect the pure products of others need to be criticized and transformed" (p. 176). Relations of power between Western art collectors and African producers, owners, and dealers of art have favored the large-scale transfer of African cultural heritage to the West from the colonial era to the present day, as seen in the example of Mali. The ritual significance of Dogon pieces, their unique esthetic appeal, and monetary value on the international market continue to fuel Western passions for acquiring these prized works of art and resituating them in museums, galleries, and private collections. Even with the passage of Malian laws banning the export of antiquities and the binational accord between the US and Mali, the loss of cultural heritage in Mali continues daily and remains a grave problem facing the nation in the twenty-first century.

In this context, the *CultureBank* of Fombori provides a pertinent case study of a local response to widespread cultural heritage loss rooted in a long historical tradition and exacerbated by the dire economic situation in which rural Malians find themselves today. In integrating the goals of microcredit and cultural conservation, the *CultureBank* extends our understanding of the possibilities for both microfinance institutions and community museums in the West African context. By extending loans to participants who place cultural objects in the *CultureBank* as collateral, the bank has turned a community's cultural heritage into a vital economic resource. Rather than selling irreplaceable antiques to antique dealers or tourists, participants have the option of using their valuable heirlooms to gain much-needed access to credit. This economic incentive has promoted cultural conservation in the community, and participants have used credit to significantly increase profits from small commerce activities in the local marketplace.

As this case demonstrates, the *CultureBank*'s success is not based solely on financial indicators such as loan repayment but also derives from the satisfaction of participants and community members in general who have benefited from the retention of their collective cultural resources in Fombori and from outreach programs that enrich the life of the community. During the course of this study, the enthusiasm of Fombori community members regarding the *CultureBank* underscored the positive impacts observed. This widespread local endorsement speaks to the perceived value of the institution by the population it aims to serve.

An important observation uncovered by this study, however, is that male borrowers have consistently benefited from higher average loans and higher average profits from loan investment than female borrowers who receive the majority of loans. This discrepancy points to the need to develop both more equitable lending practices and additional training for women to maximize their earning potential.

Finally, the *CultureBank* offers a useful model for the future of African museums. Former Malian President Konaré highlights the need to conceptualize new ways of supporting museums and institutions dedicated to the conservation of African culture:

> In effect, how can one imagine that in the coming years – which will no doubt see the economic conditions in our African countries even further deteriorated – can we conform to models [of museums] which are impossible to assume independently at the financial level? How is it possible, therefore, not to conceive of a new economy for the African museum, which is in keeping with the resources of its population?
>
> (Konaré 1992:ii)

In keeping with the local resources in Fombori, the *CultureBank* has in fact devised a new economy for the African museum better adapted to the realities of African settings. Although outside donor assistance was necessary to fund the museum's construction and initial microcredit activities, the institution has been locally managed since its inception and has maintained its financial sustainability over the past five years by assuming all operation costs with the income gained from loan interest.

In the words of Konaré, "It seems time now ... to eliminate the Western model for museums in Africa so that new methods for the preservation and promotion of Africa's cultural heritage can be allowed to flourish" (Konaré 1991:377). In conclusion, perhaps the most inspiring aspect of Fombori's *CultureBank* is the community's proactive response to material culture loss that has provided a viable blueprint for future endeavors in Mali and elsewhere that aim to keep cultural heritage in the hands of its rightful owners.

Notes

1. The African Cultural Conservation Fund (ACCF), an NGO based in Bamako, Mali, is currently working with two communities in the Bambara region of central Mali to establish *CultureBanks* based on Fombori's example with funding from the World Bank. ACCF is also working closely with the Fombori staff to improve the quality of services provided by the institution and to expand its microfinance activities to include a savings program. The phrase "banking on culture" is used by ACCF website as a thematic title for its *CultureBank* projects.
2. Through the support of the West African Research Association and the University of Arizona, School of Behavioral Sciences Research Institute, data for this study were collected in 2002 through interviews with *CultureBank* staff and a random sample of 30 participants stratified by gender.
3. Group guarantees operate in various ways: (1) by creating a fund to which all members contribute that can be accessed if one or more members fails to repay; (2) by prohibiting other group members from accessing new loans if all members are not current in their payments; or (3) by requiring group members to assume direct liability if other members default (Ledgerwood 1995).
4. According to the United Nations Human Development Index in 2004, Mali ranks 174rd out of 177 nations worldwide. Statistics are based on life expectancy, GDP per capita and literacy rates (www.hdr.undp.org). As of 2003, gross national income (GNI) was US$290 per capita in Mali (www.worldbank.org).
5. For example, a website from the Barakat Gallery in Los Angeles listed a 42.5 inch Dogon "ancestral fertility sculpture" from the nineteenth to twentieth centuries for $30,000 in 2003 (www.barakatgallery.com).
6. Mali receives about 80,000 tourists annually from Europe, North America, and Asia and tourism is rising by 4 percent a year according to Mamahadou Keita of the Office of Tourism in Mali. The main attraction for approximately 90 percent of foreign tourists in 2000 was the Bandiagara Escarpment (http://news.bbc.co.uk/1/hi/world/africa/1280076.stm).
7. Based on the results of this research, the *CultureBank* formally terminated the practice of extending uncollateralized loans as of September 2002.
8. For both statistical tests, p = 0.0005. A paired t-test was used in the first analysis.

References

Appadurai, Arjun, (1986) "Introduction: commodities and the politics of value" in Arjun Appadurai (ed.), *The Social Life of Things: Commodities in Cultural Perspective*, New York: Cambridge University Press.

Brent, Michel, (1994) "The Rape of Mali" *Archaeology* 47(3):26–34.

Buckley, Graeme, (1997) "Microfinance in Africa: Is it Either the Problem or the Solution?" *World Development* 25(7):1081–93.

Clifford, James, (1998) "Histories of the Tribal and the Modern" in James Clifford (ed.), *The Predicament of Culture: Twentieth Century Ethnography, Literature, and Art*, Cambridge, MA: Harvard University Press, pp. 189–214.

Crosby, Todd V. (1998) "The CultureBank Manual" US Peace Corps, Bamako, Mali (unpublished).
Douglas, Mary and Baron Isherwood, (1979) *The World of Goods: Towards an Anthropology of Consumption*, New York: W. W. Norton and Co.
Ezra, Kate, (1988) *The Art of the Dogon: Selections from the Lester Wunderman Collection*, New York: The Metropolitan Museum of Art.
Greenberg, James B. (forthcoming) Notes Toward an Anthropological Understanding of Credit Arrangements.
Griaule, Marcel, (1963) *Masques dogon*, Paris: Institut d'Ethnologie.
Hughes, Robert, (1981) *The Shock of the New*, New York: Alfred A. Knopf.
Imperato, Pascal James, (1978) *Dogon Cliff Dwellers: The Art of Mali's Mountain People*, New York: L. Kahan Gallery/African Arts.
Johnson, Susan and Ben Rogaly, (1997) *Microfinance and Poverty Reduction*, London: Oxfam.
Khandker, Shaidur R. (1998) *Fighting Poverty with Microcredit*, New York: Oxford University Press.
Konaré, Alpha Oumar, (1992) Preface and speech in "What Museums for Africa?: Heritage in the Future" (Conference Proceedings from 18–23 November 1991). International Council of Museums, Dijon-Quetigny: Darantiere, pp. i–ii, 377–9.
Kopytoff, Igor, (1986) "The Cultural Biography of Things: Commoditization as a Process" in Arjun Appadurai (ed.), *The Social Life of Things: Commodities in Cultural Perspective*, New York: Cambridge University Press.
Kouroupas, Maria Papageorge, (1995) "U.S. Efforts to Protect Cultural Property: Implementation of the 1970 UNESCO Convention" *African Arts* 28(2):32–7.
Laude, Jean, (1973) *African Art of the Dogon; the Myths of the Cliff Dwellers*, New York: Brooklyn Museum in association with the Viking Press.
Ledgerwood, Joanna, (1995) *Microfinance Handbook: An Institutional and Financial Perspective*, Washington DC: World Bank.
Leloup, Hélène, (1994) Dogon statuary, Strasbourg, France: D. Amez.
McNaughton, Patrick R. (1995) "Malian Antiquities and Contemporary Desire" *African Arts* 28(2):23–7.
Mosley, Paul and David Hulme, (1998) "Microenterprise Finance: Is There a Conflict Between Growth and Poverty Alleviation?" *World Development* 26(5):783–90.
Quinones, B. R. and Seibel, H. D. (2001) "Mainstreaming Informal Financial Institutions" *Journal of Developmental Entrepreneurship* 6(1):83–95.
Rahman, Aminur, (1999) "Microcredit Initiatives for Equitable and Sustainable Development: Who Pays?" *World Development* 28:617–29.
Shapiro, Daniel, (1995) "The Ban on Mali's Antiquities: A Matter of Law" *African Arts* 28(2):42–6.
Sidibé, Samuel, (1995) "Pillage of Archaeological Sites in Mali" *African Arts* 28(2):52–9.
—— (1996) "The Fight Against the Plundering of Malian Cultural Heritage and Illicit Exportation: National Efforts and International Cooperation" in Peter R. Schmidt and Roderick J. McIntosh (eds), *Plundering Africa's Past*, Bloomington: Indiana University Press, pp. 77–93.
Stanley, J. L. (1987) "The African Art Market: An Essay and Bibliography" *Africana Journal* 14(2/3):157–70.
Steiner, Christopher, (1994) *African Art in Transit*, New York: Cambridge University Press.

Van Beek, Walter E. A. (1988) "The Functions of Sculpture in Dogon Religion" *African Arts* 21(4):58–65, 91.
—— (2001) *Dogon: Africa's People of the Cliffs*, New York: Harry Abrams, Inc.
Webster, Leila and Peter Fidler, (1996) *The Informal Sector and Microfinance Institutions in West Africa*, Washington DC: World Bank.

7 The darker side to microfinance[1]
Evidence from Cajamarca, Peru

Katie Wright

Introduction

The literature on group dynamics suggests that an awareness of the tensions which exist in groups is all too often overlooked in the literature on microfinance (Marr, 2002). It is argued that microcredit programmes are open to abuse by group leaders, particularly the president and treasurer, and that there are often great differences in terms of experience and power between these agents and the rest of the members. This problem is compounded by the fact that NGOs, due to time constraints, are seldom in touch with the rank-and-file, and only have contact with the leaders. For example, Mercado has noted this trend in relation to women's groups in Mexico:

> It is worrying that preparation is limited to very few women, leaving the development of the rest of the group very problematic. Across Mexico and Central America, many NGO and government initiatives promote the setting up of women's groups and fund the training merely of the president, secretary and treasurer for each. Often these posts have gone to women who already have considerable 'power-over' ... encouraging them to misuse both power and funds ... the women may use their knowledge to personal ends rather than share it.
> (1999:119)

This point is also made by Riger who asks:

> Since when does the empowerment of vulnerable groups and persons simultaneously generate a sense of community and strengthen the bonds that hold society together? Does it perhaps promote certain individuals or groups at the expense of others, intensifying competitiveness and lack of cohesion?
> (Riger quoted in Townsend *et al.*, 1999:119)

The main objective of this research is to study the impact of microfinance on low-income groups of women in Cajamarca, Peru.[2] The theoretical literature on reasons why microfinance can fail to alleviate poverty is becoming well established (Wood and Sharif, 1997; Hulme and Mosley, 1996). However, much of the failure has been placed on issues relating to programme design such as credit disbursal and delivery. This focus is also predominant in the literature on group dynamics such as in Montgomery's study (1995) on the social costs of peer pressure in solidarity groups in Bangladesh. By contrast, the wider social and cultural issues affecting microfinance outcomes have received much less attention. The literature in Latin America on group dynamics is very sparse and emerging studies such as Marr (2002) have tended to take a broadly economistic rather than anthropological form of enquiry. In order to fill this gap in the literature, the study presented here draws on the theories of cultural anthropology (such as the work of Rosen, 1941) whereby the emphasis is placed on privileging the ideas participants themselves use to describe and determine their actions (and to document this in thick ethnographic detail) and to situate this in the wider social and cultural contexts in which individuals operate and are associated to others.

A period of 18 months was spent conducting fieldwork in Peru (April 1998 to September 2000). Informants were recruited using locally respected gatekeepers. Semi-structured interviews were conducted with different kinds of household (female-headed, married, separated, widowed etc) at different stages of the life cycle. Questions were piloted and rephrased and much attention was placed on framing questions in such a way as to minimise response bias (Wright, 2003). The majority of interviews were conducted in women's homes, allowing for the observation of relationships and interactions between family members.

In total, 119 interviews were conducted with women in the region of Cajamarca in the areas of Porcón, La Encañada, Bambamarca, Yanamango and central Cajamarca where the following information was sought: (i) Personal details – age, marital status, education, dependants, how long resident in their area, migratory history; (ii) background of the microenterprise – motivation for taking out credit, when the microenterprise was set up, with what funds, present condition, what produced, where sold, source of microcredit; (iii) main changes in the family or microenterprise; (iv) socio-economic profile of the household – income and expenditure, structure of the family, decision making, male and female roles in the household; (v) main problems relating to the political and economic climate; (vi) difficulties arising from the microenterprise activity; and (vii) perceptions, opinions and expectations/aspirations, for the future.

This paper is organised into two parts. Part one briefly contextualises the research. Part two assesses the empirical evidence from Cajamarca. Part two is divided into three sections. Section one focuses on the tensions that exist among members of group-based schemes in the northern highlands of Peru. Section two considers ways of interpreting these findings.

Section three is a detailed case study of embezzlement in one microcredit group 'Comedor La Perlita' and analyses the position of multiple stakeholders. It is argued that entrenched social and cultural structures such as kinship and patron–client relationships in rural communities influence microfinance outcomes.

Social, cultural and economic context

The case studies in part two are taken from several different communities in Cajamarca, which is located in the northern highlands of Peru. The socio-economic organisation which characterises Andean communities is highly complex and received much interest from anthropologists and economists during the 1980s (Degregori, 2000). In terms of economic production, cultivation is organised according to seasonal requirements and available labour supplies (Golte, 1987:61). Production methods have traditionally been based on the '*minga*' system, defined by Deere (in her study of households and class in Cajamarca) as 'collective work parties' (1990:78) whereby members of the community work for the common good. For example, 'each individual contributes their labour to build the house of one member of the village and receive in return food, *chicha* (a corn-based beer) and *coca*. Peasants work in the knowledge that they will benefit later in the same way should they need an act of labour involving collective work' (ibid.:78). Despite this solidarity aspect, Deere argues that with families mutually dependent on each other for services, labour and the production of goods, relations between households are 'unlikely to be unproblematic' (1990:2).

The changing significance of peasant household participation in wage labour from 1940–1980 and class relationships on the Cajamarcan *haciendas* have also been studied by Deere (1990) who cites in particular how entrenched patron–client relationships were fostered through the personalist and paternalistic nature of the hacienda system, whereby peasants tried to curry favour with *hacenderos* (landlords) in return for their protection. Other authors have focused on the closely-knit nature of communities whereby households are interrelated through kin and dense social networks (Degregori and Golte, 1973) which facilitate the economic survival of individual members (Mossbrucker, 1990:109). The basis for all personal relations is that of reciprocity – '*ayni*', which refers to the offering and granting of favours, discussed among others, in the work of Mayer (2002) and Mayer and Zamolloa (1974). Given the importance of kinship links for ensuring economic survival, it has been argued by Altamirano that the concept of poverty in Andean society is associated with a lack of these relationships (1988:27). Thus, the poorest in society is a person who belongs to no family group, has no patron and no helper – an orphan.

In terms of gender relations in Andean settings, anthropologists have written of a distinctly Andean conceptualisation of the complementarity of men and women and the roots of this lie in the pre-Inca period (Silverblatt 1980; Hamilton, 1988). However, this ideal can coexist with different kinds of gender disadvantage. For example, in Cajamarca, though women and men often accompany each other during the sale of a bull, women on their own do not generally sell bulls but rather, smaller animals which are less profitable (Wright, 2001). (This point is echoed by Harris who, in her study of gender relations in northern Potosí (Bolivia), concludes that the ideal of complementarity of the sexes can coexist with high levels of domestic violence to which women are frequently subjected.)

Rural economy and society have been profoundly transformed during recent decades due to major capitalist transformations in the countryside (Gwyne and Kay, 1999). Increasing impoverishment in rural areas is due in part to the failure of agrarian reform and also to the government's failure to support rural areas. This has meant that households are increasingly unable to sustain themselves solely with the agriculture that they produce for subsistence. As a result, as well as participating in the peasant economy, many are forced also to work in the cash economy selling products such as food, clothing and handicrafts in the urban centre of Cajamarca. It is in this context that women trade and access microcredit loans through NGOs.

Empirical evidence from Cajamarca

Clientelist practice within microcredit groups: the case of the clubes de madres *(mothers' clubs) in Porcón*

Microcredit schemes targeted at women in rural areas are generally based on the solidarity group model, whereby women participate in income generation activities in a collective group and are jointly responsible for loan repayment. Due to lack of collateral, women in the poorest rural sectors do not have access to individual loans and most have no alternative but to belong to a group in order to get microcredit.[3] Though this method of borrowing has been lauded as being highly effective (Kogan, 1998), interviews throughout the 12 months of fieldwork revealed that group microcredit schemes in mothers' clubs (*clubes de madres*) are characterised by a high incidence of corruption and self-enrichment by the leaders. For example, in 73 interviews from mothers' clubs in Porcón, 90 per cent of the informants explained that microcredit had been of no benefit to them. Moreover, they had been so exploited by the group leaders that over 70 per cent had withdrawn altogether. Responses included:

> The president kept all the money. Even today, the mothers still have not received a thing. They have now changed the group leaders. They can't work with credit any more because there is no fund left. I withdrew from the group. I would not take out credit again.

> The leaders got all the money. They did not denounce the president. They don't want to cause more hassle. If you criticise, they will attack you, meaning more hassle. They contradict you. When they didn't share anything out, I lost interest. It has not benefited me at all.
>
> There was no money. We were working in vain. The president bought pots and pans, benches and seats for her house with the profits. It became her property. They do not want to denounce her. She has threatened them. That's how far our work got us and we don't want to have anything more to do with it ... we suffered in vain.
>
> Before, I was really glad – I thought that little by little the mothers were taking out loans on their own initiative, but they just work, nothing more. They cheated them by giving only a tiny amount of food and no money. It's better if women and men work on the land.

Thus, persistently in interviews, it was revealed that rather than the dynamic being one of solidarity and group support, the relation in this case is one of exploitation:

> Again and again, washing, dyeing, they demanded we did everything. We had to find and carry firewood to dye the material. Loans are a help but it is a pity that the president takes all the money. She deceived us, and cheated us on food too, she did not give us any money at all. She kept the lot. We did not denounce her because of ignorance about how to go about it. The president shouted at us. She was very angry. She demanded that we work. She demanded everything.
>
> We worked unpaid ... we were just a form of labour ... nothing more.
>
> Nothing. They did not share out anything. With the loan we bought four arrobas of wheat, we sowed the seeds ... for her [the president]. 'On such and such a day you must come and harvest it', they told us. There was quite a lot of wheat. It was seven or eight sacks of it. They did not even give us a grain of it. My husband said: 'Why are you going just so the president can get richer? You would do better to help the children, not her'. The group withdrew and there's no more support for the club these days, not even food donations. They were supposedly setting up a place for the mothers but it's all for her! She's a family member, so they don't denounce her.
>
> The president kept all the money. Even today, the mothers still have not received a thing. They have now changed the group leaders. They can't work with credit any more because there is no fund left. I withdrew from the group. I would not take out credit again.

These different experiences of microcredit are insightful of social and cultural processes at work in rural communities. First, they highlight how relationships are of a highly personalised nature and the overriding need to fulfil kinship obligations is stressed over and above other commitments ('She's a family member so they do not denounce her'). As Rosen suggests: 'kinship is a framework for individual action and a malleable resource to be drawn on' (1984:76). Other kinds of resources may also be drawn on to cajole others into action including 'control over physical or symbolic reserves, manipulation and force of personality' (1984:112). It is argued here that these wider power dynamics which shape social interaction directly affect microfinance outcomes. In this way, individuals may be 'adversely incorporated' into a microfinance group (Wood, 2000). Rural communities like Porcón are a case in point. The president has influence in the community, experience in money management, confidence in dealing with the local authorities and is likely to be numerate and literate. The members, on the other hand, are more likely to be illiterate, innumerate and more passive, a sentiment indicated in the following statement:

> The NGO staff and the treasurer manage the money. There are no profits. Are there profits? Maybe there are. But we don't know if there are. We don't know about those kinds of things. We just go for the glass of milk programme they have. If there are no food donations, the mothers won't attend.

Given the high incidence of corruption and exploitation that appears to surround microcredit schemes in mothers' clubs, it would be logical to assume that the presidents would be denounced by the other members, with members informing the *rondas campesinas*, NGOs or government agencies that supplied them with credit about unscrupulous behaviour.[4] However, over 70 interviews with women on microcredit schemes in Porcón revealed not a single case where the rank-and-file had denounced the president or taken up the issue with the microfinance organisations. The evidence suggests that when funds are embezzled, members of the group prefer to quietly retire from the schemes, without word to anyone: 'It is better just to withdraw quietly, even though discontent.' The question remains: why do they not denounce the president? One reason voiced was that complaining may put at risk other benefits that women gain from attending the club, or jeopardise future benefits. Also, most members on microcredit schemes are related through Andean kinship networks and in these closely-knit communities there is a high reliance upon personal social resources. Fostering good relationships with kin and being loyal to patrons is essential for household survival, with the result that many women do not speak out in order to avoid creating family problems or severing good relationships with an important contact or patron. As Chambers writes, when there are injustices, keeping silent pays dividends in the long term:

Aware of the power of the richer rural and urban people and of their alliances, the household avoids activity that might endanger future employment, tenancy, loans, favours or protection. It knows that in the short term accepting powerlessness pays.

(1983:111)

In the same way, individuals in Porcón may be bound to presidents in a number of ways and on different levels and this appears to influence not only the terms on which they are incorporated into the group but the exercise of their rights within it. Thus we see how microcredit groups do not operate in isolation, but represent households embedded within communities 'where the existence of these deeper structures influence people's motivations, obligations, allegiances and informal rights' (Wood, 2000). Group members are often reluctant to criticise abuses for fear of the reprisals leaders might take and the conflict that such a course of action might cause among neighbouring households: 'The mothers are not capable of informing NGOs because of what the presidents will do to them, so it is very difficult for them to dare, to have the courage to go and inform in CARE's office ... no one does.'

The existence of sanctions as a powerful 'ordering mechanism' (Rosen, 1984:78) for not fulfilling kinship relationships also extends to other kinds of relationships such as those between of friend, political ally, important contact or patron. The relationship between client and president of a loan group in practice may mirror wider kinds of power dynamics which operate in the community at large.

Interpreting findings: no smoke without fire?

The development banks write euphorically of the advantages of the group solidarity model, stressing that group microcredit schemes work on the basis of peer pressure, mutual support and solidarity, as in the following instance:

The use of joint liability groups (solidarity groups) is an important instrument for many microfinance institutions in achieving high repayment rates. Joint liability groups substitute peer pressure for physical collateral and each one of the participants stands to lose both money and future access to credit if the group as a whole cannot meet its obligations.

(IDB, 1997:27)

However, it could be argued that this over-romanticisation of the solidarity aspect ignores other social dynamics at play in *campesino* communities. According to Gitlitz (personal communication, 1999), though peasant societies do work on the basis of solidarity (since families are dependent on other families for house construction and other kinds of labour and exchange), at the same time, individuals will try and take advantage of their neighbours if they see the opportunity. Those in positions of leadership are in the best position to manipulate.

On the other hand, other writers, such as Foster, have argued that peasant societies are characterised by criticism, gossip, envy and distrust in personal relations due to a view of the world which sees not only economic good but other kinds of good as severely limited (Foster, 1973:36). In simple terms, Foster's theory is based on the notion that in contrast to Western societies, peasant societies do not have a capitalist view of an ever-expanding economy with jobs for all, but rather, the system's resources are finite and unexpandable, thus one person's gain with respect to any good must be another's loss – i.e. I lose out if you do well (1973:36). For this reason, it is frowned upon in peasant societies for an individual to be seen to improve his or her economic situation independently of the rest. He argues that in some cases, mutual suspicion and distrust can generate conflict and make it difficult for people to cooperate together for the common good (Foster, 1973:34).[5] Thus, it is always assumed that local leaders are only interested in personal gain, with the result that a successful person or local leader (such as the president of a mothers' club) may get a lot of criticism and is likely to be distrusted. Though she may achieve positive gains for the group, she has to live with the suspicion that she is out to serve her own ends (Foster, 1973:37).

This analysis begs the question: how much of the disillusionment with microcredit expressed in section one is based on rumour or are leaders truly abusing their positions of power? The following section provides a detailed case study of tensions that arose when a microcredit loan was embezzled by the president in the *Comedor 'La Perlita'*. Accounts are presented from the perspective of multiple stakeholders.

Case study of the Comedor 'La Perlita'

The *Comedor 'La Perlita'*, set up in October 1998 was comprised of a group of low-income women living in a peri-urban area of Cajamarca and had two sources of funds, one of which was managed jointly by the NGOs CARE and IDEAS.[6] The original idea behind the group's formation, was that money could be raised from the microcredit schemes to fund the education of the daughters of the members, with members taking out small loans and paying 4 per cent interest to the president they had elected, who would then bank the funds. Initially, *La Perlita* was highly successful, outperforming other *comedores* in the area. However, as time passed by several members began to suspect that the president was embezzling funds. These suspicions heightened when she refused to disclose written accounts stating how much had been raised. Several members began to realise that although the accounts sent to CARE seemed to be in order, a significant part of the loan fund was missing. What had happened to the funds?

According to one group member, who we shall call Flor, the coordinator of the project that worked at IDEAS was contacted on several occasions, but instead of coming to discuss the problem with the rank-and-file, she telephoned the president and explained that such problems would have to be resolved by the group. After having given the president (who we shall call Rosa) ample opportunities on different occasions to account for the money, Flor accused her of pocketing 8,000 *soles* (approximately £1,600) before the Public Ministry (Quinta Fiscalía Penal) on 3 March 1999. She also challenged the president for allegedly renting the *comedor* and using it as private property when in fact it belonged to the group.

Not until 26 May did the *Ministerio Público* respond, dismissing the case on the grounds that there was evidence to suggest that the money had been distributed to the members. Undeterred, Flor accused the Fiscal Provincial (provincial judge) of the Quinta Fiscalía Provincial Penal of abusing his authority, for the delay in administering justice, as well as favouring family members on the grounds that Rosa reputedly had much social prestige and leverage given that her husband worked for the local council. It is important to recognise the 'informal potential' which holding such a position in a close-knit community is likely to have (Rosen, 1984:100). Being an actor in the local political structure would mean that over time, he could utilise his position to favour allies and friends by offering them protection. It could also be used to forge contractual or dependency ties with others.

On 17 June 1999, Flor demanded that the case should go to a higher court, the Fiscalía Superior Penal, adding to her charge against the president that she had invented the names of the members to whom she supposedly gave credit (an accusation confirmed by the fact that her own list of recipients did not match the one which she presented on a different occasion to CARE), once again repeating her demand that Rosa return the outstanding money.[7] Although CARE had supplied the credit, it did not take an active part in the legal proceedings, but did provide several documents stipulating how much the group had been given. These records confirmed that for the 4 per cent interest that the members paid, the amount banked was well below that of other *comedores* paying the same rate of interest, implying that there were significant sums missing.

Flor responded to these events by inscribing the *comedor* legally in the public register, a document which states the legal rights and responsibilities of the president and formalised procedures, such as writing receipts for payments and money transfers. It also stipulated that the *comedor* was the property of the organisation and not of an individual. The resolution of the trial against Rosa was delayed until January 2000, when Rosa along with the treasurer agreed in court to repay their share of the missing funds, totalling approximately 32,500 *soles* (£6,800). The judge ruled that the *Comedor La Perlita* should come under new management. Despite this judgement, by May 2000 – a year since the initial charge was lodged – Rosa had not repaid a penny.

THE LEGAL VIEWPOINT

When interviewed, Flor's lawyer (Vásquez), explained that he was convinced Rosa had stolen the money. Initially he felt the case would be straightforward, since they possessed conclusive evidence to prove the accusation. In practice, however, it did not turn out as he expected due to Rosa's manipulation of wider power dynamics in the community. According to Vásquez, in court, Rosa managed to avoid the question of embezzlement of funds by saying that she belonged to a different organisation from Flor and had given funds to the members of this other organisation. In this way she did not need to account for the money, because she refused to recognise the authenticity of the first organisation. Rosa added that Flor was not a member of the same community as she lived outside its boundaries. However, Vásquez argued that Rosa did not have the legal documents necessary to prove her case. One obstacle he encountered was that Flor had dealt with corrupt public officials who were not even prepared to process her claim. Only when they were pressurised by the *Defensoría del Pueblo* did they set the legal wheels in motion.[8]

Flor and the group of 15 members who backed her allegations could not pay for the services of Vásquez but they decided to be advised by a final year law student at the University of Cajamarca who offered to pursue the case gratis. Thus, whilst Flor was represented by a law student who had not yet graduated, Rosa had two fully trained barristers in her defence and had the contacts and money to pay for this because of her husband's role on the local council. Despite this disadvantage, according to Vásquez, it should have been a relatively simple case to resolve, as Rosa's evidence was seriously deficient. One tactic Rosa did employ, however, was to begin a hate campaign against Flor with the backing of 65 members, some of whom had been on the credit programme and were beholden to her. Under pressure, they stated that the president had given them loans and that they would pay back. The fact that Rosa had so much support, added weight to her case, making it unlikely that the courts would force her to repay. Once again we see how the members of the microfinance programme were bound to the president in a variety of different ways and on different levels. Some of those who supported her in her hate campaign against Flor were members of kin or other personal contacts who were beholden to her and her husband in different ways. Aware of this unequal power dimension, Rosa successfully managed to use kinship relationships and other personal contacts and resources to back her. This reflects the work of Rosen who demonstrates that where communities are close knit and relationships are highly personalised individuals can 'solidify their image as a leader' by utilising the support of those bound to them (1984:114)

Even the barrister acting for Rosa (Cruzado), realised that there had been poor management of the funds and exploitation of the members. (Vásquez added that the *comedores*[9] are well known for fraud and corrupt practice and that he has seen various cases whereby the food donations given by CARE or PRONAA have been sold by the leadership in markets in the town, who pocket the profits. Such behaviour was also commented on by mothers' groups in Porcón.)[10] Cruzado's concern was to get the two groups represented by Rosa and Flor to conciliate, while at the same time committing Rosa and other members to pay back the money they owed to the organisation, as well as arrange the forming of a new organisation with a different leadership. Having summarised the legal views, we now examine the testimonies of Flor and Rosa.

FLOR'S AND ROSA'S VIEWPOINTS

First, Flor lamented the poor treatment that she and her supporters had received throughout the legal process, in which the authorities proved unprepared to pursue effectively her claim. The favouritism shown to Rosa because she had more social leverage ('*barra*') was also criticised:

> Well, in the public ministry they treated us in a way that we, as human beings, did not deserve. As women coming from poor backgrounds, it was even worse. I recognise that the authorities are very corrupt, totally corrupt, because though there were documents giving conclusive proof, it was the last straw that they just filed the case, filed a crime, which could be proven irrefutably to have taken place. That angered us a lot.

Second, the legal battle had put a tremendous strain on family life: 'As women, we have our homes, our obligations. We abandon all of this, all the things we have to do at home, spending the most part of the day in the street.' She argued that CARE's supervision had been totally inadequate, complaining that their control procedures were so slack that it was easy to present false figures, which CARE would do nothing to correct:

> CARE only supervised the management committee, president and treasurer, but the account books were taken to CARE's office. So the leaders did the accounts, wrote whatever they wanted in the account books, in such a way that suited themselves, so CARE was completely unaware of the problems arising in the group. And due to lack of information, of the opinions of the members.

Rosa, on the other hand, maintained in interview that although the accounts were not in order, she had not embezzled the funds and criticised Flor for selfishness and enviousness. She admitted that she had wrongly lent to members outside the group, who had however repaid, but denied stealing the funds, suggesting that there had been errors on both sides: 'No one is perfect, and it is better to admit your mistakes.' She eventually tired of the animosity and legal expenses and dropped the case.

CARE'S PERSPECTIVE

An ex-CARE staff member was consulted to establish CARE's position. Why did the institution not get involved in the legal process? This informant stated that CARE had given inadequate training with respect to control of both the credit funds they operated. When interviewed, the informant argued that '*La Perlita*' was no longer the responsibility of CARE, as it had ceased to be an NGO and had become an EDPYME (a financial entity more akin to a bank).[11] As the projects and objectives of the EDPYME were different, there was simply no time nor will to get involved. They also feared a bad press:

> I can give you a personal opinion, but it is not that of CARE. As an EDPYME, as I said before, the objectives are different, it is now more of a financial institution. I would have been wasting my time if I had concerned myself with the problems of groups that have nothing to do with the objectives of the EDPYME. There's no one who will go and dedicate time, because it means dedicating time. It was a project that no longer existed for us. Now we are involved in a new project with new objectives.

She continued:

> As for CARE, there was indifference. CARE did not want the image of its institution ... to receive bad publicity, of being in legal battles, because all these things go on television, so it was really to do with not wanting to be seen to be entangled in these kinds of problems. But I am sure that there must be people out here who say, CARE gave the credit and this generated problems and now CARE won't show its face and work towards a solution.

The informant described how presidents regularly embezzled funds and stressed the powerlessness of the group to solve the problem, in addition to the reluctance of CARE staff to intervene: 'We want loans and there is no money. "How can that be, if you have saved 70,000 soles?" There is no money and they aren't accounting for it, go and speak to her.'

Thus, we see that in cases of corruption there are no formal procedures for NGO staff to follow. The loan officer added that it scared her to have to go and talk to the president about malpractice since CARE's policy is not to intervene. On the other hand, this informant felt a moral obligation to do so, because otherwise presidents get away with fraud and the group gets no benefit:

> If you don't go, the women stay that way – no one clarifies the accounts and they get irritated. The president is strong, she manages the group, she does not want to clarify the accounts because she has lent money to all her family members – in this case, to her mother, her sister...

This case demonstrates how unequal power relationships in the wider community can be reinforced, rather than challenged by microfinance interventions.

THE NEW PRESIDENT'S VIEW

An interview with the new president, Elizabeth, revealed that Rosa has finally paid 50 *soles* towards what she owes. Though initially Elizabeth was threatened by Rosa, the former president is now taking a more repentant stance. It is becoming clear that there was great family pressure on Rosa to steal, especially from her husband:

> Rosa is now paying, she paid 50 soles the other day. I told her: 'What example are you setting for your children in robbing money?' She is very influenced by her husband: 'They can't put you in jail, you don't go to jail for debt'. There is a lot of family pressure. The husband asks his wife for loans under the names of the female members of the household, but it's the husband taking the money. They have clusters of family and friends who they give to. Rosa gives to her grandmother, her mother. Her husband wants her to be president and to have this power. Presidents like her need training. They should not let their husbands interfere. The husbands beat them if they don't give them money. You have to value yourself. All the members shout at Rosa, when really, it is her husband behind it all. Rosa says her husband beats her if she doesn't give him the money.

This issue of appropriation of loan funds by male relatives is also stated in the wider literature on gender and microfinance. For example, Goetz and Gupta, in the context of Bangladesh cite how women do not necessarily control the loans that are disbursed in their names: 'A significant portion of women's loans are directly invested by their male relatives, while women borrowers bear the liability for repayment' (1996:45). Other writers, such as Mayoux have also stressed the issue of appropriation of loans by other family members (1988). Ackerly adds that where borrowers on credit programmes simply become 'a means' of credit and income earning for their husbands, this can serve to subordinate women's strategic interests in the long term (1995:59).

In the case of *La Perlita*, the loan was not only appropriated by Rosa's husband but he also had influence over the land on which the *comedor* had been built, facilitated by his links on the local council:

> The men wanted to take away our site. They have the knowledge and education and know the authorities of the area. The man thought he could humiliate us: 'We're going to oust these women from their site' – but we defended ourselves tooth and nail against the authorities. Rosa's husband has influence in the area and has access to offices. He donated the land where our women's association is based to the municipality.

Again this issue points to the necessity of understanding the wider power dynamics and gender hierarchies that exist in the wider community. Despite the problems experienced by the *comedor* '*La Perlita*', there has been a change of consciousness among members:

> Previously the mothers allowed themselves to be cheated. Now they are more vigilant. They see that there is a quantity of money in the bank. They ask, 'President, where are the profits from the *picarones* (fried chicken pieces) we sold?' They are very on the ball and so I have to be straight too. Since the trial they have woken up. I put pressure on them and they do so to me.

The president is no longer perceived as untouchable, operating like a *caudillo*. Rather, the group feels that members are on equal terms: 'Before we felt we are members. She is the leader. If I do anything wrong, she will kick me out. Now we see that she does not own the money, we have our own rights.' In terms of learning how to deal with the authorities, they have also gained confidence and experience: 'Before, we used to think: Wow! Actually going to the office of a police man or a lawyer! Now we have a better idea about how to go about getting justice. We know how to defend ourselves before the authorities.' They have also realised the importance of playing an active role in the scheme: 'Now, everyone wants a post. Before, everyone said "I don't have the time". Now, they all want posts and they carry them out very well. They don't have experience in how to do it, but they use their ingenuity and it works well.' They also attach a higher importance to the *comedor*: 'Credit should be seen as a help, an activity. At home, we feel suffocated. In the meeting, where we can look for friends, we have a space. You feel brighter, you forget your worries, you have ideas. It's a shower of ideas at the comedor.'

It should be noted, however, that in the case of Cajamarca, if there are wider social impacts of women's participation in microcredit programmes (such as reduced deference to those in power or formation of new kinds of associations based on more equal power relationships),[12] these are mostly incidental and, as in the case of *La Perlita*, they were generated indirectly in response to the problems encountered on the credit scheme, rather than as a result of direct benefits produced from microcredit interventions. Contrary to the view propagated by the main development banks, these results suggest that any 'empowering' effects on women are likely to be indirect and unanticipated rather than directly linked to their microfinance activity.

Conclusion

The evidence from Cajamarca suggests the need to re-emphasise the importance of group dynamics when conducting research on the impact of microfinance. The results suggest that entrenched social structures based on kinship and patron–client relationships in rural communities directly affect the way in which these programmes operate. Rather than being used as a vehicle to challenge these unequal structures, microcredit groups were seen to reinforce existing hierarchies and inequalities. Though disillusioned members may spread rumours to exaggerate the number of presidents who use the loan for personal gain, there is nevertheless strong evidence to suggest that this practice does exist and that there is no smoke without fire. Furthermore, the issue is not so much that embezzlement by the leaders goes undetected, but rather, that Microfinance Organisations (MFOs) do not see it as their role to intervene as it is seen as an issue which is internal to the microfinance group. It is argued here that the issue of group dynamics goes beyond the parameters of the microfinance intervention itself and that though improved programme delivery and design (raised by authors such as Montgomery) are important, it is the wider social and cultural setting in which actors are situated and relate to others that needs to be addressed and understood by MFOs and donors if microfinance programmes are to avoid reproducing the very structures of inequality that they purport to challenge.

Notes

1 Though this chapter concentrates on tensions among groups there are also other reasons why credit was not seen to be working effectively. For example, depressed rural markets limited the scope for microcredit as an income-raising strategy. Second, the importance of gender was raised by this research. For example, MFOs appeal to an ideology that reinforces women's sense of obligation to provide for their families. The very pressure of repaying loans can lead to high levels of 'self-exploitation' by low-income women. As well as being detrimental to credit users themselves, in certain cases informants voiced how this added pressure threatened the stability of the household unit and the well-being of its members. See Wright, 2001.
2 This chapter focuses entirely on microfinance in Cajamarca in the northern

highlands of Peru. The original thesis upon which this is based also compares the case of Cajamarca with that of the capital, Lima and draws out rural/urban differences. For an in-depth discussion of these comparisons see Wright 2001. I would like to thank James Copestake for his helpful comments on this chapter.
3 Leaders of mothers' clubs are elected annually by the other members. The elected posts are those of the president, secretary and treasurer. In this way, a hierarchical structure exists in these clubs.
4 *Rondas campesinas* are rural peasant organisations that from the late 1970s have been administering justice in the northern *sierra* of Peru. Among other things, they hold their own assemblies and resolve disputes over land tenure and household violence. They operate in Porcón and in the town centre of Cajamarca. For an in-depth study of the historical conditions that led to their formation, see Starn *'Nightwatch'* (1999).
5 It should be noted that the work of Foster has been somewhat discredited in recent times given that gossip and envy are not uniquely associated with peasant societies since they exist in all societies, irrespective of the economic model. Foster's approach of seeing peasant communities as 'closed static systems' has also come under fire. These criticisms do not detract however from the more general argument that where societies are inherently based on highly personalist alliances, they are likely to manifest characteristics of competitiveness and jealousy (Rosen, 1984:135). Deere also takes the view that in closely-knit communities, where people are dependent upon each other for services (such as labour exchanges for house building), these relationships are unlikely to be entirely free of conflict (1990).
6 IDEAS stands for *Instituto de Desarrollo y Asistencia Social* (Institute of Development and Social Assistance). CARE is an independent, international relief and development organisation that operates in more than 70 countries in Africa, Asia, Latin America, the Middle East and Eastern Europe.
7 Meanwhile, in the same month of May it was confirmed by the NGO CIPDER (*Consorcio Interinstitucional para el Desarollo Regional*; Inter-institutional Consortium for Regional Development) that Rosa had also been provided with credit supposedly for the *comedor La Perlita*, and that she had not paid it back.
8 The *Defensoría del Pueblo* (Ombudsman's office) was created under the constitution of 1993 and works autonomously from the state. Its mission is to protect the constitutional rights of individuals and the community at large and to ensure that state administration perform their duties. It also aims to make the public aware of local services provided by the state.
9 Women's collective strategies, such as their role in fostering community participation through the establishment of the *comedores populares* (popular soup kitchens) and *clubes de madres* (mothers' clubs) in Peru during the 1980s have received much attention (Barrig, 1998). Less attention has been paid to the subsequent withdrawal of women from these community programmes in the context of continued economic hardship and marked decreases in government subsidies for these activities.
10 Interviews in Porcón conducted in July and October 1999, revealed that many of the *junta directivas* keep the food supplied by PRONAA for their own families and only give a fraction to the members.
11 EDPYME stands for *Entidades de Desarollo de la Pequeña y Microempresa* (Entities for Small and Microenterprise Development). These are recognised as formal, fully-fledged financial institutions.
12 For further discussion of different kinds of wider social impacts see Kabeer 2003.

References

Ackerly, B. A. (1995) 'Testing the tools of development: credit programmes, loan involvement and women's empowerment' *IDS Bulletin* 26:3, 56–68.

Alberti, G. and Mayer, E. (eds) (1974) *Reciprocidad e intercambio en los Andes Peruanos* (Lima: IEP).

Altamirano, T. (1988) *Cultura andina y pobreza urbana: Aymaras en Lima Metropolitana* (Lima: Pontífica Universidad La Católica).

Barrig, M. (ed.) (1998) *De Vecinas a ciudadanas: La mujer en el desarollo urbano* (Lima: Sumbi).

Chambers, R. (1983) *Rural development, putting people last first* (Harlow: Longman).

Deere, C. D. (1990) *Household and class relations: peasants and landlords in Northern Peru* (Berkeley: University of California Press).

Degregori, C. I. (2000) *No hay país más diverso: Compendio de antropología Peruana* (Lima: IEP).

Degregroi, C. I. and Golte, J. (1973) *Dependencia y desinteración structural en la comunidad de Pacaraos* (Lima: IEP).

Foster, G. (1973) *Traditional societies and technological change* (New York: Harper & Row).

Golte, J. (1987) *La racionalidad de la organización andina* (Lima: IEP).

Goetz, A. M. and Gupta, R. S. (1996) 'Who takes the credit? Gender, power and control over loan use in rural credit programs in Bangladesh' *World Development* 24:1, 45–63.

Gwynne, R. and Kay, C. (1999) *Latin America transformed: Globalization and modernity* (London: Arnold).

Hamilton, S. (1988) *The two-headed household: Gender and rural development in the Ecuadorean Adnes* (Pittsburgh: University of Pittsburgh Press).

Harris, O. (2000) *To make the earth bear fruit: ethnographic essays on fertility, work and gender in highland Bolivia* (London: ILAS).

Hulme, D. (2000) 'Is microdebt good for poor people? A note on the dark side of microfinance' *Small Enterprise Development* 11:1, 26–9.

Hulme, D. and Mosley, P. (eds) (1996) *Finance against poverty* (Vols 1 and 2) (London: Routledge).

IDB (Inter-American Development Bank) (1997) 'Evaluation of Global Microenterprise Credit (GMC): "Who gets access? How much does it cost?" Summary of three case studies.' Ecuador, Paraguay, El Salvador.

Kabeer, N. (2003) 'Assessing "narrow" and "wider" social impacts: Conceptual and methodological notes' Presentation for global Imp-Act meeting, South Africa, 4–8 May 2003.

Kogan, L. (1998) *Practical notes: development in practice* (Oxfam, UK: Carfax Publishing Ltd).

Marr, A. (2002) 'Studying group dynamics: an alternative analytical framework for the study of microfinance impacts on poverty reduction' *Journal of International Development* 14:4, 511–34.

Mayer, E. (2002) *The articulated peasant* (Boulder, CO: Westview Press).

Mayer, E. and Zamalloa, C. (1974) 'Reciprocidad en las relaciones de producción' in G. Alberti and E. Mayer (eds) *Reciprocidad e Intercambio en los Andes Peruanos* (Lima: Instituto de Estudios Peruanos, pp. 66–86).

Mayoux, L. (1998) 'Women's empowerment and micro-finance programmes:

approaches, evidence and ways forward' *Development Policy and Practice Working Paper* 41 (London, Open University).

Mercado, M. (1999) 'Power to Do: and to make money' in J. Townsend, P. Alberti, M. Mercado, J. Rowlands and Z. Rowlands (eds) *Women and Power: Fighting Patriarchies and Poverty* (London: Zed Books).

Montgomery, R. (1995) 'Disciplining or protecting the poor? Avoiding the social costs of peer pressure in solidarity group microcredit schemes' *Papers in international development* (Swansea: Centre for Development Studies, pp. 289–305).

Mossbrucker, H. (1990) *La economía campesina y el conepto de 'comunidad': un enfoque crítico* (Lima: IEP).

Rosen, L. (1984) *Bargaining for reality: the construction of social relations in a muslim community* (Chicago: University of Chicago Press).

Silverblatt, I. (1980) 'The universe has turned inside out ... there is no justice for us here: Andean women under Spanish rule' in M. Etienne and E. Leacock *Women and colonisation: Anthropological perspectives* (New York: Praeger, 149–85).

Starn, O. (1999) *Nightwatch: The politics of protest in the Andes* (London: Duke University Press).

Townsend, J., Zapata, E., Rowlands, J., Alberti, P. and Mercado, M. (1999) *Women and power: Fighting patriarchies and poverty* (New York: Zed Books).

Wood, G. (2000) 'Prisoners and escapees: Improving the institutional responsibility square in Bangladesh' *Public Administration and Development* 20, 221–37.

Wood, G. D. and Sharif, I. A. (eds) (1997) *Who needs credit? Poverty and finance in Bangladesh* (Dhaka: University Press).

Wright, K. (2001) 'Women's participation in microcredit schemes: Evidence from Cajamarca and Lima, Peru' University of Liverpool, unpublished PhD thesis.

Wright, K. (2003) '"Problems? What problems? We have none at all." Qualitative data collection for impact assessment: getting the questions right' *Journal of Microfinance* 5:1.

8 Banking on bananas, crediting crafts

Financing women's work in the Philippine Cordillera[1]

Lynne Milgram

Introduction

Since the 1970s, the gender and development movement has put gender issues on the table. We have moved from patronizing welfare models of development to understanding that involving women in designing initiatives from the outset is integral to achieving the most fruitful outcomes. Yet, the fact that social institutions and development organizations continue to produce gendered outcomes which can be constraining or disadvantageous for women means that it can be useful to adopt a feminist perspective to examine the relationship between the institutional claim to empowerment and the capacity of program design and practice to generate social opportunity for women (see Goetz 1997). Such an approach raises questions about how theories of power underlying the concept of empowerment are currently being used in development practice. To generate debate around these issues, this chapter analyzes a new (1997) microfinance development program in the northern upland Philippines established by the Central Cordillera Agricultural Programme or CECAP.[2] CECAP's Rural Finance System is developing a local system of village savings and loan groups and connecting these to local banking cooperatives to promote economic development.

In current international development practice, issuing credit, particularly to women, has gained wide acceptance as the most effective means of reducing poverty and empowering program beneficiaries. The frequently articulated example of the empowered borrower – one who wisely invests money in a successful livelihood enterprise to better the social (education, nutritional) and economic (income) position of herself and her family – represents the fulfillment of the microfinance promise (Murdoch 2000).

Much of this enthusiasm rests on what Jonathan Murdoch (2000:617) terms the "win–win" premise: microfinance institutions that follow the principles of good banking will also be those that reduce the most poverty and provide people with more life choices. By being able to achieve financial self-sustainability in a timely manner, microfinance institutions will be able to grow without the constraints imposed by donor budgets, and will be able to serve effectively and empower more poor people. A key tenet is that poor households demand access to credit, not necessarily cheap credit; thus the income generated by loan interest will eventually cover the costs of operating microfinance programs (Murdoch 2000:619). While some find this argument to be self-evident, others are more skeptical. The latter argue instead that microfinance fails to reach the poorest (Fernando 1997), has a limited effect on income (Hashemi *et al.* 1996), and does little to address the broader socio-economic causes of poverty (Goetz and Sen Gupta 1996).

I argue that particular understandings and applications of power, such as those that privilege the market or are rooted in gender hierarchies, are built into the rules and practices of social institutions such as that of CECAP and, that this institutional climate can influence the results of programs from the outset (see Goetz 1997). The implications of such a power bias can, in turn, hold unintended consequences for social change objectives as initiatives may be actively contested and resisted by participants who are excluded from decision-making processes. In practice, CECAP's program encompasses conflicting goals; it prioritizes achieving financial self-sustainability within the short lifespan of the project 1997–2002 and thus gives little more than lip-service to realizing member empowerment and poverty reduction. Consistent with their prioritization of the market-led model of development, then, CECAP's program design leaves little space for women's voices to be heard, and thus little opportunity to incorporate women's knowledge and experience into more locally appropriate and potentially empowering livelihood enterprises.

While researchers and development practitioners debate to what extent such local systems of experience and socio-economic organization should be respected or challenged, most programs are designed partially in deference to existing values, and partially to change them. I argue, like Brooke Ackerly (1997:142), that both "deference and opposition" require understanding such organizational systems (e.g. gender and class hierarchies) to effectively operationalize social justice objectives for women, especially. By relying on the familiar theoretical distinction between formal and informal economy, rather than on the more locally appropriate understanding of intra-familial, class, and gender relationships, CECAP's initiatives have failed to address the broader discriminatory infrastructure within which women work; and their program, in many cases, has thus left women with debts resulting from inappropriate livelihood projects.

Drawing on Ackerly (1997:141) I define woman's empowerment as a function of both institutional change and individual initiative. With regard to women's institutional environment empowerment necessitates changing or eliminating the society's values, practices, norms, and laws that constrain women's activities and choices. Second, empowerment depends upon an individual woman's ability to take action and make choices. As Ackerly (1997:141) points out, the two aspects of empowerment are not easily

174 *Lynne Milgram*

differentiated from one another as a coercive environment may limit a woman's agency.

To explore these issues in women's empowerment and microfinance development, I use data on women's work in handicrafts and farming (banana cultivation and trade) at the household level. Following a discussion that problematizes the theoretical context of women, empowerment and microfinance, I explore the extent to which different women have been able successfully to operationalize CECAP's microfinance program. I conclude by discussing how microfinance initiatives in the Cordillera highlight the broader issue of gender, sustainable development, and policy formation which are currently being debated in development studies.

Accessing credit, accessing empowerment?

Since the 1990s, microfinance initiatives based on the Grameen Bank model have been increasingly adopted by development practitioners as the most prevalent intervention to reduce poverty and empower women, particularly. As heralded by the 1997 Microcredit Summit Conference in Washington DC, success stories are being written around the world from Oceania to Asia, Africa to South America. The cornerstone of these programs is the provision of subsidized access to loans, not subsidized loans per se as interest rates can be equal to those of the regular banking institutions. Through a process in which peer group pressure, rather than possession of conventional collateral (land, capital), ensures timely loan repayments, women normally marginalized from the formal banking sector receive small loans for livelihood projects (Yunus 1994). In so doing, microfinance programs provide borrowers with alternatives to usurious moneylenders and with opportunities to build or expand household enterprises. The key to microfinance's rise as the star of international development is the documentation of the positive impacts associated with lending to poor women, especially in terms of increasing their household income. Women are targeted as program beneficiaries because of their record of higher repayment rates and their prioritization of expenditure on family welfare; this, in turn, promises increased program efficiency, poverty reduction as well as a positive social impact due to improvements in women's positions within family and society (Wood and Sharif 1997).

However, a growing number of studies have questioned the validity of using increases in household income as the sole barometer for measuring improved quality of life for household members (e.g. Berger 1989; Goetz and Sen Gupta 1996; Rahman 1999). Hulme and Mosley (1997:98–101) argue that increased income does not necessarily result in a reduction in poverty. They point out that poverty is not only about having inadequate income or income below the poverty line, but is also about the inability to sustain a specified level of well-being through lack of options in work or through lack of control over earnings. Microfinance advocates who adopt a broader view of poverty suggest that strategies must move beyond offering only credit to include "protectional strategies" such as voluntary savings, emergency consumption loans, and low-risk income-generating projects that are unlikely to create indebtedness (Hulme and Mosley 1997:100, Wright 2000:15). Although development organizations now widely recognize that poverty is multifaceted and that people's own perceptions are fundamental to identifying what poverty means to them or is, many microfinance programs still fail to enhance women's socioeconomic positions because initiatives do not challenge the discriminatory and exclusionary infrastructure in which women work and live.

Addressing these debates, Linda Mayoux (1998) identifies three paradigms of gender and microfinance delivery that focus on achieving either financial self-sustainability, poverty alleviation, or feminist empowerment. Each regard "women's empowerment as a process of change in a complex system of interlinked and mutually reinforcing dimensions of gender subordination" (Mayoux 1998:6). However, their goals are differentially weighted in their prioritization of microfinance delivery, complementary services, organizational structure, and new opportunities for women (Mayoux 1998:6–7). These differences account for why certain policies and practices and not others prevail in reality.

The financial self-sustainability paradigm seeks to increase household income by providing credit to increasingly large numbers of poor people to practice economies of scale (Mayoux 1998:11, 13). Women are targeted for efficiency as they are better repayers and as such are an "underutilized resource for development" (Mayoux 1998:14). In the poverty alleviation paradigm microfinance is part of a wider integrated community development program aimed at poverty reduction as well as at improving individual well-being, decreasing vulnerability and expanding access to social services (Mayoux 1998:17–18). In the feminist empowerment approach microfinance responds to the immediate practical needs of poor informal sector women workers, but it is regarded as only part of a strategy for the wider social and political empowerment of women through social mobilization and advocacy around issues of gender equity at the macro-level (Mayoux 1998:19).

The current feminist scholarship debating issues in the field of gender, empowerment, and development provides a useful entry to identifying the role of credit programs in changing institutional environments that enable borrowers to broaden their range of action and choice. In her discussion of different institutional models of development, Goetz (1997:7), like Hulme and Mosley, argues that initiatives often focus on the "technical" matters of quantifiable input provision in a process which neglects issues of women's actual control over these inputs. She (1997:6) maintains that the business of expanding women's access to and control over resources and of revaluing their roles in the rural economy disrupts traditional interpretations of gendered need and worth upon which patterns of

176 Lynne Milgram

female exclusion and denial are based. Such hesitancy to implement gender-transformatory aspects of policy – to tackle the larger social and politico-economic context that largely restricts women to domestic sphere activities – is also reflected in the tendency to minimize the empowerment-related objectives of such programs as has occurred in CECAP's program (Goetz 1997:7).

Kabeer similarly argues that studies evaluating the impact of microfinance on women's empowerment often use the concept of "managerial control" as their index of measurement. Managerial control, she maintains, confuses two distinct aspects of decision making related to household resource allocation: "control" and "management." Control has to do with the policy making function (e.g. deciding how resources are to be utilized) while management has to do with the implementation function, putting into operation the policy decided upon (Kabeer 1998:6). By focusing on the index of managerial control, programs highlight the implementation of decision making related to the management of the loan-funded enterprise, but offer little insight into control over decision making about loan use. Women's empowerment is rooted in their obtaining the controlling position that enables them to determine "the rules of the game" (Goetz 1997:7), rather than simply how the rules are implemented. Indeed, Goetz (1997:10) points out that analyses of implementation patterns show that women's identification with policy making is often limited to those features of their lives which center on their contribution to family welfare and on their needs as dependents of men, rather than on their needs as producers and marketers in extra-household spheres.

Fraser's (1997) analysis further highlights the complexity of addressing gender injustice in development programs with conflicting goals. She (1997:28) argues that gender is a "bivalent differentiation" that suffers both economic and cultural injustice. Thus people subordinated by gender need both redistribution (redistributing and reorganizing economic opportunities) and recognition (upwardly revaluing disrespected identities), both of which need to be pursued simultaneously (1997:15–16). Changes in both spheres, most commonly implemented through "affirmation," she (1997:28) maintains, do indeed assure women a fair share of existing economic opportunities as well as respect by revaluing feminism. However, in both spheres, the larger socio-economic infrastructure remains unchanged, namely, the nature and number of jobs accessible to women and the prevailing binary opposition in which being female sits (1997:29). Fraser (1997:29) argues then that the most promising path for transforming the deep structures of both political economy and culture must encompass "transformative" measures aimed at "dismantling androcentrism by destabalizing gender dichotomies" thereby challenging gender injustice.

Some Philippine microfinance programs similarly exemplify how development incentives may be tied more closely to quantitatively measurable performance targets than to qualitative objectives such as promoting empowerment processes, regardless of the organization's official line. Sharon Miron (1997; see also Chua 1998) demonstrates this tension in her study of a southern Luzon credit program operated by CARD Bank (Center for Agriculture and Rural Development), one of the country's most successful microfinance programs. She argues that although CARD's access to credit has indeed improved women's income, savings for emergencies and personal self-confidence, it has in fact not truly "empowered" women (1997:206). Miron (1997:62) found that despite women contributing 25 to 50 percent of the household's total income and spending 40 to 50 percent of their time in productive activities, a majority of women still refer to the man as the breadwinner and to themselves as housewives, emphasizing their reproductive rather than their productive work; and in decision making, men often have the final say in cases of a deadlock (see also Kwiatkowski 1998:82–96). Thus, women often excuse men for spending 30 to 60 percent of their income on "personal wants" rather than contributing their earnings to the pooled household resources as is the usual practice (Miron 1997:55). She also demonstrates that many women spend more hours working in both spheres thus increasing income by increasing workload. Miron (1997:208) concludes then, that although access to financial resources enhances women's positions within the traditional family sphere, women must also have control of the decision-making processes governing income distribution as well as institutional alternatives to dependence on family.

Rebecca Coke (2000), in her research in the central Philippines, similarly argues that microcredit programs adhere to a feminine subsystem tied to household and community management. As such, they are geared to women's roles as small household producers and mothers which, in practice, fall short of their goal to empower women, and in fact, may lead to program failure. For the Filipino wife, family needs are often placed before her obligation to the larger community and thus to her microcredit group or institution. Female borrowers may choose to divert loan funds from bank repayments to family expenses even when her groupmates do not approve. Coke (2000:10) argues that in the Philippines, the Spanish colonial ideal of a virtuous woman means that women are customarily expected to sacrifice themselves for the good of their families (see also Chua 2001:154). In many cases then, loan funds may be diverted to cover essential family needs (healthcare and education); other women, understanding the rationale for their groupmates' delinquency may not exert the peer pressure expected by program management because they feel they themselves would have acted in a similar fashion, having little alternative, especially in a culture that validates maternal self-sacrifice (Coke 2000:13–14).

It becomes evident that facilitating women's access to physical resources through credit alone only partially addresses circumstances of social injustice. Empowerment strategies for women must build on the social embeddedness and on the multidimensionality of power to make a difference in women's ability to control these resources, determine agendas, and make decisions.

Situating the Philippine Cordillera

The provinces of Ifugao and Kalinga-Apayao are located in the Gran Cordillera Central mountain range that extends through much of northern Luzon. The main economic activity throughout the Cordillera is subsistence wet-rice cultivation carried out in irrigated pond-fields, and in many areas the high elevation and cool climate limits cultivation to one rice crop per year. Where the temperatures are warmer and the terrain gentler in both provinces, small-scale farmers can seasonally produce a limited surplus of crops such as vegetables, bananas, and coffee which they sell commercially. Most families, however, to sustain themselves throughout the year must also engage in non-agricultural income-generating work such as producing crafts, working in the tourist service industry, or operating grocery stores.

Except for the small percentage of those living in town centers, most people live in hamlets of two to four houses scattered throughout the rice fields. Many settlements are several hours' walk from the nearest road and the limited roadways are often blocked by landslides cutting off many municipalities and towns for weeks during the rainy season each year (May–December). The disperse housing pattern means that the population density is extremely low and this, coupled with the provinces' substantial distance (ten to 12 hours) from major urban markets, challenges development efforts to achieve program efficiency.

Men and women both work in extra-household income-generating activities as noted. The region's socio-economic systems of bilateral kinship and inheritance, ambilocal residence and primogeniture (inheritance based on seniority not gender) means that women own land and inherited wealth and have ready access to different economic opportunities. Most women are prominent in the management of household finances and hold power in this sphere by controlling the allocation of household's cash resources. Men, however, predominate in public positions in politics and in religious office, and although men participate in domestic tasks, women still assume the bulk of childcare and domestic responsibilities (Kwiatkowski 1998; Milgram 2001b).

Throughout the Cordillera, moreover, it is important to consider the differences among women. Depending upon factors such as their social class (landed elite, tenant, or landless) and their education, some women as artisans and vegetable traders may have more of an advantage than others to gain prestige and increase income through their involvement in microfinance programs as the following case studies demonstrate.

Financing women's work

The Central Cordillera Agricultural Programme, operational since 1989, is jointly funded by the European Union and the Philippine government's Department of Agriculture (CECAP 1997:4). Its renewed seven-year mandate began in July 1996 and contains, among other programs, a rural microfinance component charged with "increase[ing] income and strengthen[ing] resource management capabilities" through all programs in the Cordillera (CECAP 1997:6).

In their credit scheme, borrowers, primarily women, organize themselves into peer groups of between five and 15 members to receive small loans without the requirement of physical collateral (land, capital). Loans are issued in predetermined and increasingly larger amounts upon borrowers' successfully repaying their loans in 50 weekly installments. Group members provide social collateral by agreeing to guarantee and monitor the repayment of each other's loans. Program participants who have proved themselves creditworthy by meeting weekly and contributing an agreed upon amount to their pooled group savings can access CECAP's low interest loans (15 percent per annum) from local subsidized banking cooperatives.[3]

Betting on bananas

Loans from the CECAP-designated banking cooperatives are used most often to increase the scale of existing activities or to diversify into related fields. Women choose income-generating projects that can be easily integrated into the existing mix of domestic and agricultural activities in which they are already engaged. I found, however, that those who have been able to take advantage of the first round of loans (pesos 4,000 or CAN$125.00), as well subsequent loans, are women engaged in already-existing businesses such as trading bananas or crafts, running grocery stores and selling home-made snacks. Women who work solely in cultivation or in non-paid domestic work are reluctant to borrow funds for investment. For the poorest households (those not in business), the opportunities for productive use of loans are limited, and the risk of taking loans that are repayable on a weekly basis are unacceptably high (see also Fernando 1997:175).

For example, in Kalinga-Apayao, within one group, Doris Bannug[4] buys and sells bananas while many of her co-members are banana producers and Doris's suppliers. When the group qualified to take a CECAP sponsored loan, only Doris took action on this opportunity as her co-members feared that their fluctuating income, based on seasonal cultivation, would not be sufficient to meet their weekly loan repayments. Using her access to loan funds, Doris has been able to expand her business by purchasing bananas from more producers while continuing to offer farmers the same price. Traders like Doris may also own grocery stores from which they advance dry goods to producers in exchange for the delivery of bananas, thus earning additional profit on the mark up of the groceries. A similar situation occurs in some groups with regard to the production and trade of crafts.

Doris is reluctant to pass on benefits in the form of higher prices to her farmers for their bananas because she herself is not in control of the prices she receives from larger town buyers. Throughout the Cordillera, the parameters of pricing bananas are firmly established at each level of the buying and selling network. Village farmers gather and sell their bananas to their favourite local village buyer. Bananas are counted and sold per 100 pieces which consists of "hands" of bananas counted in terms of five pieces. If a hand of bananas physically holds either six or 11 bananas, for example, the extra pieces are not counted by the buyer but offered by the farmer as a "good-will" gift according to customary practice. The village buyer, in turn, sells her bananas to larger town buyers who either personally transport the bananas to large urban markets or wait for the urban buyers to pick up the produce according to a prearranged schedule. In the latter transaction, for each 100 bananas counted, the village buyer must include an extra ten bananas as insurance against spoilage, also in a good-will gesture. A similar practice of gifting produce between seller and buyer occurs with vegetable marketing. Farmers selling their vegetables to wholesalers are expected to add 1 kilogram of extra produce for every 10 kilograms sold.[5]

Ultimately, then, the prices paid for the produce at each level of this network are determined by those paid by the wholesale buyers in the main urban markets such as Manila. The dynamics of such group interaction has the effect of more firmly entrenching pre-existing fault-lines within the community; it widens cleavages among women based on age and class, determined by ownership of land, success in business and education, and, in turn, threatens the long-term sustainability of savings and loan groups.

Some village banana buyers, however, are developing their own innovative options for marketing their produce by beginning to work through Philippine fair trade NGOs such as the Association of Partners for Fairer Trade (APFTI). Fair trade practices guarantee producer groups locally appropriate prices for their products and work to maintain ongoing support services (e.g. market access, skills training) (see Milgram 2001b). Both producers and small buyers have approached CECAP to request larger loans and skills training workshops that would enable them to form producer groups and thus access APFTI's services. By facilitating such member initiatives, CECAP's development efforts could move beyond simply making credit available; they could initiate transformatory measures that challenge the discriminatory infrastructure in which some of these practices such as buying and selling bananas are so firmly enmeshed.

CECAP's prioritization of the market-led practice of development is further demonstrated in the planning staff's misguided efforts to identify new income-generating projects for women that resulted in a high percentage of delinquent loans. In one Ifugao village many women combine subsistence agriculture with their work in crafts applying basketry embellishment to carved wooden containers for the tourist market. Artisans indicate that the pesos 4,000 loan is not enough for them to independently engage in production since carvers require cash advances for their products and are often late in delivering their orders. Such risky delays may cause the prospective producer-trader to miss her buyers' deadlines (see Milgram 2001a). CECAP staff have encouraged women here to collect and sell local, organically-grown ginger which commanded a high price in urban centers in 1998 and early 1999. To meet their weekly repayments members continued to do craft piecework.

Borrowers expressed concern, early on, about possible overexposure in this new income-generating project. In 1997, only one or two women regularly bought local ginger from farmers to sell in urban markets. During the summer of 1998, however, more than 12 women were armed with bank loans to start similar businesses. Members trading ginger feared that as more loans were granted for this same purpose, competition among neighboring buyers may cause prices to decrease thus jeopardizing their projected profits and their ability to meet their schedule of repayments. This indeed occurred early in 1999 and was compounded by the situation in which many women were not able to sell the ginger they had kept in storage. Since most women retain the primary responsibility for childcare and domestic tasks, many of those who took loans to market ginger had to store their collected produce, some for up to three months, until they could conveniently travel to city markets. Others hoped to receive a higher selling price by accumulating larger quantities for volume sales. While in storage, some of the ginger decreased in weight as it started to dry out such that some women lost up to 30 percent of the weight of their stock. This situation coupled with falling prices made it difficult for borrowers to repay their loans. Indeed, nine of the 12 women dropped out of the program leaving behind delinquent loans and two disbanded groups.

By offering only credit without the provision of broader market and social support (e.g. childcare, transportation to market, agricultural training) CECAP's program, in this and in similar instances with regard to crafts, has done little to help women secure their livelihoods; nor has CECAP facilitated new roles for women such as the opportunity to move from producer to producer-trader status.

Seeking options, diverting funds

In addition to investing loans for specified income-generating projects most women also spend some portion of their CECAP funds on household consumption needs. Although this diversion of loans is contrary to the lending policy of CECAP and of the banking cooperatives, the use of CECAP loans is rarely monitored after the loan application has been approved. Given their large workload, rural field staff and bank outreach workers devote little time to loan supervision, turning their efforts, instead, to successful and timely loan collection. Many women thus divert their loans from their original investment to adjust to fluctuating market demands and prices for crafts or vegetable produce, as well as to cover unexpected family expenses (e.g. healthcare).

Susan Tayad, for example, took a loan to buy and sell bananas directly to her village neighbours in upland Ifugao, hoping to bypass the permanent vegetable traders who monopolize sales in the town center. Her proposed costs were based on the selling price of bananas grown under normal climatic conditions. When she went to purchase the bananas in the lowlands, she found that because of the lack of rain in 1998, the selling price had increased by 20 percent and the bananas were smaller than usual and thus not readily saleable. She decided on an alternate course of action and purchased, instead, bulk supplies of sweet rice, coconut, oil, and sugar to make homemade rice cakes; and subsequently she added other baked goods such as different types of muffins and fried vegetable cakes to her production. Susan and her mother sell these snacks to their neighbors, to nearby businesses, and to those living along the road to the town center. As selling baked goods reproduces a low-profit return on her time and investment, Susan transformed her remaining cash into small, low-interest loans to her basketry-producing neighbors. She hopes to gain, not only a profit on these loans, but also social capital for her supportive gesture to the artisan community. Susan remains fearful, however, that by diverting her loan to moneylending practices she will jeopardize her chances of securing subsequent loans.

Such situations demonstrate how institutional rules, structures, and practices that privilege the market and the predetermined proper behavior and work of women, continue primarily to serve the political and social interests which institutions were designed to promote in the first place (Goetz 1997:6). Given the restricted opportunities for women for income-earning activities, many borrowers have a low absorptive capacity for additional capital; businesses commonly associated with women's work, such as making and selling homemade food or crafts, exhibit sharply diminishing returns to capital after the first loan. Since the original business cannot expand beyond a certain local market context, women commonly divert their subsequent loans to other businesses or to pay for family consumption needs. As Coke (2000:13) points out, in such cases, the probability of default increases as the borrower's "discounted value of expected future loan benefits decreases."[6]

Susan's initiatives demonstrate how women carve multiple channels through which to tackle shifting socio-economic contexts and refashion information offered by development programs. The manner in which Susan has redirected her investments and nurtured social networks, challenges traditional assumptions about women's roles and capacities for self-development which contribute to women's lower entitlements. By failing to consider the input offered by women's voices, CECAP's program reproduces the ongoing cycle of women's engagement in only low-return, home-based occupations. Their policies hardly provide women with an institutional alternative to dependence on family, nor do practices demonstrate sensitivity to difference among women and commitment to outcomes which are empowering to a broader range of women.

Conclusions

In spite of the laudable gains achieved by placing gender on the policy agenda of international development, embedded within models such as CECAP's microfinance program is an understanding of women's needs that can be seen foremost to reflect the concerns of agencies for financial accountability. As Ackerly (1997:155–6) argues, when performance incentives are increasingly tied to the speed with which funds are moved, rather than to their impact on the socio-economic infrastructure within which women work and live, pressure to disburse and recover money rapidly diminishes concerns to ensure that credit contributes to women's social and financial autonomy.

By embedding social change objectives in programs driven by market forces, CECAP has tended to view its problems as technical; their policies and practices have largely ignored the pre-existing fault-lines among women, the differences that existed before project implementation. Thus, while some established microentrepreneurs have been able to use CECAP's microfinance loans to augment their existing businesses, others have found themselves marginalized by the system and scrambling to make their weekly loan repayments. Indeed, without wider socio-economic and political support for borrowers, even microentrepreneurs cannot expand their businesses sufficiently enough to justify the reinvestment of increasingly larger loans. Loan funds may be diverted then, to cover household consumption needs putting borrowers at risk of default. Entrepreneurs, moreover, hesitate to pass on benefits to smaller producers as they themselves remain vulnerable to broader market and class constraints.

CECAP's failure to develop transformatory initiatives such as work options for women other than low-paying, home-based enterprises, have enforced, rather than challenged, stereotypes about gender needs and the division of labour that institutionalizes women's domestic work. As Fraser (1997:23, 29) argues, "to correct inequitable outcomes of social arrangements without disturbing the underlying framework that generates them," not only leaves intact ideological structures that produce gender and class subordination, but also marks women as deficient as these corrections must be repeatedly administered.

The reduction of women's needs to temporary infusions of credit cannot guarantee opportunities for social change, just as idealistic expectations about women's solidarity cannot in themselves transcend hierarchies that mitigate women's collective action (Rankin 2001). The group-based framework for delivering resources to women is less problematic if one objective is its contribution to women's collective empowerment. In the Cordillera, it becomes a problem, however, if it is merely an instrument for more efficient development practice – a means of managing controlled and uniform resource delivery and recovery (Goetz 1997:12). Simply gaining access to credit institutions falls short of establishing a controlling voice in how policy and practice are decided upon as well as implemented. While CECAP group members might be able to provide information or knowledge which may eventually feed into some aspects of policy or project design, they are not actually changing any of the key program decisions.

Promoting broader debates within microfinance initiatives, as well as within other affirmative approaches, can provide a foundation for operationalizing a more normative agenda for development. Developing transformative interpretations of women's needs can lead to deeper structural communication among women within the parameters of their lived experiences. These channels, in turn, may create the most realistic opportunities for women to develop a collective social criticism of gender and class inequality to assume power over conditions of change.

Notes

1 A earlier version of this article was published in "Atlantis: A Women's Studies Journal" 2002. Special Issue: *Gender Globalization and Development*, 26 (2): 109–19. The research reported in this study was conducted over seven months in 1998 and during the summers of 2000 and 2001 in association with the Cordillera Studies Center (CSC), University of the Philippines, College Baguio, Baguio City. Funding was provided by the Social Sciences and Humanities Research Council of Canada (SSHRC) through a post-doctoral fellowship and a subsequent three-year standard research grant and by the Ontario College of Art and Design. I thank my colleagues at CSC for their guidance and generous support of my research, and the management and field staff at the Central Cordillera Agricultural Programme for their cooperation with and contributions to this study. To the participants of the microfinance program in the Philippine Cordillera provinces, I owe a debt of gratitude.

2 The Central Cordillera Agricultural Programme operates its microfinance and agricultural support programmes in four Cordillera provinces: Kalinga-Apayao, Ifugao, Abra and Mountain Province. Although I have conducted research in each of these provinces, data for this paper focuses on Ifugao and Kalinga-Apayao.

3 For a more detailed account of the design and implementation of CECAP's microfinance program, see Wright 2000. In an earlier paper analyzing different

aspects of microfinance in the Philippines, I discuss CECAP's program design with regard to its effect on poverty alleviation and women's positions (see Milgram 2001b).
4 All personal names of individuals as well specific village names are pseudonyms.
5 For a discussion of patron–client relationships in rural trade in the Cordillera, see Milgram 2001a.
6 Women most commonly divert their loan funds to pay for emergency healthcare and tuition costs. In many cases, to cover their CECAP loan repayments, borrowers took additional loans from moneylenders, at 10 percent interest per month, from their household subsistence budget.

References

Ackerly, Brooke (1997) "What's in a Design? The Effects of NGO Programme Delivery Choices on Women's Empowerment in Bangladesh" in Goetz, A. M. (ed.) *Getting Institutions Right for Women in Development*. London: Zed Books, pp. 140–58.
Berger, Marguerite (1989) "Giving Women Credit: The Strengths and Limitations of Credit as a Tool for Alleviating Poverty." *World Development* 17 (7): 1017–32.
Central Cordillera Agricultural Programme (CECAP) (1997) *Annual Report to the Central Cordillera Public*. Banaue, Ifugao: CECAP.
Chua, Ronald T. (1998) *The Performance and Sustainability of Two Philippine Microfinance Institutions*. Brisbane, Australia: The Foundation for Development Cooperation Ltd.
—— (2001) *Impact of Microfinance on Poverty Alleviation, A Philippine Study. Contribution to the World Development Report 2000/01*. Laguna, PH: CARD Bank.
Coke, Rebecca N. (2000) "Wife, Mother, Businesswoman: The Effects of Competing Social Roles on Microfinance Business Default." unpublished manuscript.
Fernando, Jude L. (1997) "Nongovernmental Organizations, Micro-Credit, and Empowerment of Women." *The Annals of the American Academy* 554: 150–73.
Fraser, Nancy (1997) *Justice Interruptus: Critical Reflections on the "Postsocialist" Condition*. New York: Routledge.
Goetz, Anne Marie (1997) "Introduction: Getting Institutions Right for Women in Development" in Goetz, A. M. (ed.) *Getting Institutions Right for Women in Development*. London: Zed Books, pp. 1–28.
Goetz, Anne M. and Rina Sen Gupta (1996) "Who Takes the Credit? Gender, Power and Control over Loan Use in Rural Credit Programmes in Bangladesh." *World Development* 24 (1): 45–63.
Hashemi, Syed M. (1996) "Sidney Ruth Schuler and Ann P. Riley. Rural Credit Programs and Women's Empowerment in Bangladesh." *World Development* 24 (4): 635–53.
Hulme, David and Paul Mosley (1997) "Finance for the Poor or the Poorest? Financial Innovation, Poverty and Vulnerability" in Wood, G. and Sharif, I. (eds) *Who Needs Credit: Poverty and Finance in Bangladesh*. London: Zed Books, pp. 97–129.
Kabeer, Naila (1998) *Money Can't Buy Me Love? Re-evaluating Gender, Credit and Empowerment in Rural Bangladesh*. IDS Discussion Paper 363, Sussex University, Brighton: IDS.
Kwiatkowski, Lynn M. (1998) *Struggling with Development: The Politics of Hunger and Gender in the Philippines*. Boulder, CO: Westview Press.

Mayoux, Linda (1998) *Women's Empowerment and Microfinance Programmes*. Discussion Paper, The Open University, Milton Keynes, London, UK: Small Enterprise Development.

Milgram, B. Lynne (1998) *(Re)Formulating Microfinance: Early Observations on the CECAP 11 Rural Finance System: A Report*. Banaue, Ifugao, PH: CECAP.

—— (2001a) "Situating Handicraft Market Women in Ifugao, Upland Philippines: A Case for Multiplicity." in Seligmann, L. J. (ed.) *Women Traders in Cross-Cultural Perspective: Mediating Identities, Marketing Wares*. Stanford, CA: Stanford University Press, pp. 129–59.

—— (2001b) "Operationalizing Microfinance: Women and Craftwork in Ifugao, Upland Philippines." *Human Organization* 60 (3): 212–24.

—— (2002) "Reorganizing Textile Production for the Global Market: Women's Craft Cooperatives in Ifugao, Upland Philippines" in Grimes, K. and Milgram, B. L. (eds) *Artisans and Cooperatives: Developing Alternative Trade for the Global Economy*. Tuscon, AZ: University of Arizona Press, pp. 107–27.

Miron, Sharon Gail (1997) "Empowering Women through Development: The Perspectives of Filipino Women in a Rural Non-Government Program." MA Thesis, University of Alberta, Edmonton, AB.

Murdoch, Jonathan (2000) "The Microfinance Schism." *World Development* 28 (4): 617–29.

Rahman, Aminur (1999) *Women and Microcredit in Rural Bangladesh: An Anthropological Study of Grameen Bank Lending*. Boulder, CO: Westview Press.

Rankin, Katharine N. (2001) "Governing Development: Neoliberalism, Microcredit, and Rational Economic Woman." *Economy and Society* 30 (1): 18–37.

Wood, Geoffrey D. and Iffath A. Sharif (1997) "Introduction" in Wood, G. and Sharif, I. (eds) *Who Needs Credit: Poverty and Finance in Bangladesh*. London: Zed Books, pp. 27–58.

Wright, Graham A. N. (2000) *Microfinance Systems: Designing Quality Financial Services for the Poor*. London and Dhaka: Zed Books and The University Press Limited, Dhaka.

Yunus, Mohammad (1994) *Banking on the Poor*. Dhaka: Grameen Bank.

9 Microcredit and empowerment
Visibility without power[1]

Jude L. Fernando

The origins of microcredit practices in Bangladesh date back to before the British colonial period. Since then, numerous governmental and non-governmental organizations (NGOs) have implemented many different types of microcredit programs in their respective development efforts. The resurgence of microcredit during the 1990s was the result of framing the development discourse vis-à-vis the empowerment of women in the light of the convergence of a number of factors. These convergent elements include decades of development failures, the mainstreaming of gender in development, shifts in mainstream economists' thinking about the role of the informal sector and the poor, the specificity of the accumulation and legitimization crises of capitalism since the end of the Cold War, neoliberal restructuring of the of the state, the emergence of NGOs as influential actors in development,[2] and finally, the emergence of a worldwide consensus that the goals of development are best achieved within the confines of neoliberal capitalism, rather than alternatives to it. Given these conditions, both the reproduction of development and of capitalism, was predicated on their ability to secure more effective and aggressive modes of intervention and representation, and to legitimate their respective agendas. The uniqueness of the post-Cold War microcredit regime lies in the ways in which these overlapping trends converged around microcredit and made it meaningful to groups with diverse interests.

This chapter, drawing from the two studies in Bangladesh, explores how the convergence of these factors shaped the discourse on microcredit-based empowerment of women as a new orthodoxy in development. It delineates the consequences of this orthodoxy for the empowerment of women, the social transformative potential of NGOs and state formation, and the trajectory of social change under the conditions of neoliberal capitalism. It also provides a critical analysis of what I call an *impasse* in current gender and development debates, i.e. how the reproduction of gender inequalities occurs through the appropriation of the language and practices utilized to eliminate them, and in the process, legitimizes the institutions that the projects of empowerment seek to transform. Finally, I will reflect on possible ways out of this *impasse*.

Framing the discourse

Empowerment is an evolving process. The current positioning of microcredit in the discourse of empowerment points to a crucial turning point in feminists' thinking about the interplay between gender and development. This section explores how feminist thinking about gender in development has historically shaped the discourse on empowerment, and therein, the role of microcredit. While exploring answers to these questions, this section analyzes the convergences of multiple constituencies such as feminists, the state, NGOs, and international donors, and reveals how they have shaped the current popularity of microcredit as a tool of empowerment.

In the early 1970s, advocates of Women in Development (WID) pointed out that the inequalities between men and women across societies and cultures were a result of "irrational prejudices" in development planning by culturally biased sex stereotypes.[3] For Ester Boserup, the marginal status accorded to women in development was a "costly mistake that the planners could no longer afford to neglect."[4] Her study was instrumental in drawing women into mainstream development and changing their status from being mere welfare recipients into becoming active participants in development. WID's success in this regard also provoked complex theoretical debates on household models that were predominantly used in economic analysis. In the early 1980s, the dominant model was the new home economics model: households were considered homogeneous decision-making units within which the members had joint utility functions.[5] Later models emphasized that household members have clearly identifiable different production systems, each one with a high degree of autonomy vis-à-vis allocation and consumption of resources. According to these models, household relationships were struggles between members trying to maximize their benefits through bargaining, contracting, and negotiation.[6]

However, these changes did not point to significant departures from the basic assumptions of neoclassical economics. First, WID's emphasis on "disembodied rationality" within households retained the methodological individualism of neoclassical economics by treating men and women as equals in the production sphere. It emphasized that women, too, are rational human beings and pointed out that the realization of their full potential in the economy, is thwarted by a lack of opportunity because of their constricting socializing process. Second, WID did not abandon the market system as the mechanism for the allocation and distribution of resources. However, critics of WID point out that the inclusion of women into the mainstream on the mere grounds of efficiency implies that "the issue was not so much that women needed development, but development needed women."[7]

By the 1980s, a large body of literature indicated that programs specially targeted towards women did more harm than good: they lacked relevance to the needs of women, and were insensitive to the specific issues faced by women, and consequently perpetuated culturally conditioned forms of subordination.[8] Feminists' disenchantment with the basic ideological underpinnings of WID, particularly with liberal theories of economy and society, further buttressed these criticisms.[9] On the one hand, the assumption of equality between men and women in the sphere of production based on individual rationality obscured the impact of women's reproductive activities on their "agency, choice, and rationality."[10] Simultaneously, however, WID ignored systemic relationships between social, economic, and political inequalities based on sex, class, and other factors, and the social process generated by the development process itself, by locating the policies to achieve equality between the sexes in the mainstream development process.[11] Furthermore, WID's exclusion of gender politics legitimized the hegemonic status of mainstream development as "a universally valid and non-ideological agenda."[12]

Among the approaches developed to overcome the limitations of WID, the Social Relations Framework (SRF) focused on the ways in which differences in "social relations of everyday life" impinged upon the structuring of social, economic, and political status between men and women.[13] These asymmetries are institutional arrangements, which typically place men in a privileged position by providing them with greater bargaining power to mobilize material and institutional resources in order to promote and defend their own interests. Men downplay the idea that gender inequities exist and make conscious efforts to thwart attempts to address such inequities. Given that these inequalities are socially constructed through the mediation of religious, cultural, and biological norms that are widely shared by the society at large, women and men subscribe to prevailing gender disparities as "biologically given or economically rational."[14]

Moreover, the interconnectedness of gender, class, ethnicity, and nationality has placed women in a complex position from which it is difficult to articulate their specific interests. These interests may not be as evident to women or to "sympathetic" policy makers as "needs emerging out of existing daily routines and responsibilities might be."[15] A way out of these dilemmas was the division of women's interests as "practical" and "strategic."[16] For example, an increase in income is considered a practical interest, which is a prerequisite for increasing their opportunities to participate in the public sphere.

Empowerment is a process and consequently that process which creates an institutional environment that enables women to take

> Control over material assets, intellectual resources, and ideology. The material assets over which control can be exercised may be physical, human, or financial, such as land water, forests, people's bodies and labor, money, and access to money. Intellectual resources include

knowledge, information, and ideas. Control over ideology signifies the ability to generate, propagate, sustain, and institutionalize specific sets of beliefs, values, and attitudes and behavior – virtually determining how people perceive and function within a given socio-economic and political environment. Empowerment begins not only by recognizing the systemic forces that oppress them, but act to change existing power relationships. This requires a recognition and awareness of these forces that perpetuate women's subordinate position should be followed by a reversal of values, attitudes, indeed, their entire worldview.[17]

According to Naila Kabeer, the demand for empowerment, however, does not "usually emerge spontaneously from the conditions of subjugation due to the women's lack of awareness."[18] Rather, "empowerment must be externally induced, by forces working with altered consciousness and awareness that the existing social order is unjust and unnatural."[19] As Kabeer suggests, "[c]onscientization is an initial step in the struggle through which women define their capacity to define and analyze their subordination, to construct a vision of the kind of world they want, and to act in pursuit of that vision."[20] Paulo Freire, while elaborating the importance of the "conscientization" approach, argued that the "oppressed suffer from a duality which has established itself in their innermost being. They discover that without freedom they cannot exist authentically. Yet, although they desire authentic existence, they fear it. They are at the same time themselves the oppressed whose consciousness they have internalized."[21] Their "vision of a new man is individualistic; because of their identification with the oppressor, they have no consciousness of themselves or as members of an oppressed class."[22] Conscientization is a form of education that strives to develop critical consciousness about themselves and the conditions that oppress them and to create a new form of social solidarity where people are free from the "existential duality of the oppressed, who are at the same time they and the oppressor whose image they have internalized."[23] It enables the oppressed groups to come to the realization that liberation is possible, when "the oppressor–oppressed contradiction is superseded by the humanization of all men."[24]

Freire's pedagogy was particularly influential among those who were disenchanted with the capitalist and radical socialist projects of social change because it promised a middle path. Within a short span of time, numerous development strategies, inspired by Freire, gained recognition from those international aid agencies also disenchanted with the mainstream approaches to poverty alleviation. The ways in which Freire's pedagogy were incorporated into the NGO ideology did not appear to present any significant opposition to the restructuring of the state under neoliberal economic reforms. Nor was Freire clear about the nature of the political economy that ought to result from conscientization programs. It promised a process for a better world, without specifying what it was. But the NGOs did recognize that, although necessary, creating awareness through education is not a sufficient condition for social change. In situations of abject poverty, the oppressed are unlikely to be attracted to such programs because women's economic vulnerability is at the center of powerlessness. Often, institutions that fulfill women's economic needs (i.e. practical) are among those that require reformation in order to realize larger goals of empowerment (i.e. strategic interests). Women are unlikely to be motivated to break away from existing institutional arrangements in situations of abject poverty and powerlessness; this is particularly the case at times when the opportunities for women to participate in activities in the public sphere are constrained by cultural and religions institutions.

Microcredit is a strategic means of initiating social change in situations where women's participation in the public sphere is constrained by the institutional environment within which they live. The argument was that microenterprises created a flexible space for women to interact as a group, initiate educational programs, and mobilize to achieve other dimensions of social change. The advocates of empowerment endorsed these claims as they thought microcredit was a practical means towards achieving women's strategic needs. Within a short span of time, microenterprises became a central component of the majority of the NGOs involved in programs directed toward the improvement of the social status of women. Even those NGOs that were at one time ideologically opposed to credit have made significant compromises. Indeed, it is difficult to find an NGO that does not have credit as a main component of its overall programs.

Sayed Hashmi, a proponent of the Grameen Bank approach, characterized this transition to credit as evidence of the demise of the conventional conscientization paradigm. Martha Chen, in *A Quiet Revolution: Women in Transition in Rural Bangladesh*, illustrates this form of economic determinism as follows:

> We believe that village women's control over and access to material resources is a necessary condition to women's exercise of social power and autonomy. If [women's] productivity can be enhanced or [their] employment expanded, women will automatically exercise greater power and autonomy within their households.[25]

Such economic reductionism, however, positioned microcredit comfortably within the ideological and institutional parameters of the evolving neoliberal economy.

Microcredit became popular during a time in which the developing countries were rapidly implementing neoliberal economic reforms, known as structural adjustments and stabilization policies. The proponents of these economic policies acknowledged that the social and economic costs of structural adjustments are disproportionately born by the poor.[26] For example, a World Bank study noted that structural adjustments might affect the poor in two different ways: "In the long run such policies reduce the real income and consumption of poverty groups [...] even in the long run some poverty groups may not benefit from the processes set in motion by the adjustment efforts."[27] Ignoring the needs of these impoverished masses presents a serious impediment to economic reforms, particularly in situations where the politicization of poverty leads to political instability. However, for the World Bank and the International Monetary Fund (IMF) these are a "symptom of a crisis, for which structural adjustments were the only cure."[28] Microcredit could create an enabling for the poor to benefit from the new economic reforms, which was epitomized by the World Bank's notion of "Development with a Human Face."[29]

These trends led international development agencies to search for new approaches to poverty alleviation that were politically and economically manageable, and conducive to the smooth implementation of economic reforms. In other words, these agencies were interested in a type of political economic regime(s) that embraced the imperatives of political pluralism (democratic politics) and liberal economic reforms. It is in this context that microcredit appeared to be a "win–win" option, promising to advance the liberal ideology of private entrepreneurial capitalism, and social mobilizations based on multiple social identities. These developments were also aided by a reappraisal of the first generation neoclassical models of credit.[30]

The school of thought that emerged in response to this debate, known as the Economics of Rural Organization,[31] pointed out two fundamental reasons for the failures of past credit programs. First, conventional approaches to credit are unlikely to overcome issues associated with information asymmetries, screening, enforcement, and high transaction costs involved in credit programs where markets are underdeveloped.[32] Second, it is impossible for external institutions to overcome a moneylender's capacity to manipulate the social, economic, and cultural network much more efficiently than external lending institutions. As an alternative, this school of thought emphasized the advantages of using cultural norms, values, shared meanings, and cognitive structures in enhancing the efficiency of credit programs. As Guasch and Braverman note, credit cooperatives that were initiated as small-scale local organizations, were successful as financial intermediaries because of their emphasis on "institutional and human development with some form of joint liability or control over members' assets."[33]

During this period, development policies under the influence of neo-institutionalism and the corresponding new political economy emphasized the need for appropriate institutional prerequisites to achieve successful outcomes from economic reforms.[34] In other words, underdevelopment was viewed as an institutional problem. Consequently, the emphasis of development shifted towards overcoming the limitations of the state and informal sector organizations in development. The emphasis on institutions was buttressed by changes in the mainstream economists' attitudes towards the role of the informal sector in development. This was in response to the expansion of the informal sector due to the dismantling of state investment in social welfare and development, structural adjustments and stabilization policies, massive rural–urban migrations, and most importantly, a decline in overall living standards. The way out was not to expand the labor absorptive capacity of the formal sector, but to improve the "legality, security, and financing of the formal sector."[35]

The informal sector in mainstream development circles is now, no longer considered a temporary condition – it is unlikely to disappear from the economy. It is, in fact, a structural outcome of neoliberal economic policies. The very survival of the formal sector now hinges on the market's friendly activities towards the informal sector. The latter is important for the former in a number of respects. Under neoliberal economic reforms, the informal sector absorbs the cost of adjustments, provides cheap labor, subsidizes the low wages paid by industry, and provides subcontracting services to the formal sector. At the same time, politically destabilizing distributional struggles are mostly located in the informal sector, given that the majority of the poor live in it.[36]

In this scenario, NGOs emerged as the most favored institutions due to their claim to have a comparative advantage vis-à-vis the state. NGOs typically operate on a small scale, with flexible approaches, and have proven they can successfully overcome the problems faced by conventional approaches to credit by using existing traditions, indigenous knowledge, and social networks. The social contexts of marginalized groups are diverse and require flexible institutions to respond to their problems. State programs have failed because of their top-down and bureaucratic nature of planning and implementation. Proponents of transformative approaches to empowerment argued, "grassroots, non-governmental organizations tend to be less rule governed and their face-to-face interactions with their constituencies have given them a greater advantage in [...] promoting innovative strategies and less scope for sidestepping the issue of subordination."[37]

During the Cold War period, the state was the most important institution in development, whereas now, it is viewed as a hindrance to it. Criticism of the state came from all directions of society, and changes in its role in development were urgently needed. Under the conditions of globalization, this has proved to be an extremely difficult task, as its worldwide expansion continues to be spatially uneven, with diverse institutional/political expressions in various state formations. Yet, abandoning the state altogether, was not a feasible proposition. Rather, it required transformation, because in the final analysis, it bears the responsibility of managing the accumulation and legitimization crises of capitalist development.

Post Cold War capitalism has been far more aggressive in terms of its search for new markets to secure cheap labor, natural resources, and consumers. Inevitably, one of its main targets was the Cold War discourse of development given that the majority of the world population experiences capitalism in the language and practices of development. However, development historically has demonstrated tendencies to converge and deviate from capitalist interests and even to become a counter-hegemonic force against capitalist interests. Development could not be abandoned; it needed to be reconfigured in the light of new challenges. On the one hand, development should continue to should hold its promises to improve the standards of living of the poor in ways not threatening to the reproductive needs of capital. On the other hand, development should accommodate the new demands of diverse interests groups e.g. environmentalist, feminist, culturalist, post-modernist, post-structuralist etc. It was in the interest of capital to ensure these social movements would not emerge as a counter hegemonic force. Development needed a "facelift" with new language, modes of representation and policy interventions so that it would be an effective instrument in dealing with the accumulation and legitimization crisis of capital. Historically, development far from being a simply Western imposition on the Third World has contained multiple voices and has shown the potential to threaten the expansion of capitalist development.

At this conjuncture microcredit promised to be a win–win potion for development and capital. They both embraced the importance of women in the respective agendas. The ways in which leading feminists articulated the claims about empowerment through microcredit showed promising potential to respond to multiple demands of the development, without threatening the interests, of capital. It is empowerment, not revolution based on class interests. It is about addressing the gender equality via empowering the agency of women. The shift from WID to Gender and Development (GAD) did not challenge the capitalist interests, because the mainstream GAD advocates' emphasis of power relations did not challenge how they are structured within the capitalist economy.

Initially, some NGOs on ideological grounds rejected microcredit as a means of empowerment. Particularly, they wanted to maintain a distance from the large-scale commercial banks, international donors, and the private sector in general, as such collaborations were perceived to undermine the autonomy and social transformative capacities of the NGOs. Within a short period of time, however, ideological tensions subsided; claims by the pro-microcredit NGOs became more acceptable to international donors – as opposed to those NGOs that believed in land reform, education, healthcare and building social movements as prerequisite for empowerment. The proponents argued that "Increased income earned by a low-income mother translates into a chain of positive improvements for her family. This chain starts with her capacity to purchase more food. A better diet and improved nutrition stimulate better family health. Improved health results in greater resistance to disease, higher energy, greater capacity for work and learning and thus enhanced productivity. As family nutrition and health are stabilized, incremental investments in the education of children are almost certain to follow. Close behind education expenditures comes investments in home improvements. And finally, these outcomes are paralleled by a near-total transformation of the borrower's self-respect."[38]

In response, many NGOs converted their "rural development programs" to "rural credit programs," and some of them began to function like a bank. The values, ethics, ideological orientation, and internal management structures of the NGO sector saw radical changes as the rapid success of microcredit programs became the key indicator that measured their successes and survival. Analysis of the links between high rates of loan repayment by women and their empowerment became a new field of social inquiry and research.

Concepts, methods, (mis)representations and issues

Income is the most critical and most simple variable used in measuring the impact of microenterprises. Despite this usefulness, income is extremely difficult to measure accurately, and there are numerous problems in explaining the relationship between income and empowerment. Households derive income from multiple sources, including both marketed and non-marketed goods and services. Microenterprises are one of the sources of income: the costs and income pertaining to them are mixed with other sources of income and expenditures. It is extremely difficult to collect data on all the production and consumption activities of a household and then isolate the costs and incomes associated with the given microenterprise as separate from other activities.[39]

The term "household" does not necessarily mean homogeneous units in terms of distribution of economic and social power between its members. Men and women undertake a wide range of income generation activities and it is difficult to separate the costs and incomes incurred by them individually.[40] Income of a household at a given moment in time often is not accurate to regular (e.g. expected seasonal changes) and irregular factors influencing income (e.g. unexpected natural disasters, changes in income) over time. In most cases, households do not maintain written records. Recall data from direct interviews is often subject to distortions and inaccuracies resulting from sampling, measurement, and response errors.[41] The respondents far from being naive are sensitive to the value of information they provide.[42]

As a way of addressing these limitations, some studies have used alternative indicators such as expenditure and consumption. First, the total assets of a household can be used as a proxy based on the assumption that they are purchased from income. Apart from the difficulty of measuring the short- and long-term changes in the stock of assets, it is difficult to assign monetary values to assets and make linkages between them and the income derived from microenterprises.[43] Second, households can be ranked according to wealth. An index of wealth can be prepared on the basis of selected assets based on the assumption that income determines the amount of assets. Therefore, households with higher income will own more assets than those with lower incomes.[44] A major difficulty with formulating this relationship is that assets change more gradually compared to variations in income and changes in income do not lead directly to corresponding changes in assets. Third, those who believe that household expenditure can be used as an alternative measure for income argue that it provides a more accurate picture, and especially that it is less subject to seasonal changes, less sensitive a topic, and hence likely to be more accurately reported.[45] However, it is difficult to attribute changes in expenditure directly to changes in overall income of the household or from a given microenterprise. Increases in income can come from dissavings and negatively impact on household welfare. Also, increases in income can come from the fact that there are fewer propensities for relative changes in consumption compared to changes in income; consumption is not an accurate proxy for variations in income.[46] The main difficulty with proxy variables is that they do not measure the same phenomena as income because "relationship between proxy variable and the income," and income and family welfare is complex.[47]

The outcomes of microenterprises involve a multiplicity of social actors and networks, partly because NGOs do not provide all services necessary for microenterprises. These actors and networks have associated with the people for a longer period than the NGOs, and are deeply rooted in the social and cultural life of the communities. They therefore have a greater influence on people's lives. The dilemma faced by the NGOs is that on the one hand, the success of NGO programs in microcredit to enroll women and to maintain high rates of repayments are attributed to their ability to utilize local traditions, values, and institutions. On the other hand, empowerment means transformation of some of these institutions that are considered oppressive to women and creating alternative ones. Successful outcomes of the microenterprises may be mainly a result of the very "oppressive" institutions that the NGOs desire to transform. Similarly, income and repayments of loans do not necessarily explain the reasons behind the role of institutions that are not directly associated with a given NGO project. For example, a reason for increased school attendance of female children of families with high rates of loan repayment may be due to increased availability of government subsidies, rather than the assistance provided by the NGOs. Therefore, the loan repayment rates and earned-income neither explain the nature of institutional changes resulting from the NGO investments in microcredit projects, nor allows us to identify the specific contribution made by the NGOs as opposed to other institutions that assist them in these projects. Then the fundamental issue of evaluating the impact of NGO programs is to separate the impact of NGOs from that of other institutions that are directly and indirectly involved in a given project, given the fact that a multiplicity of institutions e.g. donors, local government, informal organizations etc., interactively shape the outcomes of NGO programs.

Another limitation of current methods is the difficulty in explaining the differential impact of credit on men and women. Pitt and Khandeker's study departs from earlier notions of a homogeneous household with unified preferences to heterogeneous and divergent preferences, among households.[48] The study argues that credit has actually contributed to the empowerment of women by increasing their contribution to household consumption expenditure, the hours devoted to the production for the market and the value of their assets, and consumption. However, Pitt and Khandeker do not make it clear how these changes lead to empowerment because their notion of a gender-differentiated household model has ignored the intra-household power relations; power is treated as an "ephemeral variable." The study does not take into account a great number of aspects, such as contextual variations in socio-economic and demographic backgrounds, the size of farmland, per-capita income, the number of living children, age, ownership of assets, etc. This is a result of Pitt and Khandeker basing their analysis on non-unified and differentiated utility functions that do not take account of the fact that power differentials between men and women are shaped by factors that are not necessarily responsive to change in income.[49]

These studies although concerned with the link between empowerment and income earned from microenterprises and loan repayment rates, do not make a distinction between ownership and control aspects of microenterprises; therefore, such indicators are of limited use in explaining the institutional and power relations in microenterprises. By substituting "control" as a proxy of "power," Ann Marie Goetz and Sen Gupta have examined the "degree to which women actually control loans once they have gained access to credit institutions."[50] They revealed that a significant portion of credit given to women was actually controlled by men, thereby challenging the claims made about empowerment based on repayment of loans. However, this study does not make clear how and under what conditions one can separate the control of income by men and women. It seems this separation is based on a problematic a priori assumption of the possibility that women act independently of men in utilization of credit and income. This is possible only if it is assumed that within the context of the South Asian family and society such institutional separation is "feasible" and that women are "passive and voiceless subjects." In other words, Goetz and Sen Gupta ignored the possibility of women exercising agency and the complex ways that women subvert forces oppressive to them without having direct control over the income of the household. The reason for such limitations is that their analyses are not grounded in systematic theorizing of the function of patriarchy in relation to relationships between the welfare state and the family and how they are influenced by microcredit, because the family unit is the primary means through which the private domains of women are brought into the public domain.[51]

Goetz and Sen Gupta also observed "men coming to women's weekly meetings and submitting the loans on behalf of women. This deprives women of the benefits of regular group attendance and social contact."[52] Moreover, loan repayments come from sources other than income from microenterprises, such as reduction in women's consumption level. When women cannot repay, they are forced into a supplicant relationship with their husbands. Goetz and Sen Gupta pointed out evidence where conflicts over loans have led to violence within the family. However, it is unclear how control over income mitigates these adverse impacts or brings the types of institutional changes that empowerment projects desire. The question also needs to be raised as to whether the women perceive that control over income is a necessary factor for their empowerment. It also needs to be clarified whether the meaning attributed to empowerment by the women is similar to what Goetz and Sen Gupta imply.

The link between repayments and increased income due to NGO credit is not clear. There is at least a three-month gestation period between the disbursement of credit and earning income in the majority of the microenterprises. However, borrowers are required to begin loan repayments the week following obtaining the loan. It is doubtful that the microenterprise will begin to yield income from the very first week, unless it is used in ongoing projects and commercial activities. The present studies have not probed into the methods people use to meet their repayment requirements during this period and their consequences on the overall welfare of the family.

The overall impact of credit on women and their families also need to be analyzed in relation to total welfare gains and loses suffered by families due to the neoliberal agricultural reforms by the state. How is it possible for those who borrow from NGOs to maintain such high rates of employment when, during the past decade, neither agricultural productivity, nor income derived from it, show any significant improvements? This situation is further exacerbated by the withdrawal of state subsides from the agricultural sector. Off-farm employment created by microenterprises cannot absorb all the consequently unemployed. Food-aided employment schemes, which accounted for a significant portion of non-agricultural employment, also declined. There has been only a modest improvement in poverty levels, while income inequalities have actually widened. Also economic uncertainties and insecurities continue to increase in response to both agricultural- and non-agriculture-based incomes becoming exposed to vicissitudes of the global economy. How does microcredit impact the ways in which women cope with these externally imposed constraints and maintain high repayment rates?

Recent studies critical of microcredit have focused on how microcredit has led to the reinforcement of patriarchal norms of women's subordination, including violence against them, and led to their disenfranchisement.[53] The arguments are more convincing than the claim about "increase income and time spent in income-generating activities as automatically enhances women's influence over household decision-making."[54] While these studies have provided important insights, their analyses and claims would have been far more convincing if they had taken into account how the use of essentialized notions of gender, public–private dichotomy, and household in current studies frame their research questions, methodologies and outcomes particularly within the context of the imperatives of neoliberal political economy.

According to Kabeer, empowerment may occur at different levels, encompassing different dimensions, materializing through multiple processes involving the realization of preconditions of choice and resources, the exercise of choice or agency, and the uniqueness of choice or achievement that enable women to transform structures of women's subordination.[55] She also correctly points out that most studies do not take into account borrowers' perspectives of empowerment, and the possibility that in certain situations, joint decision making can be more empowering for women than individual decision making.[56] Simeen Mahmud, while elaborating on Kabeer's work by incorporating a definition of empowerment developed by Chen and Mahmud (1995), has shown that empowerment is a process that involves three dimensions: the conditions for empowerment, the route to empowerment, and the achievement of empowerment. While these are analytically useful insights, they are also based on some problematic assumptions, particularly when they were applied to the Bangladeshi context.[57] However, the broadening of the meaning of empowerment has not been accompanied by improvements in concepts and methodologies to evaluate their applications.

Mahmud's analysis is based on the assumption, that "access to the public domain enhances choices for women regardless of whether they use purdah or not."[58] Here she seems to impose a public versus private dichotomy on localities of women involved in microcredit, and uncritically assumes the former is superior to the latter. The histories of social struggles show that the advantages of private and public domains are context-dependent. Often there is correspondence between the two domains. The successes of microcredit are in fact based on complex articulations of relations between the two. What determines their relative merits for empowerment depends on women's control over the ideologies and institutions that shape the power relations in their private and public domain. Perhaps, we need to explore the question as to whether women's entry into public domain through microcredit (and/or articulation of relations between the two domains) undermines the opportunities for their empowerment in their private domain, which is now partly regulated according to the imperatives of microcredit. The questions that need to be posed are: how do the discourse and practices of empowerment through microcredit shape the power relations in public and private domains? What are the consequences of women's participation for their empowerment? Mahmud also makes the rather obvious point that the "socio-economic status of women respondents were more strongly related to household poverty than to participation in a microcredit program."[59] She then argues that the potential for improvement of women's material base by their participation in microcredit is small "because women's access was limited to resources that do not expand women's choice a great deal."[60] However, she fails to explain why it does not happen. The reason for this is that her study does not probe into how the institutional framing of women's entry into, and participation in, the public domain through microcredit, reproduces the structural forces that are oppressive to them. The answer to this question requires an analysis of the incorporation of household production and consumption into the larger political economy in the light of women's involvement in microcredit.

Kabeer's emphasis is on the necessity of analyzing empowerment at different levels and the differences in the meanings of empowerment between researchers, which raises several issues. How can we explain the implications of microcredit with such different impacts on various levels, and the relations between them? Who are the ultimate beneficiaries at each level? Second, women's perceptions of empowerment may be different from that of the researcher or the NGOs providing credit. Such cultural relativism however is not an excuse for employing a notion of empowerment that is alien to the women, as a means of evaluating the impact of credit. The underpinnings of such claims rest on the assumption that there are no shared concerns about empowerment between women in different spatial locations. This latter point might be completely fallacious and might provide traditional notions of empowerment that prove to be an obstacle to the improvement of women's social and economic status. Such cultural relativism, akin to conceptualizations of empowerment by those development theories with post-structural, post-colonial and post-modern sympathies borders on nihilism that might lead to what is known in human rights circles as "the tyranny of traditionalism."[61] Institutions that are oppressive to women may exploit the cognitive and spatial gaps constructed or legitimized by such relativism. The very act of providing microcredit frames brings local and "foreign" notions of empowerment into contact with each other. It is possible that women appropriate and transform to achieve their culturally specific goals of empowerment according to their needs. However, such possibility does not give legitimacy to the kind of relativism that I discussed above. We need to analyze the nature of these the institutional and power relations that shape the trajectories of empowerment both local and "alien," how relations between them are articulated by microcredit, and consequences for lives of poor women.

Current studies do not systematically analyze how the relations between the NGO and the borrowers are shaped in relation to how they are positioned within the larger local and global economies. They simply evaluate microcredit as a relationship between the borrowers and the NGOs. In practice however, borrowing, utilization, and repayment of credit involve the tightly controlled social networks of the community and global political economy. Analyses of these institutional relations are important to identify clearly the ultimate beneficiaries of credit projects are in terms of who controls the decisions regarding borrowing, investment, repayment, and utilization of incomes. Microcredit should be viewed as a social relation that mediates between women borrowers, their household, and the local, national, and international environments that matters to their lives. The challenge is to identify how the discourse of microcredit structure gender relations in these different environments

The two case studies in this chapter analyze the institutional processes, the social, economic, and institutional relationships, that shaped, and resulted in, the final outcomes.[62] It systematically identifies and analyzes the institutional relations in the different phases of the NGO operations. These phases are social histories of NGOs, community's perceptions about NGOs, point of entry, program implementation, program evaluation, and post-evaluation program changes. The reason for such a detailed and systematic analysis is that at each phase NGOs interact with diverse institutional actors, the international donors, the governments, informal institutions in the communities, local government authorities, and other NGOs working in a given area. The information on the impact of some institutions in one phase may not be visible at another phase and in the final outcomes. For example, the way in which outcomes of a given project are shaped by the type of indictors desired by the donors may not be visible in the repayment rates, and the role of the government at initial stages of the project may not be visible in the later stages. Inability to identify these institutional dynamics casts serious doubts over the current claims of NGOs successes and has led to attributing the successes and failures of microcredit programs to the wrong institutions.

By combining actor-oriented research with structuralist political economy, the following case studies analyze how different institutional actors interact in different phases of microcredit, through negotiations, compromise and conflict between them, and the impacts of these interactions on institutional relations within and beyond a given locality. The moments of "interface" during these interactions are used to separate the specific roles and impacts of individual institutional actors in a given phase, and their impact on the final outcomes of the project. From a theoretical point of view, such method of analysis is a hybrid theoretical approach that allows us to overcome the limitations of universal and particularistic narratives of social change or, differently put, to capture the complex interplay between structure and agency without becoming victims of essentializing either of them. It also makes it possible to simultaneously probe into the questions of how instrumentality of microcredit, and therein the agency of women, is framed by larger political and economic environment and the consequences for empowerment of women.

Association for Social Advancement (ASA)[63]

ASA was established in 1979. It is one of the five largest NGOs in Bangladesh to date. The initiative to establish ASA was taken by a group of "like-minded" people led by Shafiqual Chowdhuri. Shafiqual's father was the son of a provincial landowner. Shafiqual began his career as an officer of the Bangladesh Academy for Rural Development (BARD).[64] Initially, Maoist thinking about the issues and organization of peasants influenced Shafiqual and his colleagues.[65] While at BARD, Shafiqual's main interest was in social mobilization for collective action among the landless peasants, which was then known as the "conscientization" approach to social development. Subsequently, he worked as a program director in Manikgonj for the Christian Development Commission of Bangladesh (CCDB), which had a significant impact on the development of Shafiqual's ideas about development. Subsequently, the CCDB sent him for a training course at the Center for Development Studies in Bombay, where he was exposed to more radical ideologies about social change through organizing "peasant activism, and was shown how such ideas might be incorporated into the work of the NGO by setting up peoples' organizations."[66] This was the period in which the liberation theology was having a significant impact on the activities of the Christian NGOs, particularly in the developing countries. Initially, the CCDB gave approval for this type of agenda on an experimental basis in Manikgonj, "but warned him against stirring up conflicts in the village, where he proposed to work."[67]

Eventually, Shafique became critical of the activities of the CCBD. He asked, "How can an NGO promote a pro-poor radical analysis of the village political economy if it is not prepared to support landless people in their consequent struggle against their oppressors?"[68] According to his view, NGO action should lead to "organization of the rural poor and prepare them for conflict with the landowners."[69] However, he failed to convince the CCBD to provide assistance to experiment with his ideas. Eventually, he met an Australian liberation theologian, Harvey Perkins, who during that time was conducting seminars and workshops on the "[c]hurch role as one of leading the poor in their struggle for Liberation from poverty and oppression."[70] Subsequently, Golum Chowdry and Shafiqual, both employees of the CCBD, held discussions with Harvey Perkins in Barisal in order to explore the possibility of starting a separate NGO. Subsequently, ASA was registered formally as an NGO in 1979. The radical approach to social development ASA advocated through mobilization, attracted the Christian donors who were more in favor of the social gospel – a form of theology heavily influenced by Liberation Theology.

During 1985–1987, ASA's main goal was to bring broad-based structural change to society through the mobilization of landless people. Income-generation projects were mainly supported by interest-free loans with an equal emphasis given to participation of both the men and women in them. Moreover, adult education, primary healthcare, legal aid for the landless, and eye-clinic camps comprised a major component of its programs. This radical approach to social change by ASA took a "secret society" atmosphere, where ASA members took a secret oath in the night in committing their lives to the people's movement. Harvey Perkins noted that during this period, ASA *samiti* (local society), "Looked like the early stages of an emergence of a landless peoples' movement" where men and women share a common vision of communal ownership of land. Yet, ASA did not even come close to fulfilling this vision. A spokesperson for Mongol Sheikh *samiti*, one of the ASA *samities* that lasted for almost eight years, noted that, "I had a dream. In that dream, all our members made great strides and became very rich. But we never achieved that victory."[71]

> *We learned in* the *samiti* that the land was meant for the landless poor. Encouraged by ASA, we plowed that land and sowed wheat. But at the harvest time, the rich men hired a gang of roughs and cut our wheat. They also filed a case against us. We fought for two years: we ran out our money ... and most of us paid more out of our own pockets. By that time, ASA was no longer interested in supporting us. Reluctantly, we closed down our *samiti*, our Chairman deceived us, and that caused us a great pain and suffering.[72]

Similar sentiments were expressed by the other ASA samities, particularly after they lost many legal battles involving land ownership. Soon the top leadership of ASA came to realize that their approach to mobilization of poor peasants for radical social change was a misguided one. ASA's present Executive Director and Shafiqual admitted that,

> We realize that may be what we are doing is a wrong thing – not only theoretically wrong, even practically wrong, because people didn't like our advice. When we said to them "Please come and fight with the moneylender or with the landlord" they would say "no." Why? They are helping us in some way at least. But you are not helping [us]. You are giving only a sermon or a lecture. [We gradually realized] that when we talk about systems, about changing society, people do not listen to us, they are not thinking of us [as] their good friend.[73]

Initially, ASA's first governing body consisted of "like-minded" persons who took the night-time pledge at Uttali expressing their commitment for social change through the mobilization of landless people. As ASA was moved away from its original vision toward a more gradual approach to social change, K. Jhangir, one of its popular leaders, wanted a reorientation of ASA samities into a federation that would consist of volunteers, which would give each samiti a high degree of autonomy. He argued that this change was essential if ASA was to maintain the spirit of a true peoples' movement. Sahfique opposed the idea because it was, according to him, an attempt by some samities to grab ASA's assets. Later, Jhangir was dismissed on the grounds of a technical irregularity. Jhangir responded by taking over one of the samities and establishing his own NGO called Mouchak.

Since 1980s, ASA's emphasis on credit increased to the extent that the other social development programs became marginal, and the legal aid program that was established for the assistance for landless people, was abandoned. Shafiqual, defending ASA's shift to credit, noted "[w]e did not understand credit at that time. Rather we criticized the Grameen Bank, all banking activities, and World Bank. We said these people are exploiting us, running the economy."[74] Today, ASA is considered to be one of the "big four" leading NGOs and a success story in the area of microcredit. By the end of 1996, ASA was expected to have 600,000 members in 30,000 samities and disburse US$44.5 million. It had 263 unit officers managing its branches and employed 2,103 field workers. Two hundred and forty ASA samities reported a loan recovery rate of 98 percent.

Stuart Rutherford, a member of the ASA's board of governors, noted, "[m]any people still have difficulty in coming to terms with the fact that ASA is now largely a quasi-bank. To put it simply, people are embarrassed. Lending money to poor women at high rates of interests, and sometimes having to put a good deal of pressure on them to repay doesn't always make you feel good."[75] There were indeed serious differences between the ASA and the donors at the 1994 donor consortium meeting. Donors proposed the idea of establishing a bank, specifically in order to deal with the increasing volume of loans. ASA rejected the idea, as it would tarnish the organization's image as a development organization and, as a result, may not be in a position to concentrate on its social programs. Donors preferred the consolidation of ASA's credit programs, rather than expansion. According to ASA "Development = economic change," but the donor consortium preferred "Development = social change."[76]

Meanwhile, ASA has become one of the major borrowers from the Polli Karma Sahayek Foundation (PKSF); a semi-government agency established to provide financial resources for NGOs involved in microcredit. In addition, ASA also borrows from commercial banks at commercial rates of interest. However, the increasing collaboration between the government and ASA and handling of credit programs by ASA were not accepted favorably by the donors. Some donors who were apprehensive about emphasis on microcredit at the expense of education, advocacy, and structural reforms argued that,

> It seems that ASA has become an extension of the government and that it runs a parallel agenda rather than empowering the poor according to the definition of the consortium members: In view of the consortium members, the empowerment of the beneficiaries through sustainability of the groups and their control over resources is a vital criterion.[77]

Consequently, traditional Christian donors who shared ASA's radical philosophy reduced their funding to ASA. Furthermore, the donor consortium of ASA suggested that ASA should separate education from credit, as it was seen that the education program had suffered as a result of the organizations' emphasis on credit. ASA, while agreeing that there was a need to improve the education aspect of its programs, pointed out that education could only work if it was combined with credit facilities; and ASA preferred this combination as it "[d]oes not want to be a just a bank, but a development organization."[78] ASA has postponed is radical goals of empowerment, until its clientele and the organization become self-sufficient. According to Stuart Rutherford, credit may prove to be ASA's strength, "[o]f the big four, ASA is likely to be the first to accept that rural banking and political mobilization are two different things – and decide to concentrate on the former."[79]

The Grameen Bank

The Grameen Bank originated as an alliance between the Bangladeshi government, banks and two economists at the Chittagong University in Bangladesh. In 1976, Dr H. I. Latif and Muhammad Yunus, who were faculty members of the Department of Economics at Chittagong University, Bangladesh, convinced a local bank to lend to small-scale farmers on an experimental basis. According to Bishwapriya Sanyal, the bank agreed to provide the capital, "Not because he [Yunus] was leading a grass-root based effort, but his family had a long-standing relationship with the bank where, at the time, his father kept a fairly large amount of money on deposit."[80] The bank lent the money on the condition that borrowers would borrow at commercial rates of interest. But the founders of the Grameen Bank were interested in making loans available to those who could not provide conventional types of collateral, which constituted the majority of the Bangladeshi population. Ideologically, Yunus is critical of the Capitalism. He argues capitalism is about making rich richer. The essence of capitalism is expressed in two of its basic features: a) profit maximization and b) market competition. In their abstract formulations none of them was supposed to have anything conspiratorial against the poor. But in real life they turn out to be the "killers" of the poor by making rich the richer and poor the poorer. [In this] capitalist world we have installed a greedy (almost blood thirsty) person to play the role of profit-maximizer. Not only we have deprived him of all human qualities, we have empowered him by giving him all the institutional support he can use depriving the same support to everybody else.[81]

Yunus offers an alternative vision to the capitalist world where, "instead of one motivating factor (greed) to keep it in motion, we can introduce social consciousness or social dreams as another motivating factor. Both types of people can be in the same market place, using the same tool and concepts of capitalism, but pursuing completely different goals."[82] In Yunus' world of humanized capitalism, "the role of social-consciousness-driven entrepreneurs in the new configuration of the capitalist world is assigned to the state in a socialist framework."[83] He effectively marginalizes the state, and humanizes the capitalism: "The state did not do a good job in this role. Can capitalist concepts, tools and framework allow, support and promote economic activities parallel with narrow personal objectives? My answer is emphatic 'yes.'"[84]

Yunus' articulation of capitalism with its pro-poor sympathies made a significant contribution to the re-structuring of the post Cold War economy in Bangladesh and other developing countries. His attempts to humanize capitalism through microcredit provided ideological justification for the withdrawal of the state from the economic activity, on the one hand: on the other hand, Yunus' criticism of the traditional NGO activity provided the ideological justification for channeling aid for more market-oriented activities as they promised more self-reliance. As Yunus noted, "Charities and handouts help maintain and deepen poverty. These do not give equal chances to the poor. Handouts take away the initiative from people, Human being thrive on challenges not on palliatives."[85] Grameen's style capitalism gained even more credibility when it became the key policy instrument of addressing gender inequality.

By the early to mid-1990s, the Grameen Bank had established itself as the leading NGO in Bangladesh. To date, it has a clientele of over two million and approximately 95 percent of them are women spread over 34,000 villages.[86] By October 1993, donors had disbursed US$85.92 million to Grameen, which makes it the highest recipient of international aid. In 1989, donor disbursements accounted for only 10 percent of its budget. By 1992 and 1993, it had accelerated to 92 percent and 160 percent respectively.[87] Grameen's successes in lending forced many NGOs to shift their emphasis from conscientization and social mobilization to microlending. Sayed Hashemi, of Grameen Bank, characterized this shift as the "demise of conscientization paradigm."[88]

During the formative period, the relationship between Grameen and the international community was tenuous. Muhammad Yunus, at the International Conference on Action to Reduce Global Hunger, organized by the World Bank, criticized the Bank for "causing misery and pain for people, and to nations." The World Bank on a number of occasions tried to incorporate Grameen as one of its partner agencies. At times, it went so far as to ask the government of Bangladesh (GOB) to pressure the Grameen to accept World Bank funds. One of the reasons for this was that, "Every so often, a [the World] Bank-funded project that failed received unfavorable media attention, and the project, or the World Bank itself, was compared unfavorably with Grameen. To many people at the World Bank, Grameen represented an increasingly well-known success story in which the Bank had no role."[89] After a period of resisting calls for collaborating with the World Bank, in 1995 the Grameen became a member of the Consultative Group to Assist the Poorest (CGAP), a multilateral donor program established by the Bank to increase microfinance allocated to the poor. Yunus was also elected as the Chair of the Policy Advisory Group (PAG), which is an advisory body without power for decision making. Subsequently, Grameen played a leading role in the Microcredit Summit, held in Washington DC, in February 1997, and Yunus was also a one of the keynote speakers at the International Women's Conference held in Beijing, China.

The analysis

Different social actors that are directly and indirectly associated with the microcredit programs share different views about the final objectives of microcredit programs. For the international donors and the high ranking NGO officials, the final goal of microcredit programs is to empower women through changes in institutions and power relations. They explain empowerment in a language similar to mainstream discourse on gender and development debate, and the discourse on empowerment that is dominant in academic and policy circles.

During interviews, terms such as "empowerment" and "institutional change" were never used by the Field officers (FOs). What is even more surprising is that even though over 90 percent of the beneficiaries of credit are women, FOs rarely mentioned women as their main target, but the family and the community. Their main concern was the technical and economic efficiency of credit programs. The communications between the FOs and their higher ranking officers are mainly on the quantitative aspects of credit programs. Given the complexity of issues involved in repayments, there is no time to discuss the social impacts of credit. With the increasing emphasis on the professionalization of NGOs along the lines of commercial banks and financial self-sufficiency, FOs are mainly trained to be efficient credit managers of credit programs. Once a program is in place, they have hardly any time left other than to ensure loans are repaid on time, as their employment security is purely based on performance.

The relationship between the NGOs, local institutions, and women who directly benefit from NGO programs is nothing more than a straightforward relationship between debtors and creditors. For the people in Madhupur, Bangladesh, NGOs are one among many institutions in the area and they are "outsiders" that bring in foreign money to help the "poor." When women were questioned about their reasons for participating in credit programs, they pointed out that it enabled them get some additional money for the family. Women, who have been in the credit programs for nearly five years, never referred to the notion of empowerment in any way similar to those shared by the NGOs and their donors. Whenever I discussed empowerment by using the local terminology understood by the women, they pointed out that credit programs are unlikely to change their situation unless they provide large amounts of credit, education for their children, agricultural inputs at cheaper prices, and marketing facilities. These facilities are needed to create new types of employment and help them to redeem their land from the moneylenders. However, they pointed out that these "facilities are not provided by the NGOs, therefore both ASA and Grameen Banks are nothing but moneylenders. In terms of their lending practices NGOs are less sympathetic towards us [women] than the local moneylenders."[90] But the general consensus in the village was that redemption of land from the moneylenders, agricultural subsidies and better schools and hospitals are crucial for them to improve their standard of living.

There is no systematic and collaborative participation of (FOs and) target groups in planning, implementation, and evaluation of credit programs. These procedures are decided through the negotiations between the international donors and the top-level management of the NGOs; and they are standardized and applied on a national scale. In the final analysis, NGOs are primarily accountable to the international donors. The villagers are told that their non-compliance with the stipulations of the NGOs will result in donors withdrawing their financial assistance. In the 1990s, the main themes in these NGO–donor consortia were raising professional standards (e.g. accountability and transparency) and financial self-sufficiency, and their direct emphasis on educational and social development programs has progressively declined.

Several factors have contributed to the increased pressure on NGOs by international donors to make a compromise between the financial self-sufficiency of the individual institutions and other social development goals. First, there are difficulties in measuring the outcomes of NGO interventions that cannot be quantified, which makes the accountability and transparency of NGO activities a difficult task, particularly in the light of the attempts to harmonize the practice of the NGOs with other market institutions. Second, NGOs have not been successful in fulfilling reporting requirements set by the donors, which has made it difficult to evaluate their targets and achievements. A project evaluation report of the Grameen Bank (GB) in 1994 noted that, "GB has failed to predict loan growth accurately and [it] did not use the annual budgets to control the lending program, when the demand for loans, especially new seasonal loans and housing, escalated." Consequently, GB was asked to introduce sophisticated systems of ratio analysis to monitor performance of its 1,000 branches. By following internationally recognized accounting practices GB's performances will stand scrutiny by the international banking and donor community. Such a consideration is important with the international interest in GB replication and GB approach to rural poverty alleviation.[91]

Third, donors became increasingly concerned about the risks to the long-term viability of the organizations resulting from the rapid growth in the number of borrowers and in the amount of internal financing to cover the outstanding debt. The practices of internal financing increased the number of loans taken by the individual borrowers, and some "borrowers with large loans may already borrow elsewhere, or from the GB adjusting their subsequent loans, so that they can pay interests on time." The report further cautioned the Grameen on the long-term sustainability of the program.

With the introduction of new loans, GB has greatly increased opportunities for members to continuously use new loans to repay an existing one, resulting in credit pyramiding. The problem remains concealed until, and if, GB has to introduce credit rationing and borrowers have insufficient funds to cover repayments. Then, if credit pyramiding occurred, defaults cascade and compound through a system that has experienced a rapid growth. The result can be an institutional collapse. There is no way for the mission to find out if such pyramiding is occurring; GB might direct it with more rigorous branch level monitoring.[92]

Consequently, the evaluation reports submitted by FOs are increasingly limited to quantifiable performance of NGOs. Often during my fieldwork, it was puzzling how these quantitative data submitted by FOs are translated into detailed descriptive accounts of NGO performance. For example, in planning and evaluation meetings and in the reports submitted to the international donors by the NGOs, "Islamic fundamentalism" and resilient local power structure are cited as main obstacles to successful implementation of NGO programs. When questioned about the issue of fundamentalism, however, the FOs who actually implemented the programs pointed out that there are a number of female members of the families of *mullas* (religious leaders) involved in NGO programs, and they haven't experienced any instances where religious institutions or practices have obstructed the scope of their programs. FOs pointed out that the scope of their credit programs does not in any way threaten the religious values of the community and, a few conservative religious leaders are happy with the NGOs because provisions of credit prevent women working outside their homes and allows them to take care of the needs of the family."[93]

The credit programs are implemented by the FOs appointed to the research area by their respective central offices. FOs are recruited from outside the area where they work, and they are required to have, at minimum, a college level education. None of the FOs are permanent residents of the area in which they work; generally it is the policy of an NGO to recruit FOs from outside a given locality in order to avoid mismanagement and corruption. Only three out of 12 FOs interviewed were women. The discrepancy of the ratio of men to women does not have much impact on overall programs because all FOs follow the standard approach and function according to the instructions given by their superiors.

The first step taken by FOs, after having been appointed to the area, is to make contacts with "influential" persons in the village, such as the elected persons, traders, landlords, and school teachers. These people are told that the aims of the NGOs are to help the poor and the community by improving their income, education, and health standards. In addition, as a "precautionary measure," FOs inform the leaders of the village that participation of women is an essential precondition for receiving assistance from the NGOs, and it is a condition imposed by the international donors. However, there was no evidence of any protest against credit in the area. In fact, some of the Islamic religious leader's wives were involved in the credit programs.

A noteworthy feature at this phase is the lack of interaction between the local government authorities and the other NGOs working in the area. One local government officer at the *Thana* (local government) office said,

> We have no control over the NGO, because they have support of the higher authorities in the government, and they have established good relations with the local leaders. If we try to interfere with the activities of these NGOs, not only the government, but also the people will be against us. As you probably know that in this country [Bangladesh] Union Chairman [person elected by popular ballot], has more power than the civil servants – and the NGOs collaborate with the Union Chairman, rather than with us. This is the reason why we cannot respond to villagers' numerous complaints regarding malpractice of NGOs such as coercion used for recovery of loans, particularly by means of withholding of savings in the event that there is failure to repay loans by persons concern or by any one of their group members.[94]

Generally, NGOs and their members share similar views about the inefficiency and corruption of the government authorities. However, women members pointed out that the existing government programs benefit the community more than the NGO programs. Most of the women are of the view that they have more opportunities for demanding what they want from the government officers as well as protesting against their actions. Such actions are not possible with the NGOs. Some of the villagers also pointed out that at times the government officers refused to provide any assistance to those who borrow funds from the NGO. In other instances, both the NGOs and the members have sought the mediation of the government offices to settle disputes regarding repayment of loans. Some FOs with the help of government officers threaten potential loan defaulters with law suits, arrests, and withholding of whatever government assistance is available to them. People respond to these threats because they might lead to loss of land and houses if they have to mortgage them in order to raise funds to cover the legal fees or to bribe the policemen or local government officials.

The locations for credit programs are decided by the central officers of the NGOs. The general tendency among the NGOs is to concentrate in the areas where the social and physical infrastructure is relatively developed. As a result, the majority of the NGOs are concentrated in a small geographical area. Surprisingly, during the last four years, NGOs attempts to expand their geographical coverage have failed as they try to coordinate their activities in order to increase the number of people they could assist and reduce their members borrowing from more than one NGO. NGOs and the people in the area attribute this to the competition among the NGOs to maintain high rates of repayments of loans.

After an area is selected, FOs strictly follow the targets set by their superiors as to the number of credit groups to be formed within a given period of time There was no evidence that these targets were based on systematic feasibility studies. FOs complained that the application of uniform criteria and standards were applied to execute and evaluate programs throughout the country without taking into account the diverse problems FOs face at the field-level. The FOs have no option, but to organize the credit programs in order to generate information required by the predetermined indicators used by their head officers to evaluate their programs. They pointed out that their,

> job security depends on running profitable credit programs. We get extra benefits if we achieve these targets. If we don't, we are either transferred or we lose our jobs. The head office set the targets, and we follow them. There is hardly any consultation with us in setting these targets. However, so far we have the flexibility to use whatever means we need to maintain the required rates of return from the credit programs.[95]

From the perspective of the common people, the relationship between them and the NGOs is nothing more than one of lender and borrower. However, in order to safeguard themselves from prevailing criticisms about NGOs, FOs take the initiative in informing the villagers that credit programs are not intended to disrupt Islamic religious practices or convert people to Christianity. In general, the discussion of the impact of credit on religion was not at issue in the community or among the religious organizations at the national level as it was among the donors and some academics. Whenever, I tried to discuss matters pertaining to religion, I was told by the FOs and the community leaders that "[c]redit programs are open to everybody, and no villager is going to oppose them as the eligible borrowers are selected by themselves."[96]

The NGOs believe that the seclusion (*pardha*) of women from participating in the public sphere is the major obstacle to the improvement of women's social status. However, perceptions of both men and women about *pardha* are contradictory. Some are of the opinion that an improvement in the income of their families would mean that women no longer have to do "backbreaking" work outside their homes, and they would be able to maintain *pardha*. In turn, this would enhance the social status of the family and thereby increase the prospects of their daughters getting married to good husbands. Very few objected to women migrating to the city for work in the garment sector or working in public works programs, provided that women were educated and secure working conditions were available. My discussions with the FOs revealed that the main advantage of lending to women is that they are "easily contacted in relation to the high mobility of men, and they are better managers of the spending patterns of the household."[97] One FO pointed out that, "[i]n our culture, mothers are the ones who maintain the subsistence of the family. They will find one way or another to make sure loans are repaid. They make enormous sacrifices for the welfare of the family." With the exception of the two educated teachers in the village, most of the borrowers at least in public said that are proud of such sacrifices.

The traditional elites who were mainly marginal farmers, showed less resistance towards women joining the NGOs. These elites are also the ones who were seriously affected by the deterioration of the agricultural sector. They became rich through trade (e.g. they became new suppliers of agricultural inputs after the government withdrew agriculture subsidies), government contracts, and income earned from employment in Gulf countries. They are relatively more educated and their lifestyles are more modern than the traditional elites. More importantly, they tend to be more aggressive in revitalization of Islam in the village. Generally, new elites tend to look down upon the traditional elites due to their "backwardness" and "ignorance," and collaboration with the Pakistani government and other anti-Bangladeshi elements. Similarly, the traditional elites are antagonistic towards the elites because the latter monopolizes the government subsidies, trade, and moneylending. Women are generally caught between the NGOs' negotiations between traditional and new elites; partly intra-elite lending resulting from the NGO credit.

Although new elites insist on women maintaining *pardha* and were critical of NGOs for having hidden agendas that are un-Islamic and anti-Bangladeshi, the impact of these objections seemed to be limited to legitimizing their claims to status and leadership in the village, and there is no evidence that such claims obstructed activities of the NGOs. Interestingly, NGOs seem to collaborate more with the new elites than with the traditional ones. Perhaps the reason for this is that new elites are more closely aligned with the state power, and they are powerful in the areas where the NGO programs are located.

Before, the FOs enter a given locality, the feasibility of their projects are negotiated with the village hierarchy through their networks at national level. Through these negotiations a few women are selected to lead the credit groups. The majority of these women maintain close economic relations with the new elites. Once the FOs are confident of meeting the financial targets set by their superiors, they assign the responsibility of forming the groups to the group leaders. Then they either rent or build an office space in close proximity to the group. These premises typically belong to influential persons in the village who consider renting to NGOs to be more profitable and reliable than renting to traders. Some of these proprietors consider providing facilities to NGOs as a "philanthropic activity" and as a service to the poor. On several occasions, they represented themselves as being responsible for bringing NGO credit to the village; hence they have an obligation to ensure that their community will not default NGO loans.

Generally, credit groups consist of about 20 women. The majority of these women live close to the main road where infrastructure is relatively developed compared to the interior parts of the village. They also participate in state-sponsored employment schemes such as food-aided public works programs and now are severely affected by the decline of these employment schemes and the withdrawal of state food and agricultural subsidies. They also have better access to resources and employment due to their relationship with new elites and surplus households. Those living in the interior parts of the village are relatively poor and live in areas where the infrastructure is less developed.

In my research area over 90 percent of the borrowers were members of more than two NGOs. Generally, NGOs and the group leaders are reluctant to lend to those who live in the interior sections of the village as they are considered to be a high risk group. At the same time, those in the interior of the village, generally in areas that are far away from the main road and commercial centers, are reluctant to participate in the credit programs. This is due to negative accounts of NGOs that were circulating in the area and the reluctance of the group leaders to include them as they are considered to be high risk and time consuming in terms of management. Those in the interior pointed out that NGOs used coercive methods on them, more than those living in well-developed areas, in order to ensure regular repayment of loans, including forcing people to sell their moveable and immoveable assets to repay loans. However, those excluded from the credit groups are not entirely deprived of the NGO programs since their members lending to non-members is a common practice highly encouraged by the NGOs and group leaders.

During the first group meeting, members formally elect their leaders. Nine out of 12 group leaders were closely linked to those with whom the NGOs made initial contacts. Generally, group leaders belonged to "surplus households" and men in their families played a leading role in economic and political activities in the locality. The majority of the group leaders had at least five years of experience in dealing with NGOs and they hold membership with more than two NGOs. Seven out of 12 leaders came from families who lend money. NGO officers gave a number of reasons as justification for providing women the responsibility of implementing the credit programs. Some of these include:

1. Group leaders are closely linked with the village hierarchy because they (women) are surplus households, or through dependent relationships with the surplus households. This makes NGOs less susceptible to public criticism in the event of conflict between the group members regarding credit related matters.
2. The group leaders have personal knowledge of the group members and their surroundings. This allows the NGOs to spend less time investigating the backgrounds and payment potentials of the members. This also reduces NGOs' costs involving the secreting of the borrowers repayment potential and the enforcement of loan recovery.
3. The fact that group leaders use existing social institutions that are more familiar to the people to implement credit programs prevents the NGO from being perceived as an outside agency.
4. Some group leaders function as moneylenders, employers, and suppliers of input necessary for the income generation projects. This allows them to control use of loans and regulate the entire production and consumption behavior of the households. This allows the NGOs to assess the profitability of lending.

The need for credit is unanimously agreed upon by men as well as women because there is no other source of employment available in the locality. However, there were significant differences in poverty alleviation strategies followed by the NGOs and those preferred by the women. NGOs firmly believe the best strategy for poverty alleviation is small-scale income generation projects based on credit. Women, however, argue that their traditional home-based income generation activities have failed to improve their standards of living. Instead, they would be better off if they were provided with employment with regular wages, legal and financial assistance to redeem mortgaged land, agricultural inputs at cheaper prices, and water pumps at cheaper prices. For example, lack of financial and institutional resources have forced poor households to rely on traditional means of litigation (e.g. *samaj* and *salish*) in order to resolve land disputes. People dislike these institutions, as their decisions favor landlords and moneylenders. The main demand of the women, however, is the education of their male and female children because the future prospect of them having employment in the village is slim. Even the poorest women argued how education for the female children increases the family income, enhances their prospect of getting married, and reduces the amount of dowry.

NGOs use extremely strict and seemingly arbitrary criteria to determine the credit worthiness of the potential borrowers. Although, the Grameen strategy is to provide credit for those without conventional types of collateral, the following criteria illustrate a system of collateral far more elaborate and exclusive. The borrowers should be able to earn cash income for a "reasonable" number of days during the year; they should possess physical assets such as a bicycle, a radio, jewelry, and animals that have a reasonable market value. The borrowers should also have the presence of at least one male who earns a regular income residing in the family or helping the needs of the family, and prove the possibilities of borrowing from different sources. In some groups, borrowers should be willing to maintain savings with the group leaders, in addition to three months of mandatory savings in order to qualify for credit. Immediately after they satisfy these conditions, the information about the income, consumption and other expenditure patterns of the households of the borrowers are closely monitored by group leaders, moneylenders, and members.

Generally, widows are excluded unless they have the guarantee of the group leader or a male relative. Unmarried daughters also are not preferred since they are likely to leave home after marriage in order to prevent a high probability of loans being used for the purpose of dowry. However, these rules are waved when another member of the family or the potential bridegroom underwrites the repayment of NGO loans. In these situations the families of the borrower continue to make repayments, while the credit is entirely transferred to the families to which their daughters got married. When both their daughters and sons-in-law live in the same village, the responsibility for repayment becomes more complex and contentious.

In the case of Grameen Bank the group members are required to take an oath which includes sixteen decisions (see below). It was not possible to evaluate the impact of these decisions. The majority of the members of the Grameen Bank and villages in general are extremely cynical about women taking the oath. Some consider it is unnecessary and simply a formality to satisfy the "foreigners." A number of women pointed out that, "If they have the resources, there is no need for outside agencies (NGOs) to remind them of their domestic and moral responsibilities." Women consider the oath as an insult to them, but do not blame the FOs since they are told by the FOs that it is a condition imposed by the international donors. From the perspective of the FOs, the oath is important means of educating the "ignorant women" and maintaining discipline within the group.

The 16 decisions of Grameen Bank:
1. We respect the four principles of the Grameen Bank – we are disciplined, united, and courageous workers – and we apply them to all our lives.
2. We wish to give our families good living standards.
3. We will not live in dilapidated houses. We repair them and work to build new ones.
4. We cultivate vegetables the whole year round and sell the surplus.
5. During the season for planting, we pick out as many seedlings as possible.
6. We intend to have small families. We shall reduce our expenses to a minimum. We take care of our health.
7. We educate our children and see that they can earn enough money to finance their training.
8. We see to it that our children and homes are clean.
9. We build latrines and use them.
10. We only drink water drawn from a well. If not, we boil the water or we use alum.
11. We will not accept a marriage dowry for our son and we do not give one to our daughter at her marriage. Our center is against this practice.
12. We cause harm to no one and we will not tolerate that anyone should do us harm.
13. To increase our income, we make important investments in common.
14. We are always ready to help each other. When someone is in difficulty, we all give a helping hand.
15. If we learn that discipline is not respected in a center, we go along to help and restore order.
16. We are introducing physical culture in all centers. We take part in all social events.

In the majority of the cases, there was no direct correspondence between the stated-purpose in the credit application forms and the actual uses of credit. Credit is generally used for the immediate financial needs and ongoing income-generation activities of the family. In deciding the eligibility of loans, the main concern of the group leaders is the repayment capacity of the borrowers rather than the actual investments. In most cases, the microenterprises are managed by the entire family, and therefore the responsibility of repayment of loans is shared. It appears that women's direct ownership of microenterprises is neither required by the NGOs nor by the women. One of the reasons is that the real ownership of these microenterprises are determined by who helps the women to become creditworthy, make regular repayments, and provide inputs for their investments and employment for other family members.

Over 85 percent of the women borrow from more than one NGO in addition to borrowing from informal sources. Despite the presence of over 12 NGOs, only a small percentage of the credit requirements of the members of the two NGOs are met by the institutional sources. Estimated credit from these sources include: friends and relatives 10 percent, surplus households 55 percent, traders 25 percent, and NGOs 10 percent. The terms and conditions attached to these sources vary according to the relationship between the borrower and the lender, the nature of collateral, urgency of need, availability of alternative sources, and size of the loan. The NGO loan is only one among many sources of credit, and people are generally eligible only for one loan per year. When they have outstanding loans, the amount they can invest from the new loans is even less. Generally, people consider conditions attached to NGO credit as much harsher compared to those of the moneylenders. Lending strategies of moneylenders are flexible and easily negotiable as they provide a multiplicity of services to the families. Therefore, it is highly impractical for women to harm their relationship with the moneylenders. This is reinforced by the fact that different sources of credit and the methods of repayments to the NGOs are linked. Loans from the NGOs are invested in combination with loans from other sources and used for repayment of all outstanding loans.

Given the requirement for repayment of loans on a weekly basis, the majority of loans are directly used by men, mainly because male-dominated employment generates cash income on a regular basis compared to that of most women. Although some women expressed their desire to control the loans themselves, such a possibility is prevented by the fact that loan repayment is a responsibility of the entire family. Given the fact that peer-group pressure is applied on the entire family, they become inevitably dependent on men for utilization of credit. Individual control over NGO credit and income generation projects are alien concepts to most women because they believe that "no income-generation project can be carried out without the assistance of the entire family."

Neither the FOs nor the group leaders were interested in ascertaining economic feasibility of the stated projects prior to lending. Women clearly pointed out that they rarely used loans toward the purpose for which it was allotted. FOs are only interested in repayments. The NGOs consider such monitoring an unnecessary interference in internal affairs of households, and it would lead to conflicts in the groups. The fact that NGOs are not in a position to provide any services other than one loan per year prevents them from dictating how the loans should be used. Instead, the group leader, in consultation with the NGO officers, plays an important role regulating the entire consumption and social expenditure of the families of the borrowers. Women dislike these interventions. They complain that,

> Since we joined the NGO everybody in the village can tell us what to eat and what not to eat. When we failed to make repayments our group members asked, "Why did you eat chicken yesterday? Why did you send your son for a movie? Why did you buy new clothes? Why are you making plans for the wedding of your daughter?"

This leads to conflicts between and within households.

Peer group pressure is a substitute for conventional types of collateral used by the banks. It is created by using existing social and cultural institutions and the power relations embedded in them to make the poor creditworthy. Contrary to the rhetoric, peer group pressure not only incorporates a broader material base (for example, all forms of physical assets) than the conventional types of collateral used by the banks, but it also regulates and disciplines all the productive activities and consumption patterns of the households even before the women borrow their loans. Interestingly, a reason that the women prefer to lend to married women is that, according to some FOs,

> [m]others [in this culture] know how to manage the household. Men are useless when it comes to meeting day-to-day needs. It is well known that, mothers will even forgo their own quota of food in order to meet the needs of the rest of the household. Moreover, men can easily escape from the responsibility of loan repayment by leaving their home and the village, but most women stay at home and it is easier to deal with them. This is why we can maintain high rates of loan repayment.

The amount and timing of the loan delivery are not determined according to the need or the expectations of the people, but by their ability to satisfy conditions required for loan eligibility and the financial targets of NGOs. The value of the loan is determined by the NGO head officers and, in the majority of the cases, all members receive a fixed amount during each loan cycle. Of the 350 women who have been members of the NGOs for a period of four years only 5 percent received high-value loans during the fourth borrowing cycle. However, given the fact that over 75 percent of the borrowers have outstanding loans extending from their first loan, it was difficult to ascertain the exact amount available for new or ongoing investments. The actual amount going to the borrowers is further reduced when the group leader keeps a certain portion of the loan, particularly from the high risk members, to maintain the regular repayment of the entire group.

A number of reasons forced women to borrow from these sources and to maintain a dependent relationship with them. To begin with, the NGO credit was used in ongoing income-generation activities for which they had already become dependent on moneylenders. The group leader plays an important role in deciding the type of projects in which members should invest. Six group leaders are moneylenders and also suppliers of inputs for income-generation projects. Often, loans are given on the condition that women purchase these items from the group leaders. Some women complained that often they are not aware of the monetary value of their loans because the group leader provides them with cows, goats, and chickens instead of cash. Similarly, in most cases, in order to start new income generation projects, women are forced to borrow additional funds from the moneylenders/traders/landlords.

These sources also happen to be the ones who provide inputs for the income-generation projects and to whom outputs are ultimately sold. In these situations, inputs sold to women, output from microenterprises, and NGO loans are used as collateral by moneylenders. The weekly loan repayment requirement forces them to invest in projects that would yield "instant" income. For example, instead of buying a calf, borrowers are forced to spend their money on a dairy cow which can produce milk from the first week. Generally, an NGO loan is not always sufficient to buy a dairy cow. In the absence of alternative means, women are forced to purchase inputs at higher prices and sell their output at lower prices from local sources. These sources consider NGO credit has enabled them to purchase inputs needed by women in bulk and sell them at cheaper prices, thereby helping the poor in their community. One trader in the village bazaar pointed out that, "No NGO will be able to make profits, unless they [local traders] do not co-operate with them." However, traders and moneylenders are generally reluctant to invest the funds they accumulate from NGO members in activities that would generate employment and income within the village, instead they prefer to invest them in buying real estate and invest in the education of their own children.

The relationship between borrowers and lenders is a multifold and complex one. Moneylenders provide employment for women and other members in the household, and these relationships are long established; there is no logical reason why people would sever them. Moneylenders are considered to be more open and flexible in terms of negotiating the terms and conditions of loans. This is partly a result of the significant difference in the ways in which women and NGOs assess the cost of the loan (the interest rates). Women decide the cost of borrowing from the NGOs and the moneylenders on the basis of flexibility of loan repayment and the other additional benefits from sources of borrowing. Their main question is who is more reliable in terms of securing their subsistence needs. At the field-level, however, FOs have devised creative ways of working with the moneylenders given that they are the lender of last resort for repayment of NGO loans. Also from the perspective of moneylenders and landlords NGOs bring cash to the village.

Theoretically, the interest rate charged by the NGOs is lower than that of the moneylenders. However, from the perspective of the borrowers, NGO interest rates are considered to be higher and more burdensome. There were significant discrepancies between the interest rates stated in the NGO record and what was really charged by the FOs. First, an important determinant of the interest rate charged by the NGO is the amount required to maintain any given credit program as self-sufficient and profitable. Although the official interest rate charged by the NGOs is between 16 and 20 percent, the actual cost of the loan is much higher. It includes the official interest, burden of compulsory savings group funds, pressure to purchase inputs at higher prices, lack of autonomy over the use and control of loans, regulation of consumption and expenditure patterns of the entire household, and the need to maintain regular repayment rates irrespective of household income flows. Second, the actual interest paid by the borrowers is much higher when they borrow additional loans which are given to repay their outstanding loans or to supplement the NGO loans. Third, in practice, borrowers do not have access to the entire amount of the loan, as a portion of it is withheld by the group leaders and the NGOs as a security deposit. However, borrowers pay the interest on the principle allocated to them. Fourth, interest rate is arbitrarily increased on loan defaulters and more restrictions are imposed on the consumption and social expenditures of the family of the borrower. For these reasons, women consider moneylenders to be far more flexible than the NGOs despite the fact that women are well aware of the oppressive practices of moneylenders.

The majority of borrowers have mortgaged their land fully or partially to the moneylenders and were on the verge of foreclosure. Although, the landlords/moneylenders are not interested in obtaining legal ownership of land by maintaining de facto ownership they can both avoid land tax and force the debtors to invest NGOs' loans in land. However, landlords/moneylenders retain right to the all produce of the land, and borrowers pay the minimum monetary wage or a share of the produce. Not only are these poor people being reduced to little more than tenants on their own land, but they are also required to invest their borrowings from the NGOs in these lands. For these borrowers, investing NGO credit in off-farm income-generation activities is not an option because it would risk permanent loss of the land and employment. Several families pointed out that the NGO loans have been useful in terms of negotiating and maintaining employment contracts with the landlords. In these situations, moneylenders and landlords make decisions about the distribution of wages between monetary wages and in-kind wages and the timing of their payment according to repayment requirements set by the NGOs. They also take into account the amount they can appropriate from women's additional borrowings from the NGO if they maintain regular repayments.

Given the fact that weekly loan repayments come mainly from wages from agriculture-related activities, the behavior of the wage market(s) is an important determinant of the level of loan repayment. Employers increasingly prefer to remunerate work with in-kind payment as opposed to monetary wages. This is a choice they attribute to the increase in costs of agricultural production due to the withdrawal of government subsidies on agriculture inputs such as fertilizer and chemicals. Interestingly, after privatization and liberal economic reforms, some of these employers became the new suppliers of these inputs as a result of the state patronage they enjoy. The ability of the households to obtain these supplies on easier terms depends upon maintaining good relations with these suppliers. In addition to conventional types of dependency relationships, deficit-households deposit the entire amount or part of NGO loans with these suppliers so that they can obtain agricultural and consumer necessities inputs as needed. In other cases, purchases are made by using the NGO loan as collateral and women are obliged to sell the produce to these suppliers.

In response to the intense competition for employment and increasing labor costs, employers use a number of methods to keep wages down. The majority of the households prefer longer labor contracts, but maintenance of such contracts often means more work for lower payment. The reluctance of the employers to pay monetary wages and the increasingly short duration and the uncertainty of contracts have forced some to opt for shorter contracts so that they can have a greater flexibility to explore cash-generating alternative employment. In this context, the need to repay NGO loans in terms of cash has become an important determinant of negotiating these employment contracts and wages. Often families are forced to accept rigid work conditions and low wages as long as the employer promises to provide cash for timely repayment of NGO loans.

The wage contracts are not merely economic relationships but involve multiple transactions between the employers and the employees. The employers prefer to hire those who live in close proximity, which means those in the areas serviced by the NGOs. These decisions are also shaped by terms of social prestige, local politics, and security of property. This pattern of employment is common in situations where borrowers have mortgaged the land and several members of their family are employed in them. In these situations, the employers require the investment of NGO loans in the mortgaged land as a pre-condition for employment. The majority of women-borrowers belong to this wage category. Generally, NGOs are reluctant to provide loans for those with daily wage contracts, unless the group leader (often in collaboration with the employers) can retain control over a certain portion of the wages to ensure weekly repayment. It is a common practice by the group leaders to enter into a contract with the borrowers and landlords that stipulates the borrowers investing their credit in land have a mortgage with the landlord, and the landlord taking the responsibility for timely repayments to the NGOs.

The amount of time allocated for marketed and non-marketed activities by women has increased due to depletion of cash incomes and an increase in the price of basic necessities. This has increased the pressure on women to allocate more time for means to cope with the basic survival of the family. In situations where the husband and the wife, as well as other family members, are working for the same employer, female workers and children are paid in-kind wages and male workers are paid in cash wages. Generally, employers require women to work for in-kind as a condition for paying cash wages for their husbands. Women prefer non-marketed activities because of their greater flexibility as they allow women to simultaneously engage in productive and non-productive activities, to prevent depletion of cash reserves and to increase their leisure.

Women consider the lack of flexibility on the part of the NGO in terms of loan repayment as a greater burden. One woman said,

> We are constantly under pressure to think of ways in which we could raise money for weekly repayment requirements. Often, we have to sell homegrown vegetables that we earlier used for our own consumption, and forgo buying books for our children and medical treatment. We are forced to go to the forest and collect firewood and sell it in the market. The forest officials constantly harass us, as collecting firewood is illegal. We cannot send our men because they get arrested. Forest officers normally do not arrest women.[98]

A number of women pointed out that the need for cash income increased after they began borrowing from the NGO programs. They need cash to repay their loans and to purchase their daily food items after government withdrew food and agricultural subsidies. In addition, NGO loans were also considered as a main reason for the rapid depletion of rice, *dhal* (lentils), and firewood reserves, which worsens the situation during the slack season. These impacts of credit programs on different households depend on a variety of factors such as the structure and size of the household, the number of opportunities for earning incomes, and the availability of alternative means of income and substitutes for marketed as well as non-marketed goods.

In broad terms, households in the researched area can be divided as surplus households and deficit households, and the majority of NGO members belong to the latter group. Surplus households are those that maintain some amount of surplus of income on a regular basis. Deficit households are those that are in debt for a long period of time and who face much of the difficulties in repayment of loans. Debt obligations force deficit households to quickly process their surplus produce and convert it into cash more quickly than the surplus households. Consequently, they often sell their produce at a time when the prices are lower, whereas surplus households are able to hold their produce until the price level increases. The deficit household's cash incomes are higher during the harvest season because they can secure maximum days of employment. However, outstanding debt obligations and the reluctance of employers to provide monetary wages prevent them from accumulating sufficient savings for lean periods. This may well be the reason some women use the entire loan obtained from NGO for repayment of debts acquired through the purchase of basic necessities. Some families deposit the entire loan obtained from the NGO with the traders in the bazaar in return for a supply of daily rations. Suppliers on the other hand pointed out that, "NGO loans are helping people to survive since one of the main issues faced by the poor in the village is shortage of cash. We (traders) have the infrastructure to obtain supplies on whole sale and sell them at cheaper prices to the poor. How can we help the poor forever, when they do not have cash?"

The traders in the village bazaar and moneylenders maintain detailed information about their clients' transactions with the NGO. Several traders pointed out that, they often help people make their loan repayments, "[a]fter all, if they repay their loans on time they can obtain additional loans. We do not lose by helping them to repay their loans since we are guaranteed of repayment in cash instead of payment in kind. This really helps us to continue with our business." Interestingly, traders and moneylenders are not interested in investing these accumulated funds in ventures that would generate employment locally, but in real estate and education of their children. Those who are involved in retail trade brings in cheap imported products that encourage a negative impact on local industries that are unable to compete such imports, and further encourages to draining outflow of resources from the communities.

The communication between the FOs at the local level and the central office is mostly limited to the financial aspects of the program. According to one FO, during his five years of service, empowerment and other social goals were discussed twice, once during his first orientation and training program that were held in their head office and second with researchers like me. From the perspective of the FOs, they do not have enough time, resources or a mandate to engage in any matters other than achieving financial targets set by their superiors. Consequently, FOs unwittingly resort to various methods that are distasteful to the members, such as withholding a portion of the loan as compulsory savings and emergency funds. There is much ambiguity as to the exact amount withheld, but it was clear from the respondents' replies that they do not receive the entire amount designated for a loan. The most common practice, however, is that the defaulting members are given additional loans to pay off the outstanding loans. Thereafter, assets purchased from refinanced loans and produce from investments are used as collateral, and the entire economic and social activities of the borrower's family are directly regulated by the FOs in collaboration with the group leaders.

There are two recorded cases where borrowers were forced to sell their houses to a trader in the bazaar in order to repay the loan. Increasingly, it is a common practice for the NGOs to withhold members' savings, including the savings of those who already repaid their loans, until the entire group has completed their repayments. None of the members are permitted to exit the group until everyone has completed repayment. In addition, the group leaders withhold a portion of the loan to cover the repayments in emergency situations. When all of these funds are exhausted and a significant number of borrowers are likely to default, the group leader borrows a large loan from the moneylenders. When group leaders themselves are moneylenders they assume the responsibility for repaying the entire loan. Additional loans the members of the group obtain thereafter are directly transferred to the group leaders.

It is not possible for members to exit from the group until all its members have repaid their loans. First, given that most of the women have borrowed new loans to repay their outstanding ones will force those who have repaid their loan to remain in the group as the repayment of loan is a responsibility of the entire group. Second, the availability of NGO loans is an important component of the household's yearly cash flow, which includes maintaining employment contracts, regular supplies of daily needs and inputs needed for their income-generating projects. There is much pressure from the moneylenders on their borrowers to continue to borrow from the NGOs because NGO loans are important sources of their cash flow. Third, there is a fear of losing the amount women contributed to the savings and emergency funds, which cannot be withdrawn until the entire group has repaid their loans.

Group meetings are held once a week in the household of the members or in the NGO office. Generally meetings last for approximately one hour, out of which 45 minutes are allocated for matters concerning savings and credit. The remaining time is used for educational programs such as basic hygiene and literacy. The amount of time allocated for these programs progressively declines as the group enters into loan repayment phase. After each member fulfills their financial obligations, i.e. handing over savings or weekly installments, the tendency is for them to leave the meeting to attend to domestic duties or for employment. Women's attendance at meetings, especially, after they obtain their first loan, becomes irregular and the interaction between members as a group declines. Attendance drops even further during the harvest season when women are able to gain maximum days of employment. Thereafter, interaction between the FOs and the borrowers takes place mainly through group leaders; participation in group meetings is just a formality.

During these meetings the NGO officers and group leaders question women about reasons for their failure to repay their loans and women are forced to disclose information about the activities of their families in public. Potential defaulters are publicly ridiculed and told how to organize their economic and social expenditures. This is a deliberate strategy used by Grameen Bank. One FO pointed out that, "Group meetings held away from their home premises is the best way to obtain information about the reasons for failure to repay loans because usually men do not participate in these meetings. At the same time, this leaves less room for the women to lie because of the fear of members of other groups providing the correct information."

NGO officials gave two reasons for their limited emphasis on education, health, and awareness-building in their credit programs. First, funds for such programs are not available as the international donors are increasingly concentrating on credit programs. Second, until the organization becomes financially self-sufficient, they cannot afford to spend on programs that will not earn them returns to their investments in the short-run. Third, the women are not so enthusiastic about educational programs, although there is a high demand for health-related programs. It is not feasible to introduce such programs until they are ready to do so. However, women argue that they prefer education for their children as a priority, and the reasons given by the NGOs about the lack of interest among the members for such programs, are false.

It is very common among the villagers to compare the benefits from different NGO programs. One woman pointed out, "CARITAS and the World Vision invest so much on education and health. As a result, children of the members of these NGOs are more educated and in a better position to obtain employment in the city. Even foreigners (a good number of them happen to employees of NGOs and foreign embassies) hire them as domestic servants because they can speak English and know how to work in rich homes." Other women argued that, "Education is an asset. It gives status to the family when there are educated children, even if they do not get jobs after knowing how to read and write. Especially when our daughters can read and write, they can find good husbands, and we need not give high dowries." The already high indebtness further execrated by borrowing from the NGOs are not helping them to improve the opportunities of education for the children.

Interestingly these local perceptions do not appear in the written reports from FOs to the NGOs or in their final evaluation reports. Part of the reason is the nature of information the FOs are expected to report to the head offices that are only concerned with quantitative indicators such as the number of women participating in the credit programs, rates of repayments, and information about the loan defaulters. There is hardly any evidence of flow of qualitative information between the field and the NGOs that are sufficient to evaluate the impact of credit on empowerment. Given that job security of FOs are predicated on loan repayment rates, FOs are forced to make significant compromises between the financial and social goals of microcredit. Making structural changes in the microcredit programs in light of the legitimate complaints made by FOs, borrowers, rural communities, governments and researchers, has become an increasingly difficult task given the importance of financial self-sufficiency for survival of their organizations.

Conclusion

The analysis of the two case studies in Bangladesh contradicts the most widely held claims about the impact of microcredit. Current positive claims about microcredit are not only misleading, but they also disguise how the lives of the women borrowers have become even more rigidly imprisoned within the power structures that oppress them. The funds do not reach the poorest of the poor. The claim that loans are given to those without collateral is far from the truth. The assessment of collateral by the NGOs covers the total material wealth and social life of the entire household. The peer group pressures exerted deprive borrowers of control over their household assets, on the incomes of borrowers and of other members of the household, and on their "freedom" to make economic and social decisions. Now, the entire household is framed as a public domain and placed under the control of the entire community, local government officials and the NGOs.

Credit given to women, and their incomes, are appropriated by the moneylenders and traders who play an important role in helping women to be creditworthy, to invest their funds, and to repay their loans. Credit simultaneously strengthens the pre-capitalist modes of production as the income-generating programs are based on them, and subordinate them to the general accumulation of capital worldwide. Credit intensifies the drain of household wealth in both monetary and non-monetary forms, from less productive families and locations, to more productive members and locations. This mostly occurs through conversion of the moveable assets and items for subsistence into cash, reduction of their nominal and real incomes, and restricting the borrowers of their freedom to control their production and consumption decisions. The ideology of empowerment also, at least for now, provides the ideological legitimacy for the state to reduce investments in social welfare and development for the poor. Through repayment rates, the consumption and social expenditure patterns of the poor are disciplined so that they can bear the costs of structural adjustments and other neoliberal economic reforms.

Loan defaults are subject to harassment by the village elite for whom the repayment of loans is important to maintaining the continuous flow of financial resources as they are an important source of their cash flow. Although, such harassment occurs even in informal lending practices, women think that is it extremely difficult to negotiate with the NGO given the fact that NGOs involve the traders and local moneylenders who want to ensure that the NGO loans are paid in cash. High rates of repayment are predicated on the same institutions that the NGOs consider as oppressive and necessary to transform in order to empower women. The resulting configuration of institutional relations in and between public and private domains of women has imposed more restrictions on their social and economic freedom as they are now guided by the imperatives of loan repayment. Unlike the NGOs, women borrowers consistently pointed out that they would be better off with state subsidies on education, healthcare, and agricultural subsidies. The general consensus in the village is that the investments in health care, education, and agricultural subsidies outweigh the benefits from microcredit provided by the NGOs.

Microfinance has increased women's responsibility over domestic economy and their interactions with the wider society. Increased responsibility, however, has not resulted in conditions positive for their empowerment. The necessity of maintaining regular repayment has forced women to make numerous sacrifices in terms of time available for leisure, education, personal consumption etc. Such sacrifices are further worsened by the reductions in government spending in social welfare and free market economic policies. In addition women also face verbal and physical harassment from their peer groups and members of their families. Here one finds two overlapping trends. On the one hand, the gender disparities continue to widen within the economically disadvantaged households. On the other hand, such disparities have also widened the economic well-being between rich and poor households, given the fact that the borrowings of the poor households benefit the rich households. Women's participation in microcredit programs has simultaneously widened the gender and class disparities, and in particular the poor women's control over their lives and households has declined.

The negative impact of women bearing the sole responsibility of loan repayments and the necessity of participating in micro credit program-related activities are manifested in the reduction of time available for leisure, education, consumption, and welfare. Women are simply used as instruments to discipline household behavior according to the imperatives of loan repayments. Their increased responsibility for economic activities and their forced participation in micro-credit related activities have not translated into an overall improvement of their social position. Instead, these activities have resulted in *less* freedom and autonomy, particularly for poor women. The fault lies not in them assuming responsibilities, but rather, in responsibility being subordinated to the logic of capital. The failure to understand this is, in part, due to the persistence of general hesitation of gender and development studies in particular, and feminist studies in general, to assign a central place to the class function of gender relations in the contemporary trajectories of social change.

A closer analysis suggests that the initial euphoria over the success of microcredit does not seem to be sustainable. The emerging threat of a mass default of microcredit proves to entail challenges for both the NGOs as well as the state. Should such a situation occur, would the state be forced to intervene either on behalf of the NGOs or in support of the borrowers? State intervention is highly unlikely, given the fact that NGOs have not been successful in changing the local power relations that are crucial for political parties competing for state power. Furthermore, NGOs have not developed their own political constituencies and alternative forms of political mobilization. Instead, they have further strengthened the traditional patterns of political mobilization at the local level. Despite this, NGO intervention has not changed the popular perception of the majority of the population; that the state is the primary agency responsible for social development.

NGOs cannot be certain that they can use peer group pressure as a means of efficient credit program management, indefinitely. Peer group pressure is not a static, but a dynamic phenomenon. If the majority of the borrowers opted to default on their loans, peer group pressure might turn against the NGO. Unless the state is able to withstand international donor pressure, it is unlikely to mediate on behalf of NGOs. Similarly, it is unlikely that international capital will rely on NGOs as opposed to the state, as a means for creating and securing the social, economic, and political conditions conducive to its expansion. However, state intervention or non-intervention on behalf of NGOs would lead not only to a legitimization crisis of the state, and NGO sector as a whole, in terms of their respective relations with the society: unlike the NGOs the state cannot abandon its programs or escape from its responsibilities towards the poor. The state would find it far more difficult to re-establish its conventional roles in social development or to compensate for what the communities have lost due to the exit of NGOs. The exit of NGOs from these communities would only further complicate the resolution of legitimization and accumulation crisis of capital. What this suggests is that microfinance has undermined the social transformative capacities of both the state and NGOs as they are now imprisoned within the logic of capital.

The successes of microcredit programs – defined as high rates of loan repayment – are a result of women's recourse to the very institutions that are oppressing them, and which NGOs ostensibly work toward transforming. Such an outcome, which I refer to as the "commodification of feminist consciousness," is yet one among many examples of capitalism's creative capacity to subvert and undermine challenges to its continuity, by appropriating the language and practices of its opponents. Several consequences follow.

The discourse of "empowerment of women through microcredit," configure gender as a de facto class relation. In formulating policy, NGOs and their donors treat women borrowers simply as clients whose regular repayment of loans is the crucial indicator of financial sustainability of the NGOs and their empowerment. This process which is referred to as "clientification of gender," the notion of the rational, utility maximizing man (*homo economicus*) in mainstream economics, is simply reconfigured in feminist language of empowerment without any substantive changes of its role in social change. On the one hand, within the emerging political economy, gender relations serve a class function according to the reproductive needs of capital. Such feminization of surplus value accumulation is an important source of global expansion for capitalist development and its popular legitimacy. On the other hand, the failure of empowerment projects to come to terms with the centrality of the logic of capital (i.e. class relation) to the production of gender inequalities, make such projects subservient to the reproductive needs of capital. These impacts have further constrained women's freedom and capacity to use their private and public domains as a means of resistance against oppression of their own lives and families. Women's freedom to negotiate the relations between private and public domains are now regulated by institutions that are generally considered as oppressive to their empowerment. As a consequence the awareness-building and education programs associated with microcredit also frame the women's consciousness and means towards empowerment within the ideological and institutional parameters of neoliberalism. The reason for such a predicament, which I call the "feminization of capitalist modernity," is a direct result of gender theorists' inability to articulate a clear vision of a social order outside of the fundamental ideological and institutional parameters of capitalism.

The current notions of empowerment are ambiguous about the ideal nature of property rights, exchange and production relations, and the nature of the state, for an empowered social order. Consequently, their interventions in empowerment inevitably get framed by the very forces that they seek to transform. Microcredit therefore, has been least helpful in dealing with the issue raised by Pearson and Jackson, who ask: "How do we conceptualize gendered identities and subjectivities in a manner that avoids both essentialism and the unproblematic assumption of the self-determination of the individual?"[99] The outcomes of microcredit programs, points to a continuing dilemma in feminist theory: "Recovering the female subject risks essentialism; refusing a female subject risks erasing gender difference."[100]

Contrary to its expectations, the empowerment of women through microcredit as a new orthodoxy of development has not radically altered, but has reinforced, the impact of development on poor women since its inception. The social, economic, and political processes that underlie microcredit should therefore, not be "seen as a matter of scientific knowledge, a body of theories and programs concerned with the achievement of true progress, but rather as a series of political technologies intended to manage and give shape to the reality of the Third World."[101] Such technologies establish connections between diverse communities around the globe and ensure that their reproductive processes are configured and disciplined within the ideological and institutional parameters of neoliberalism.

As Arturo Escobar suggests, these impacts cannot be simply considered as "global [processes] of domination defined by power and the accumulation of normalized individuals" that run "parallel to the global process of capital accumulation."[102] At the most basic level, the former cannot be understood outside the logic of the latter. My point is not to reduce the power to capital accumulation. Rather as my analysis shows, the attempts by microcredit programs to transform relations of power and domination in diverse social locations that are scattered throughout the world cannot escape the centrality of the logic of capital in the reproduction of their social environments. The empowerment projects fail because their concerns about power and domination are imprisoned within the logic of capital and consequently the subjects of these projects are not able to critically engage with the dilemma that Paulo Freire identified as that "they are at one and the same time, themselves and oppressor whose consciousness they have internalized."

Ironically, the result of "cultural turn" in development, as evident in the organization of microcredit projects, is the consolidation of neoliberalisms' hold over development, by providing substance to the theoretical turn to imperfect market conditions as opposed to perfect market conditions in mainstream economics. The shift away from the perfect competitive model that occupied a central position in mainstream economics, toward models of imperfect competition underpinned by "new micro-foundations" and information, opened the possibility of rational and efficient allocation of resources in imperfect market conditions that was once considered a main source of market failure. This means that rural women and their informal social and cultural environments are brought into the mainstream neoclassical theoretical framework. It is simply a matter of "feminizing" the mainstream economics rather than fundamental changes of its basic ideologies, assumptions and methodologies.

Despite the withdrawal of the state from and expansion of NGOs in social development, people continue to consider the state and political parties as the final guardian of their social needs and security. Increasingly, the NGOs also seek the intervention of the state mediation to maintain the efficiency of credit programs. Towards this end the states are also under pressure by the international donor agencies to transform the legal frameworks. In several instances, NGOs used the local police and the state officials to pressurize women to repay their loans. The conflicts that resulted were organized along the lines of traditional political rivalries and intra-household differences. Often, credit related issues triggered other conflicts within the community as people drew the links between the burden of loan repayment and their decline in living standards.

Generally, women did not directly participate in these conflicts, although their names were often mentioned as an important source of such conflicts. NGOs, however, do not claim any responsibility for, or mediate in these conflicts; instead they either maintain a distance from them or simply blame "politics" as the main source of program failure. The ritual of blaming the state for the all the ills of development is reproduced here. Failures are attributed to political factors that need to be explained independent of global capitalist development. Embedded in the claim about political failure is a demand for the state to ensure the financial self-sufficiency of NGOs by enforcing legal framework to discipline the borrowers to maintain regular repayment of loans.

Microcredit provided much needed empirical substance to the endogenization of the cultural/social into the mainstream economic development models that, in turn, enhanced the popular legitimacy for the neoliberal restructuring of the state interventions (e.g. fiscal reduction in education, and health care) in social development. In the process, it has impacted the has impacted the changes in the *form* of the state in its attempts to realize its capitalist *nature*, in response to the reproductive needs of capital in its neoliberal phase. Historically, these changes in the *form* of the state are shaped by ideological and institutional strategies used by the state to cope with and manage the accumulation and legitimization crises of capitalism.[103] In these situations, NGO activities have contributed to a generation of ideological and institutional infrastructures for the state to discipline and organize the social order, to consolidate its capitalist *nature* by changing its *form*.[104] However, it is unlikely that the blurring of the boundaries between the *form* and the *nature* of the state is a permanent condition in terms of public expectations of the state. The state is unlikely to escape from bearing the main institutional responsibility for managing the accumulation and legitimacy crises of capitalism. Large-scale failures of microcredit might fuel much deeper societal crises and negatively impact the popular legitimacy of the NGOs as viable alternatives to the state and for-profit organizations.

NGOs' encounters with microcredit and empowerment is yet another instance of how historically the activities of NGOs, both radical and otherwise, have generated and facilitated conditions for both the "centralization" and "domestication" of state power.[105] In this process, states have not only subverted and exploited the counter-hegemonic agendas of the NGOs by using their own language and practices, but have also progressively narrowed the impact on social change desired by these organizations. The fundamental reason for this is that the NGOs operate on a basic concept of "state" that is ideologically and institutionally similar to the capitalist state.

The NGOs' encounter with microcredit has also contributed to a decline in the much celebrated diversity and plurality of NGOs in terms of their relations with neoliberalism. Simultaneously, the mobilization of "culture" in their programs, reproduces its diversity (or diversity of cultures around the world) and disciplines it according to the imperatives of neoliberal capital. Consequently, although NGOs – both historically and contemporaneously, have dominated the public discourse (often to the discomfort of the state), they have never been able to evolve as a counter-hegemonic force against the state, as they both function within the same fundamental logic and institutional boundaries. In other words, reasons for popular legitimacy of NGOs' claims regarding the credibility of the state in terms of its failures in social development and the reasons for failures of the NGOs to make a difference, are in fact, two sides of the same coin. The reason is that NGOs lack both the imagination and the political commitment to envision a political economy different from the one that is governed by ethics of neoliberalism.

My conclusions are, in many ways, similar to the ones echoed for nearly a decade by a number of feminist scholars concerned with women, nationalism, and development.[106] Development has always been a project of the nation state. Historically, gender ideology and nationalism have been intertwined, as one provided the framework to pursue the interests of the other. As Shrini Rai eloquently puts it, women "while remaining central to the project of nation building they were made invisible through universalized discourses of citizenship and economic development."[107] The empowerment of women through microcredit was another moment of struggles against women's invisibility and gender inequalities in the domains of the state, economy, and society. Contrary to such expectations, microcredit has provided a gendered framework for the reproduction of state power in response to accumulation and legitimization crises of capital. In this process, poor women continue to be marginalized and disempowered in the discourses on development and nation building. The difference today is that women have attained "high public visibility," without a corresponding increase in power. If we are to overcome this impasse, in the light of my analysis, I think Capitalism and Gender (CAG) ought to be the thematic and policy focus of debates concerning gender and development, once that began with Women in Development (WID). Such an exercise is unlikely to bear fruit, unless we are willing to imagine and commit ourselves to an alternate political economy capable of challenging the creativity of the capitalist system to reproduce itself, often by appropriating and disciplining the languages and practices of its opponents.

Notes

1 The funds for this research paper provided by the Aspen Institute, Washington DC and the Social Science Research Council, New York.
2 Sanyal, B. Bishwapriya, (1994) *Cooperative Autonomy: the Dialectic of State – NGO Relationship, International Institute for Labor Studies Geneva*, Research Series 100; N. Uphoff, (1989) "Grassroots Organizations and NGOs in Rural Development: Opportunities with Diminishing States and Expanding Markets" in *World Development*, Vol. 21, no. 4, pp. 607–22; "Women, Environment and

Development Organization World Women Congress for a Healthy Planet" Miami, Florida, November 8–12 1992; Nafis Sadik, "Investing in Women: Focus of the Nineties, The State of World Population," Maria Mies, "Patriarchy and Accumulation on a World Scale: Women in the International Development of Labor," and Julia Kristeva, "Women's Time," in N. O. Keohane, M. Z. Rosaldo and B. C. Gelpi (1982) *Feminist Theory: a Critique of Ideology*, Chicago University Press, Chicago; Karen Levy, (1992) "Gender and the Environment: The Challenge of Crosscutting Issues in Development Policy and Planning" in *Environment and Urbanization*, Vol. 4–1, April, pp. 134–49; Lourdes Beneriaand Gita Sen, (1998) "Accumulation, Reproduction and Women's Role in Economic Development: Boserup Revisited" in *SIGNS* Vol. 7, no. 2, Winter, pp. 279–98; Gita Sen and Caren Grown, (1988) "Development Crises and Alternative Visions: Third World Women's Perspectives" *DAWN*. Vandana Shiva, (1988) *Staying Alive, Women, Ecology and Development*, Zed Books, London; Mela Spar, (ed.), (1994) *Mortgaging Women's Lives, Feminist Critiques of Structural Adjustment*, Zed Books, London.
3 For a debate on WID, see Ester Boserup, (1976) *Women's Role in Economic Development*, St Martin's Press, New York; I. Tinker and M. Bramsen (eds), (1976) *Women and World Development*, Washington DC, Overseas Development Council.
4 Boserup, 1976, p. 26.
5 G. S. Backer, (1981) *A Treatise on the Family*, Harvard University Press, Cambridge, MA; Louise Fresco, (1985) "Food Security and Women: Implications for Agricultural Research" a paper presented at the International Conference on Women's Role in Food Sufficiency and Food Strategies, Paris, January 14–19.
6 E. P. Faqhunda, (1989) "The Nuclear Household Model in Nigerian Public and Private Policy: Colonial Legacy and Socio-Political Implications" in *Development and Change*, Vol. 18, pp. 281–95; N. Folber, (1996) "Household Production in the Philippines: A Non-Neoclassical Approach" *Economic Development and Cultural Change*, Vol. 32, pp. 303–430.
7 B. Rogers, (1980) *The Domestication of Women: Discrimination in Developing Societies*, Kogan Page, London. Naila Kabeer, (1994) *Reversed Realities: Gender Hierarchies in Development Thought*, Verso, London, p. 25.
8 J. Tendler, (1988) "What Happened to Poverty Alleviation?" A paper presented at the World Conference on Micro-Enterprises, Washington, DC 6 June 1988, CSM/No. 04, World Bank.
9 Kabeer, 1994; J. S. Jauqette, (2001) "Women and Modernization Theory: A Decade of Feminist Criticism" *World Politics*, Vol. XXXIV, no. I, pp. 14–26; A. Bandarage, (1984) "Women in Development: Liberalism, Marxism and Marxist-Feminism" *Development and Change*, Vol. 15, no. 3, pp. 495–515.
10 A. Jagger, (1983) *Politics and Human Nature*, Harvester, Brighton, Kabeer, 1994, p. 28.
11 L. Benaria and G. Sen, (1981) "Class and Gender Inequalities and Women's Role in Economic Development – Theoretical and Practical Implications" in *Feminist Studies*, Vol. 8, no. 1, pp. 157–76; Kabeer, 1994.
12 Shrini Rai, (2002) *Gender and Political Economy of Development*, Polity Press., Cambridge.
13 The other approaches are: first, the Gender Roles Framework (GRE) focused on efficiency of resources allocation, emphasizing the differences in bargaining power within the households, K. Cloud, (2001) "Women's Productivity in Agricultural Systems: Considerations for Project Design," in C. Overholt, K. Cloud and J. E. Austin (eds) *Gender Roles in Development Projects*, Kumarian Press, West Hartford, CT; second, Triple Role Framework draws attention to multiple demands placed on women which includes their productive, reproductive and childcare and collective activities, C. Moser, (1989) "Gender Planning in the

234 *Jude L. Fernando*

Third World: Meeting Practical and Strategic Needs," *World Development*, Vol. 17, no. 11, pp. 1799–825. As Kabeer noted a weakness in Moser's triple role framework was its failure to "integrate the ways in which social differences between women structure the performance of their roles"; Naila Kabeer, (1992) "Triple Roles, Gender Roles, Social Relations: the Political Sub-text of Gender Training," A Discussion Paper, Institute for Development Studies, Sussex, UK, p. 13; third, Social Relation Analysis (SRA) drew attention to distribution of power relations between men and women as derived from socially constructed institutional arrangements, K. Young, (2001) "Introduction," in *Women's Concerns and Planning: A Methodological Approach for their Integration into Local, Regional and National Planning*, UNESCO, Paris; R. Whitehead, (2000) "Gender-aware Planning in Agricultural Production" *Module 7, Gender and Third World Development Modules*, Institute For Development Studies, Sussex, UK. The significant aspect of SRA is that it sees "the issue of strategic gender interests as an issue of politics rather than of better information (GRF) or more enlightened planning (TRF)" ibid. Kabeer, 1992, p. 37.
14 Kabeer, 1992, p. 299.
15 Ibid.
16 The differences between women's strategic and practical interests are based on specificity of positioning of women in the society on the basis of gender attributes. According to M. Molyneux, "strategic interests are derived from the analysis of their subordination and from the formulation of an alternative, more satisfactory set of arrangements from those which exist." Practical interests are derived from "concrete conditions of women's positioning within the gender division of labor. The practical interests are usually a response to immediate perceived need. And they do not generally entail a strategic goal such as women's emancipation or gender equality." The microenterprises, by responding to practical interests, are believed to be capable of meeting strategic interests, thereby transforming women's subordinate position. M. Molyneux, (1989) "Mobilization without Emancipation: Women's Interests, State and Revolution in Nicaragua" *Feminist Studies*, Vol. 11, no. 2, pp. 232.
17 Srilatha Batliwala, (1994) "Meaning of Empowerment: New Concepts Form Action" in Gita Sen, Adrienne Germain, and Lincoln Chen (eds) *Population Policies Reconsidered: Health Empowerment and Rights*, Harvard University Press, Cambridge, MA, pp. 129, 130–1.
18 Kabeer, 1992.
19 Ibid.
20 Kabeer, p. 299.
21 Paulo Freire, (2000) *Pedagogy of the Oppressed* (trans. M. Bergman Ramos), Continuum International Publishing Group, New York, p. 13.
22 Ibid., 14.
23 Ibid., p. 47.
24 Ibid.
25 Martha Alter Chen, (1996), *A Quiet Revolution: Women in Transition in Rural Bangladesh*, BRAC, Dhaka, Bangladesh, p. 80.
26 *The OXFAM Poverty Report*, (1995) An OXFAM Publication, UK, p. 77.
27 T. Addison and L. Dermery, (1986) *The Poverty Alleviation Under Structural Adjustment*, Overseas Development Institute, London, p. 1.
28 Oxfam Report, 1995, p. 78.
29 F. Stewart, (1989) "The Many Faces of Adjustment" in *World Development*, Vol. 27, no. 12, pp. 1843–64; L. Taylor, (ed.), (1993) *Rocky Road to Reforms: Income Distribution and Growth in Developing Countries*, MIT Press, Cambridge; R. Jolly, (1985) *Adjustment With a Human Face: Context, Content and Economic Justification for Broader Approach to Adjustment Policy*, UNDP, New York, Mimeograph.

30 For critical studies on rural credit, see: Karal Hoff and Joseph E. Stiglitz, (1993) "Introduction: Imperfect Information and Rural Credit Markets – Puzzles and Policy Perspectives" *World Bank Economic Review*, Vol. 4. no. 3, pp. 235–51; Dale Adams, Douglas Graham and J. D. Von Pisshe, (1984) *Undermining Rural Development With Cheap Credit*, Boulder, CO., Westview Press; M. Rosenzweig, (1985) "Neoclassical Theory and the Optimizing Peasant: An Econometric Analysis of Family Labor Farms in a Developing Country" in *Quarterly Journal of Economics* XCIV, pp. 31–55; Joseph Stiglitz, (1989) "Peer Group Monitoring and World Markets" *World Bank Economic Review*, Vol. 4 no. 3, pp. 351–66.

31 K. R. Hoff, A. Braverman and J. E. Stiglitz, (1993) *The economics of rural organization: theory practice and policy.*

32 J. Yaron, (1992), "Successful Rural Financial Institutions" Discussion paper 150, World Bank, Washington, DC. Available at www.worldbank.org/research/journals/wbro/obsaug98/pdf/article1.pdf Von Pishke, J. D., D. Adams and G. Donald (eds), (1984) *Rural Financial Matters in Developing Countries*, Baltimore, MD, Johns Hopkins University Press.

33 Avishay Braverman and Luis Guasch, (1993) "Administrative Failures in Government Credit Programs" in Karla Hoff, Avishey Braverman, and Joseph E. Stiglitz (eds) *The Economics of Rural Organization: Theory, Practice, and Policy*, New York, Oxford University Press, p. 60.

34 For discussions on new political economy, see: "Is the New Political Economy Relevant to Developing Countries?" *PPR Working Papers* World Bank, Washington DC; for critical evaluation of new political economy, see R. Bates, (1989) "Some Skeptical Notes on the 'New Political Economy of Development'" Duke University, Durham, NC; Bardhan, P. (1989) "The New Institutional Economics and Development Theory: A Brief Critical Assessment" in *World Development*, Vol. 17, no, 9, pp. 1389–95; R, Bates and A, Krueger, (eds), (2001) *Political and Economic Interactions in Economic Policy Reforms*, Basil Blackwell Press, Oxford; J. Nugent and M. Nambli, (1998) "The New Institutional Economics and its Applicability to Development" in *World Development*, Vol. 17, no, 9, pp. 1333–47; W. V. Ruttan, (1974) "Institutional Innovation and Agricultural Development" in *World Development*, Vol. 17, no. 9, pp. 1375–89; Douglas North, (1985) "Institutions and Economic Growth: A Historical Introduction" in *World Development*, Vol. 17, no. 9, pp. 1319–22; Allen Gruchy, (1977) "Institutional Economics: Its Development and Prospects" in Rolf Setppacher, Brigitte Zogg-Walz and Hermann Hatzfeldt (eds) *Economics in Institutional Perspectives*, Lexington Books, Lanham MD.

35 Ibid., p. 10.

36 For discussion on the relationship between informal sector and capitalist development see, Faruk Tabak and Michaeline A. Crichlow, (2000) *Informalization: Process and Structure*, Johns Hopkins University Press, Baltimore.

37 For critical studies on activities of NGOs, see: Johan Farrington and Anthony Babington (1992) *Reluctant Partners? Non-Governmental Organizations, The State and Sustainable agricultural Development*, Overseas Development Institute Study, Routledge, London; A. Fowler, (1990) "Where and How NGOs have a Comparative Advantage in Facilitating Development" University of Reading: AERDD Bulletin 28, February; Thomas Carroll, (1992) *Intermediary NGO: The Supporting Link in Grassroots Development*, Kumarian Press, West Hartford, CT; Samuel Paul and Arturo Israel, (1992) *Non-Governmental Organizations and the World Bank: Corporation for Development*, World Bank, Washington DC; D. Korten and R. R. Klauss (eds), (1994) *People Centered Development*, Kumarian Press, West Hartford, CT; Michael Cernea, (1983) "Non-Governmental Organizations and Local Development" World Bank Discussion Paper, no. 40,

Washington DC; John Clark, *Non-Governmental Organizations; Democratizing Development: The Role of Voluntary Organizations*. Kumarian Press, West Hartford, CT; Aubry Williams, (1990) "Growing Role of NGOs in Development" *Finance and Development*, December, 1990, pp. 31–3.
38 John Hatch, founder and director of research, FINCA International Inc., Washington, DC, available at www.villagebanking.org, p. 1.
39 Susan Goldmark and Jay Rosengard, (1985) "Manual for Evaluating Small-scale Enterprises Development Projects" AID Program Design and Evaluation Report no. 6. Washington, DC, USAID.
40 Stephen Devereux "Collection of Production and Income Data: A Commentary" AID Program Design and Evaluation Report no. 6. USAID, Washington, DC, pp. 202–6.
41 Carl Liedholm, (1991) "Data Collection Strategies for Small Scale Industry Surveys." GEMINI: Development Alternatives, Inc., Bethesda, Maryland, Working Paper no. 11.
42 Harold Alderman, (1993) "Obtaining Useful Data on Household Incomes from Surveys" in J. Von Braun and Detle Puetz (eds), *Data Needs for Food Policy in Developing Countries: New Directions for Household Surveys*, International Food Policy Institute, Washington DC.
43 Krishna Kumar, (1989) "Indicators for Measuring Changes in Income, Food Availability and Consumption, and the Natural Resource Base" USAID Program Design and Evaluation Methodology no. 12, Washington DC.
44 Shirley Buzzard and Elaine Edgcomb, (1987) "Monitoring and Evaluating Small Business Projects: A Step by Step Guide for Private Development Organizations" PACT, New York.
45 Carol Levine, (1991) "Rural Household Data Collection in Developing Countries: Designing Instruments and Methods for Collecting Consumption and Expenditure Data" *Working Papers in Agricultural Economics*, no. 91 Department of Agricultural Economics and Food and Nutrition Policy Program (CFNPP), Washington DC; D. J. Casley and D. A. Lury (1981) *Data Collection in Developing Countries*, Clarendon Press, Oxford; Peter Littler (1989) "A Report on Methodologies for Survey Research. Institute for Development Anthropology," Binghamton, NY.
46 Ann Inserra, (1996) "A Review of Appropriate Approaches for Measurement of Micro-enterprise and "Household Income, Assessing the Impact of Micro-enterprise Services" AIMS, Washington, DC.
47 Ibid.
48 a) Mark Pitt and Shaidur Khandeker, (1995) "The Impact of Group–Group Based Credit Programs on Poor Households in Bangladesh: Does the Gender of Participants Matter?; b) "The Household and Intra-Household Impact of the Grameen Bank and Similar Credit Programs in Bangladesh" Unpublished Manuscripts, World Bank.
49 Ibid.
50 Ann Marie Goetz and Rina Sen Gupta, (1996) "Who Takes Credit? Gender, Power, and Control Over Loan Use in Rural Credit Programs in Bangladesh" *World Development*, Jan/March, p. 44.
51 For discussion on welfare state and family, see E. Wilson, (1977) *Women and the Welfare State*, Tavistock, London; C. Cockburn, (1989) *The Local State: Management of Cities and People*. Pluto Press, London.
52 Ibid., p. 54.
53 Jude L. Fernando, (1997) "Disciplining the Mother" *Ghadar*, a bimonthly publication of the Forum of Indian Leftists, Vol. 1, no. 1, 1 May, p. 37; Jude L. Fernando, (1998) "Nongovernmental Organizations, Microcredit and Empowerment of Women" in Jude Fernando (ed.), *The Role of NGOs: Charity*

and Empowerment, The Annals of the American Academy of Political and Social Sciences, pp. 150–76; Ann Marie Goetz and Sen Gupta, M. (1995) "Who Takes the Credit? Gender, Power and Control over Loan Use in Rural Credit Programs in Bangladesh" *World Development* Vol. 24, no. 1, pp. 45–63; Rahman, Aminur (1999) "Microcredit Incentives for Equitable and Sustainable Development: Who Pays?" *World Development* Vol. 27, no. 1, pp. 67–82; L. Mayoux, (1999) "Questioning Virtuous Spirals: Micro-finance and Women's Empowerment in Africa" *Journal of International Development* Vol. 1, no. 7, pp. 957–84.

54 M. Pitt and S. Khandker, (1995) "Household and Intrahousehold Impacts of the Grameen Bank and Similar Target Programmes in Bangladesh" paper presented at workshop on Credit Programmes for the Poor: Household and Intrahousehold Institute of Development Studies, Dhaka (19–21 May) in Simeen Mhamud, (2002) *Development and Change* (42(4): 577–605), Institute For Social Studies, Blackwell Publishing, Oxford, p. 583.

55 N. Kabeer, (1999) "The Conditions and Consequences of Choice: Reflections on the Measurement of Women's Empowerment" UNRISD Discussion Paper DP108, United Nations Research Institute for Development, Geneva; N. Kabeer, (2001) "Conflicts over credit: Reevaluating the Empowerment Potential of Loans to Women in Bangladesh" *World Development* Vol. 29, no. 1, pp. 63–84.

56 Ibid.

57 M. Chen and S. Mahmud, (1995) "Assessing Change in Women's Lives: A Conceptual Framework. Working Paper No 2, BRAC_ICDDRB, B Joint Research project at Matlab, Dhaka, Bangladesh, in Simeen Mahmud, *Development and Change* (42(4): 577–605), Institute For Social Studies, Blackwell Publishing, Oxford, p. 583.

58 Mahmud (2002), p. 589.

59 Ibid., p. 592.

60 Ibid., 2002, p. 587.

61 For a discussion on the tension between Universal and relative rights see, Ken Booth, (1999) "Three Tyrannies" in Tim Dunne and Nicholas J. Wheeler (eds), *Human Rights in Global Politics*, Cambridge University Press, Cambridge, MA, pp. 11–71.

62 For an introduction and applications of actor-oriented concepts, methods and analysis see, Norman Long and Ann Long, (eds) (1992) *Battlefield of Knowledge: The Interlocking of Theory and Practice in Social Research and Development*, Routledge, London, New York.

63 The research site is located in the Gachabari *mouza* of Madhupur Thana; Tangail district – situated 120 miles north of Dhaka, the capital city of Bangladesh. Gachabari Mouza is approximately two miles away from the Thana administrative center.

64 Stuart Rutherford, (1995) *The Biography of an NGO*, Association for Social Advancement, Dhaka.

65 Ibid., p. 50.

66 Ibid., p. 55.

67 Ibid.

68 Ibid., p. 56.

69 Ibid., p. 58.

70 Ibid.

71 Ibid., p. 59.

72 Ibid., p. 60.

73 Ibid., p, 61.

74 Ibid.

238 *Jude L. Fernando*

75 Ibid., p. 50.
76 Association for Social Advancement (1994) "Donor Consortium Report," unpublished, p. 3.
77 Ibid.
78 Ibid.
79 Ibid.
80 Bishwapriya Sanyal, (1994), p. 9.
81 Grameen Bank, Bangladesh: (1992) "Does the Capitalist System have to be the Handmaiden of the Rich?" a speech given at the 85th Rotary International Convention held in Taipei, Taiwan, available at www.soc.titech.ac.jp/icm/grameen-keynote.html), p. 2.
82 Ibid.
83 Ibid.
84 Ibid., p. 3.
85 Ibid., p. 3.
86 Grameen Dialogue, 1994. A newsletter published by the Grameen Trust, Bangladesh. Available at www.grameen-info.org/dialogue/Dialogue61/technicalreport.html.
87 The Donor Consortium of Grameen Bank consists of CIDA, FF, GTZ, KFW, IFAD, NORAD, SIDA.
88 Stated in a talk given at the South Asia Regional Studies Departments, Seminar on Non-governmental Organizations, March 19th, 1997.
89 Ibid.
90 Ibid.
91 "Grameen Bank Phase III Project: Project Completion Report Mission, Final Report" (1995) Grameen Bank, 1995, pp. i–ii.
92 Ibid., p. iv.
93 Ibid.
94 Personal interviews, February 1995, Tangail, Bangladesh.
95 Personal interviews, February 1995, Tangail, Bangladesh.
96 Jude L. Fernando, (forthcoming) *Political Economy of NGOs: Modernizing Postmodernity*, Pluto Press, London.
97 Ibid.
98 Personal interviews, March, Tangail, Bangladesh.
99 Ruth Pearson and Cecile Jackson, (1998) "Introduction: Interrogating Development, Feminism, Gender and policy" in Cecile Jackson and Ruth Pearson (eds), *Feminist Visions of Development*, Routledge, London, p. 10.
100 Ibid., p. 8; Also see, Cicilie Jackson, (1996) "Rescuing Gender from the Poverty Trap" *World Development*, Vol. 24, no. 3, pp. 489–504.
101 A. Escobar, (1985) "Discourse and Power in Development: Michel Foucault and the Relevance of His Work to the Third World" *Alternatives* Vol. 10, no. 10, pp. 387–90.
102 Ibid., p. 393.
103 Fernando, forthcoming.
104 Ibid.
105 Ibid.
106 Jayewardene Kumari, (1986) *Feminism and Nationalism in the Third World*, Zed Books, London; Cynthia Enloe, (1989) *Bananas, Beaches, and Bases: Making Feminist Sense of International Politics*, Pandora Press, London; Sangari Kumkum and Sudesh Vaid, (1993) *Recasting Women, Essays in Indian Colonial History*, New Delhi, Kali For Women; A. Mclintock, (1993) "Family Feuds: Gender, Nationalism, and the Family" in *Feminist Review*, 44, Summer, pp. 61–80; Shrini Rai, (2002).
107 Ibid., p. 15.

Index

ACCION International 2, 40
accumulation and legitimization crisis 13, 15, 19, 187, 193, 231, 232; *see also* crisis of the state
Ackerly, B. 100, 103, 108, 170, 183, 185
Adams, D.J. 40, 235
African Cultural Conservation Fund (ACCF) 151n
Agarawal, B. 96, 105, 108
Amin, A. 108, 109
Amin, S. 44, 50
APFTI 108
Appadurai, A. 144, 151, 152
Ardener, S. 113, 128, 131, 132
Association for Social Advancement (ASA) 202, 205, 208, 237

Bakker, I. 98, 108
Bangladesh 10, 23, 202, 205–207, 226; Bangladesh Academy For Rural Development (BARD) 202; Bangladesh Rural Advancement Committee (BRAC) 32, 234, 237
Barret, M. 24, 42
Bebbington, A. 42, 131
Bebbington, D.H. 37, 102, 106, 114, 128, 138, 141
Beneria, L. 98, 237
Benjamin, M. and Ledgerwood, L. 52, 58, 59
Besson, M. 113, 131
Bolivia 52, 60, 113, 131, 137; Bolivian 47, 48, 56
Bornstein, D. 79, 87
Boserup, E. 188, 223
Bouman, F.J.A. 9, 39
Bourdieu, P. 36, 90, 94, 96, 98, 108
Braverman, A. 192, 235
Brenner, N. 57, 59
Brent, M. 137, 138, 151

Brigg, M. 36, 41, 64, 66, 68, 72, 86, 88
Buckley, G. 134, 135, 151
Bukharin, M. 20
Burawoy, M. 30, 42

Cagatay, E.N. 98, 108
Cajamarca 154, 157, 171
capitalism and gender(CAG) 38, 232
CARE 161, 162, 164, 165
CARITAS 225
Carmen, R. 72
Carpenter, S. and Sadoulet, L. 41
Carroll, T. 121
CECAP 172, 173, 179, 180–186
CGAP 48, 59, 207
Chambers, R. 72
Chen, M. 191, 234, 237
Chiapas 66
Christian Development Commission of Bangladesh (CDCB) 200
Chu, Michael 2
Chua, R.N. 177, 185
Clark, J. 15, 41, 236
Clark, S. 14, 19, 231
class 7, 12, 19, 22, 184, 187, 190, 229, 233, 235
Clifford, J. 149, 151
Cohen, M. 54, 59
Coke, R. 177, 182, 185
Coke, R.N. 175, 180, 183
Coleman, J. 112, 131
collateral 147, 158, 172, 213, 219, 224; social collateral 50
conscientization 188
Consultative Group to Assist Poorest (CGAP) 48, 50, 59, 207
Cordillera 178, 182, 184, 185
Cornia, G.A. and Stewart, A. 45, 59
Cruikshank, B. 74, 86
Culturebank 133, 139, 149, 151, 152

Cutler, C. 45, 59

Davis, S.H. 125, 131
Deere, C.D. 156, 169, 171
default 27, 35, 39, 115, 116, 134, 141, 151, 182, 183, 206, 223; defaulters 39, 211, 220; loan default 226, 228
Degregori, C.I. 156, 161
Deleuze, G. 69, 80, 84, 85
Denters, E. 47, 51, 58, 61
Desptoif 67–71
Deubel, T. 37, 133, 136, 138, 148, 150, 152
Dhakhwa, U. 101, 108
Dirlik, Arif 11, 40
Dongon Culture 144
Douglas, M. and Isherwood, I. 144, 152

education 6, 58, 101, 103, 105, 112, 117, 121, 127, 135, 167, 155, 195 210, 219, 229, 231
Ehlers, T.B. and Main, K. 104, 111
Elson, E. 98, 108
Emergency Social Fund (SEF) 47, 48
empowerment 1, 2, 5–8, 12, 19, 23, 31, 35, 53, 55, 64, 66, 70, 74, 75, 86, 90, 99, 125, 158, 170, 173, 175, 178, 235–237; political empowerment 175
Escobar, A. 11, 16, 39, 67, 68, 69, 84, 85, 230, 238
Esteva, G. 10, 39, 84, 89
Evens, P. 92, 108

FAFIDESS 126, 127
Fergusson, J. 11, 40, 65, 67, 68, 84, 85
Fernando, J.L. 39, 42, 104, 108, 174, 228, 234, 236, 238
financial sustainability 172; financial self-sustainability 173, 185, 186, 189, 208, 230
FINCA 114, 125, 126, 129–132
Fine, B. 18, 19, 40
Foley, M.W. and Edwards, M. 92, 107, 109
Fombori 133–144, 151
Foster, G. 152, 157, 161, 170
Foucault, M. 36, 65–67, 82–85, 107, 109, 236
Fraser, N. 41, 176, 183, 185
Freire, P. 190, 230, 234
Fukuyama, F. 97

Geertz, C. 99, 109
Gender and Development (GAD) 4, 17, 24, 36, 39, 172, 187, 188, 194, 197, 207, 231
Gertler, M. 92, 109

Ghana 135
Gill, S. 44, 60
Girillo, R.D. 40
Goetz, A.M. and Sen, Gupta 39, 104, 109, 166, 172, 182, 195, 198, 202–207, 223, 235–237
Golte, J. 156, 161, 170
Gomez, A. 37, 112, 123
Gonzalez-Vega, C. 32, 40
Goonewardena, K. 97, 106, 109
governmentalization 71, 76
Grameen Bank 1, 17, 32, 39, 75, 109, 135, 174, 186, 191, 196, 203, 209–215, 236–238; oath 215, 216; secret oath 203
Griaule, M. 137, 139, 152
Guasch, L. 190, 232
Gwynne, R. and Kay, C. 157, 170

Hardt, M. 12, 13, 40
Hartwick 40, 41, 42
Hashemi, S.M. 173
Hashemi, S.M. and Shuler S. 87, 185
health 29, 58, 71, 195, 210, 225, 227, 234; health care 35, 98, 134, 172, 185, 190
Hilferding, R. 13, 40
Honneth, A. 108n, 109, 111
Hospes, O. 115, 133
Hughes, R. 139, 154
Hulme, D. and Mosley, P. 54, 62, 121, 134, 136, 172, 176, 187
Humphrey, D. 37, 116, 118, 122, 124, 126, 132, 134

IDEAS 163, 164, 171
IMF 19, 35, 42–47, 58–63, 72
Imperato, P.J. 137, 152
income 8, 9, 17, 26, 28, 133, 134, 136, 137, 139; income generation 42, 48, 59, 77, 104, 222, 223, 234, 236
indebtedness 10, 28, 95, 175
informal sector 6, 8, 17–19, 29, 34, 40, 123, 134, 135, 138, 173, 185, 187, 193, 235
interest rates 27, 28, 32, 51, 54, 154, 207, 220, 231
Islam 110, 139, 210, 212, 213; islamization 138

James, C. 151
James, C.L.R. 7, 39
Jenson, J. 106n, 109
Johnson, R.J. 109
Johnson, S. and Rogaly, R. 60, 134, 136, 152
Jorgensen, S. 47, 60

Index

Kabeer, N. 41, 42, 99, 109, 156, 170, 191, 232, 233, 235
Kandyoti, D. 107, 109
Kapur, D. 48, 60
Kenya 135
Khandeker, S. 197, 236
Khondkar, M. 52, 58, 60
Kogan, L. 157, 170, 232
Konare, A.O. 138, 150, 152
Kopytoff, I. 144, 152
Kwiatkowski, L.M. 177, 178, 185

Latif, H.I. 205
Laude, J. 137, 152
Ledgerwood, J. 52, 58, 134, 151, 152
Leloup, H. 137, 138, 152
literacy 99, 120, 121, 136, 149, 151, 224
livelihoods 42, 46, 56, 57, 120, 126, 131, 141, 181
loan repayment 4, 25, 27, 29, 32, 114, 196, 217, 219; default 29, 99, 115, 118, 135, 227, 228; defaulters 27, 220, 225

McMichael, P. 66, 70, 82, 83, 85
McNaughton, P. 144, 145, 152
Mahmud, S. 199, 200, 236
Malawi 137
Mali 37, 133, 136, 152, 162
Marcel, G. 139
Mare, D. 41
Marr, A. 154, 155, 170
Martin, L.M. and Halstead, A. 58, 61
Marx, K. 11, 12, 16, 36, 38, 40, 63, 82; Marxian 90, 95, 98, 100, 101, 104; Marxism 232; Marxist 36, 64; Marxist Feminism 232
Mayer, E. 97, 98, 106, 107, 156, 170
Mayer, E. and Zamolla, A. (1974) 156, 171
Mayoux, L. 104, 175, 186, 261
Mexico 126
Meyer, R.L. 54, 61
Microcredit Movement 65, 70
Microcredit Revolution 2
Microcredit Summit 1, 7
Microcredit Summit Secretariat (MSC) 75, 80
Microenterprises 47, 191, 195, 196, 198, 219, 232
Microfinance Institutions (MFI) 52, 99, 112, 134, 144, 159, 160, 172
Microfinance Organisations (MFO) 168
Milgram, L.B. 37, 172, 180, 182, 184–186
Mintz, S. 99, 110
Mohammad, Y. 1, 18, 76, 77, 87–89, 205–207

Money lenders 192, 203–208, 213–219, 223–227
Montgomery, R. 155, 160
Moron, S.J. 177, 186
Mossbrucker, H. (1990) 156, 170
Murdoch, J. 99, 172, 173, 186

Negri, A. 12, 13
Nelson, J. 92, 110
neoclassical economics 19, 33, 74, 108, 192, 232
neoliberalism 5, 12, 19, 20, 30–36, 53, 57, 72, 76, 77, 82, 99, 111, 186, 229, 230; Neoliberal 6, 13, 43–51, 56, 58, 64–66, 72, 75, 81, 83, 97, 98, 99, 187, 190, 230
Nepal 35, 90, 95, 101, 104, 107, 108, 109
New Economic Program (NEP) 47
New Social Movements 10, 17, 20, 30, 66, 82
NGOs 4, 5, 8, 17–20, 28, 30, 36, 48, 52, 53, 59, 73, 82, 83, 91, 114, 120, 131, 135, 196, 197, 200, 230, 231, 234, 236

Olson, M. 91, 110
Otero, M. and Rhyne, E. (1994), 52, 61, 100, 111

Pait, S. 124, 125, 128, 129, 132
pardha 208, 213
pedagogy 200, 233; peer group 220, 228, 230; peer group pressure 24, 25, 52, 78, 100, 155, 160, 167, 175, 177, 217, 218
Peet, R. 40, 41, 42
Perkins, H. 203, 222
Peru 36, 112–114, 119, 120, 123, 131, 154, 155, 170
Pitt, M. 197, 225
Portes, A. and Landolt, P. 92, 110
post development 67, 69, 70, 91
postdevelopmentalists 10, 11, 34; postmodernism 24; postmodernization 84
Potapchuk, W. 91, 110
Powell, C. 1
power relations 9, 19, 30, 56, 84, 105, 166, 168, 190, 194, 200, 207, 218, 227, 232; *see also* empowerment
Puttnam, R. 89, 90, 91, 92, 94, 102, 106, 110, 116, 132

quinta fiscalia penal 162

Rahman, A. 39, 52, 78, 80, 86, 87, 105, 119, 152, 174, 237
Rahman, R.I. 39
Rai, S. 42, 229, 232, 233, 234, 238

Rankin, K. 98, 102, 103, 104, 107, 110, 186, 207
repayment rates 4, 6, 7, 25–28, 35, 80, 134, 138, 196, 219–221, 226; *see also* loan repayment
RESULTS 52, 61
Rhyne, M. and Otero, Maria 52, 61, 100, 111
Risman, B. and Ferre, M. 92, 111
Robinson, M. 32, 39, 42, 57
Robinson, W.I. 61
Rogaly, B. 51, 60–61, 136, 152
ROSCAs 113, 114, 116, 128, 113, 132
Rosen, L. 155, 159, 162, 163, 169, 171
Rosengard, J. 235
Rosenzweig, M. 235
rotating community saving groups 135
Ruggie, J.G. 44, 61
Rutherford, S. 62, 203, 205, 207

Sadoulet, L. and Carpenter, S. 41
Schneider, H. 52, 62
seclusion 104, 112; *see also* pharda
self-sufficiency 8; financial self-sufficiency 21, 31, 208
Sen, Amartya 11
Sen, G. 231, 232, 233
Sen, Gupta 197, 198, 239
Servon, L.J. 97, 111
Shafiqual, C. 202–205
Sidibe, S. 136, 137, 152
Skocpol, T. 92, 107, 111
Smith, N. 14
social capital 92–107, 147–149, 182
Social Relations Framework 189
Sparr, P. 96, 111
Sri Lanka 23
Srivastava, K. 11, 39
state 1, 4, 5, 11, 15, 17, 92, 98, 162, 165, 169, 228–235; crisis of the state 228; form and nature of the state 228; neoliberal state 33; state-society relations 95; Welfare state 95; *see also* accumulation and legitimization crisis
Stirrat, R. 40
structural adjustments programs (SAPs) 44–49, 191, 192, 193
sustainability: financial sustainability 134, 135, 150; self-sustainability 172, 173, 175; sustainability of the groups 205, 209; sustainability of NGOs 228

Teivainen T. 45, 62
Tellem 138; Tellem civilization 142; Tellem people 143
Todd, H. 52, 58, 59
Todd, V. 152
Truman, H. 14
Tsikata, D. and Kerr, J. 98, 111

United Nations 29, 126, 132, 151
United Nations Research Institute 110
Unnithan, M. 12, 39
USAID 38, 141, 234–235

Van Beekn, E.A. 137, 153
Velez-Ibanez (1983) 113
violence 20, 54, 67, 84, 95, 112, 126, 199, 169, 198; physical violence 54

Wallerstein, I. 66, 83
Walters, K. 38
Walters, W. 96, 98, 107, 110
Walton, J. and Seddon, D. 45, 62
Washington Consensus 44, 45, 58
Weber, H. 45, 52, 54, 56–60
Webster, L. and Fidler, P. 135, 153
Wilson, E. 91, 106n, 110, 235
Woller, G. 54, 62
Women and Development (WAD) 22, 41
Women in Development (WID) 24, 25, 108, 111, 188, 189, 194, 231
Women, Environment and Development (WED) 22
Women's Association of Fombori 140, 146
Wood, G. 159, 160, 161
Wood, G. and Sharif, I. 52, 174, 185, 186
Woolcock, M. 92, 93, 96, 105, 107, 116, 132
World Bank 17, 23, 33, 43–48, 52, 58, 232
World Vision International 225
Wright, G.A.N. 186
Wright, K. 37, 154–56, 162, 164, 168, 171, 175
Wright, S. 39
Wright, W.C. 109
WTO 17, 44, 49, 58, 59

Yunus, M. 1, 17, 76, 77, 80, 86, 88, 119, 132, 186, 205–207

DATE DUE			